Opening Doors: Orchestras, Opera Companies and Community Engagement

What is the role of classical music in the 21st century? How will classical musicians maintain their relevance and purpose?

This book follows the working activities of professional orchestral musicians and opera singers as they move off stage into schools, community centres, prisons, libraries, and corporations, engaging with their communities in new, rich ways through education and community engagement programmes. Key examples of collaborative partnerships between orchestras, opera companies, schools and music services in the delivery of music education are investigated, with a focus on the UK's Music Hub system. The impact of these partnerships is examined, both in terms of how they inspire and foster the next generation of musicians as well as the extent to which they broaden access to quality music education. Detailed case studies are provided on the impact of classical music education programmes on social cohesion, health and wellbeing, and the education outcomes for students from low socio-economic communities. The implications for the future training of classical musicians are analysed, as are the new career paths for orchestral musicians and composers straddling performance and education.

Opening Doors: Orchestras, Opera Companies and Community Engagement investigates the ways in which the classical music industry is reinventing its sense of purpose, never a more important or urgent pursuit than in the present decade.

Emily Dollman is the Head of Music Education and Pedagogy at the Elder Conservatorium of Music, University of Adelaide, and founding Artistic Director of the Open Music Academy. Emily's background combines extensive experience as an international professional violinist with a long-standing commitment to music education and instrumental pedagogy.

Opening Doors: Orchestras, Opera Companies and Community Engagement

Emily Dollman

LONDON AND NEW YORK

First published 2023
by Routledge
4 Park Square, Milton Park, Abingdon, Oxon OX14 4RN

and by Routledge
605 Third Avenue, New York, NY 10158

Routledge is an imprint of the Taylor & Francis Group, an informa business

© 2023 Emily Dollman

The right of Emily Dollman to be identified as author of this work has been asserted in accordance with sections 77 and 78 of the Copyright, Designs and Patents Act 1988.

All rights reserved. No part of this book may be reprinted or reproduced or utilised in any form or by any electronic, mechanical, or other means, now known or hereafter invented, including photocopying and recording, or in any information storage or retrieval system, without permission in writing from the publishers.

Trademark notice: Product or corporate names may be trademarks or registered trademarks, and are used only for identification and explanation without intent to infringe.

British Library Cataloguing-in-Publication Data
A catalogue record for this book is available from the British Library

ISBN: 978-1-032-05645-6 (hbk)
ISBN: 978-1-032-05646-3 (pbk)
ISBN: 978-1-003-19851-2 (ebk)

DOI: 10.4324/9781003198512

Typeset in Sabon
by Deanta Global Publishing Services, Chennai, India

This book is dedicated to my children, Joshua and Isabelle. It is for the coming generation that we need to preserve, strengthen, and renew our creative culture.

With thanks to the performers, composers, teachers, students, and arts administrators who each play such a valuable role in the ecosystem featured in this book: it has been a privilege to share your stories here.

With deep thanks also to all my family for their support, in particular to my parents for their lifelong encouragement and for the countless hours of driving me to music lessons and rehearsals as a child. Thank you for opening the doors to music for me.

Contents

Introduction	1
1 Musicians Offstage: An Overview of the Aims and Activities of Orchestral and Opera Education and Community Engagement Programmes	18
2 Origins and Development: Understanding the Early History of Orchestral and Opera Education and Community Engagement Programmes	30
3 Working Together: Models of Partnership Delivery of Music Education	56
4 Leading the Way: Case Studies of Orchestral and Opera Education and Community Engagement Programmes	67
5 Orchestras Building Communities: The El Sistema Model and Its Global Influence	104
6 Creative Music Making: The New Role of Animateurs and Teaching Artists	115
7 New Roles, New Skills: Implications for the Tertiary Training of Classical Musicians	133
8 Virtual Music Making: Classical Music Engagement Utilising Digital and Online Technology	150

viii   *Contents*

9 Music, Health, and Wellbeing: Benefits for Both
Musicians and Participants   165

10 A Second Pillar, or Working on the Fringe? A Summary
of the Current Situation and Examination of Future
Developments   173

Conclusion   184

Index   *189*

Introduction

This book is a study of the activities, aims, and vision of education and engagement programmes operated by symphony orchestras and opera companies. Over the past four decades, there has been a steady revolution in the day-to-day activities of orchestral musicians and opera companies across the globe. Today, we find orchestral and opera musicians working "off stage" in venues as disparate as schools, hospitals, prisons, nursing homes, conservatoriums, shopping centres, museums, art galleries, public libraries, and even train stations and car parks. You will now find an education or community engagement department centrally placed in all major orchestras and opera companies across the world. In some of the world's leading classical organisations, the managing director began their career path in the education department, bringing the perspective they gained through community and education work directly to the engine room of decision-making. In this book, we gain a firsthand perspective into this career trajectory from industry leaders including Kathryn McDowell, CBE, the managing director of the London Symphony Orchestra and Stephen Langridge, the artistic director of Glyndebourne Opera.

Education and community engagement programming has evolved to be a crucial counterpoint to main stage performance programming for orchestras and opera companies. These programmes have a range of extremely important aims and outcomes: to maintain and improve the status of music education in schools; to consolidate the relevance of classical music in 21st-century society; to develop the musicians, composers, and audiences of the future; to increase access to the proven health and wellbeing benefits of music; and to improve social equity in low socio-economic communities.

The title of this book, *Opening Doors*, refers to what I feel is the most essential goal of these programmes: to open the doors to music for the widest possible spectrum of society. By breaking through barriers, some real and some only existing in perception, the programmes allow more people to establish a personal connection with classical music. It is in this personal connection that the value of the music is felt, and it is also the key to the future of the industry – a future that requires great efforts across the industry to protect.

DOI: 10.4324/9781003198512-1

2 Introduction

At the time of writing, the classical music industry is facing one of its most severe tests. As the COVID-19 pandemic rippled across the world in 2020, concert houses across the world switched off the stage lights and closed the doors. Musicians' income streams abruptly ceased and the jet-setting life of conductors and soloists suddenly became untenable. While the pandemic experience has varied in different countries there has been a common global story of previously stable arts organisations confronting the threat of bankruptcy and of live performances silenced overnight. The vulnerability of arts organisations is being keenly felt, with the arts at risk within a society suffering from financial pressure. Therefore, the urgency for musicians to engage with their audiences and to ignite community support has never been so strong. Musicians need to advocate for the value of their art form: with national budgets in crisis, governments must be convinced of the importance of music to society in a bid to consolidate and sustain funding. The twin arguments of the innate importance of the musical art form and its many proven extra-musical benefits across health and community must be made clear.

Yet, alongside this crisis, there is an alternate storyline of hope, strength, and vitality. This lies partly in the fact that as a live shared cultural experience was taken away from us, we valued what we had lost more than ever before. Even as communities were forced into isolation, through music they found ways to reconnect. Connection through lockdown music-making across Italian apartment balconies, through shared tributes in song for health workers, through online projects bringing strangers together into a choir from their couches. People forced into indoor idleness found that learning a musical instrument brought an emotional outlet as well as a physical and intellectual occupation, bringing catharsis through an anxious time.

Hope also lies in the energy, creativity, and grit of the musicians and management staff of music organisations. Throughout this period of upheaval, there has been a strong and concerted effort by the music industry to continue to connect with communities, to reach out and open the door to music. Behind the concert stage, there has been a rethink of the role of symphony orchestras, opera companies, and choirs. Questions have been asked as to how, and why, musicians connect with communities. The question of the value and community relevance of music organisations has been the topic of boardroom meetings, of conference proceedings, and journal articles. This questioning, of course, did not commence in 2020; classical music has long been engaged in a battle against preconceptions that it is outdated, elitist, and irrelevant. While some may feel that performances should and can speak for themselves, others believe it is the work of education and community engagement departments that will maintain the social relevance of the art form. It is this work that we will explore in this book – its aims, activities, historical development, and future directions.

Despite the clear importance of these programmes and the lofty goals placed upon their outcomes, there is at present a lack of studies undertaken on this field of work. It is my goal to address this imbalance here by highlighting the work undertaken, its goals, its historical development, and future areas of growth. This is the first book to cover international best practice in the education and community engagement activities of orchestras and opera companies, and it is my primary aim to shine a light on the hugely important, yet often overlooked, work that lies beyond main stage concert performances. *Opening Doors* examines the various areas of activity of orchestral and opera education and community engagement programmes: education for school-aged students; programmes with a health and wellbeing focus; creative-based programmes; digital engagement programmes; programmes inspired by El Sistema with a social equity mission at heart; and programmes to help young emerging musicians to make the transition to the profession. We follow the working activities of professional orchestral musicians and opera singers as they move off stage, engaging with their communities in new, rich ways. We examine key examples of collaborative partnership in the delivery of music education between orchestras, opera companies, schools, and instrumental education services, with a focus on the UK's Music Hub system. We look at music programmes aiming to help young offenders to get back on track; at programmes aiming to rectify the gender and race imbalance in the classical music industry; and at programmes linking with health services to combat long COVID. We look at orchestras setting up schools, at opera companies working in prisons, at programmes working with dementia patients.

The links between orchestral and opera education and community engagement programmes and social equity and regeneration programmes are examined. Music education programmes led by classical musicians have led directly to substantial health and societal benefits in low socio-economic communities. The leading influence here is Venezuela's pioneering El Sistema, known worldwide as the music programme that replaced guns with violins. The extraordinary impact of El Sistema has been felt around the world. Several global orchestral education programmes inspired by the Sistema model are investigated and analysed in this book, and possibilities for future development are considered.

We look at the implications for the tertiary training of musicians in conservatoriums and degree programmes. The working life of an orchestral musician or an opera singer in the 21st century requires an increasingly diverse skillset. This new skillset comprises expertise in education, public speaking, improvisation skills, presentation, and workshop leading – in addition to attaining technical and artistic excellence on their instrument.

We also examine the larger picture of issues commonly faced in the field of music education across the world. A common picture is of uncertain funding for school music departments, of the patchy provision of music education experts in schools; of instrumental tuition predominantly available to children of high socio-economic families. Music is being crowded out of the curriculum in schools across the globe, with principals focusing

4 Introduction

their sights on science, technology, engineering, and mathematics (STEM), literacy, and coding in their quest to train the future workforce. Tertiary general teaching degrees often allocate a pitifully low number of hours to music as they train the next generation of teachers – leading to a workforce that feels nervous when confronted with a quaver or a middle C. "Classical" music, in particular, faces issues in schools. This is, of course, related to the larger issues surrounding this genre. It should be noted at this point that even the use of the term "classical" is itself problematic, with criticisms of the term as ambiguous and overly broad – that it does not reflect the true diversity of music performed by orchestras, opera companies, choirs, and smaller instrumental ensembles. The term itself, of course, naturally directs our thoughts towards music from the Classical period, and the great composers of that era, rather than being a term that encompasses the immense diversity of music performed by "classical" organisations. However, at the time of writing, an alternate term has not yet emerged with sufficient clarity – "art" music has its own connotations of elitism, "composed" music is also ambiguous. For the purposes of this book then, "classical music" will be used to refer to the industry in which symphony orchestras and opera companies operate.

In the face of these challenges and gaps in music education, the role of orchestras and opera companies in reaching out to and connecting with all levels of the music ecosystem takes on a new level of urgency. We look at specific programmes connecting orchestral and opera education programmes with school-aged students – including flagship programmes where an orchestra is a key partner with the school management. These programmes inspire children who are already learning an instrument or singing to further develop their skills by connecting with professional musicians and engaging in stimulating activities. The programmes also enable students with limited previous experience of music to engage in participatory music making and creative activities. Investment in this grassroots level of music making has significant benefits for the entire music ecosystem; these programmes are impacting on the development of future performers, composers, audience members, and arts administrators. The programmes are also key to helping to achieve greater equity in access to music education, with many programmes specifically focusing on under-represented sectors and helping to level the "playing field."

The proliferation of education and community engagement programmes by symphony orchestras and opera companies is intertwined with adaptations in the delivery system of music education. The UK's Music Hub system is a leader internationally in terms of a structured partnership system delivering impactful, sequential music education to children through their developing years. The intentions, operating systems, and outcomes of the hub partnership model of music education are investigated here, with examples of best practice identified. These partnerships see professional musicians working alongside instrumental Music Services, schools, arts organisations,

Introduction 5

and youth music ensembles with truly outstanding and impactful results. The possible application of similar models of music education partnership delivery in other international education systems is also considered.

All children are born creative. This simple statement is the heart of the message from the late, treasured, Sir Ken Robinson, a statement that resonates with the millions who have watched Robinson's TED Talk or bought his books. While few would argue with this statement, the education system is still often one that does not foster – indeed it actively stifles – the natural creativity of children. Music education offers a rich and natural area of activity in which children's creativity can truly be developed within the school system. From the 1960s onwards, composer-teachers such as Sir Peter Maxwell Davies, R. Murray Schafer, John Paynter, and George Self brought fresh thinking to the question of how children can connect with music in the school curriculum. They rightly noted that we do not restrict children from painting until they have learnt the techniques of chiaroscuro and perspective; nor then should we restrict children from improvising and composing until they have learnt the rules of four-part harmony. From this standpoint, creativity took place front and centre in the school music curriculum through the late 20th century. Due to hesitancy in the delivery of the creative content, many schools looked to an external creative workshop leader for assistance. This new role of a music workshop leader is chiefly known as an animateur in the United Kingdom, and a teaching artist in the United States. Here, a new career pathway for composers and creatively minded practising musicians developed: that of igniting and giving voice to children's musical creativity as they play with the musical building blocks of pitch, rhythm, texture, sound, and silence. We look at the creative music workshop format, and how this can help to find a direct connection to the heart of some of the most challenging of modern compositions.

I should note that it was not possible to include the full field of endeavour of education and community engagement across the world's professional musical bodies. Key case studies of orchestras and opera companies have been selected, with an eye to creating a varied picture of the field and of highlighting interesting approaches to the work. It was not possible to include an examination of the outreach work of choirs, chamber orchestras, or chamber music groups in this study for reasons of space and focus, although I am, of course, aware of the excellent work that groups in these areas are achieving. This is an area that may, and should, be covered in future research in this field.

In the same spirit of full disclosure, there is a personal aspect to my research. I am a professional violinist, music educator, and university academic working in both Australia and the United Kingdom. Through my career, I have developed a personal understanding and insight into the links between music education and orchestral and opera education programmes. As an Australian, currently working for the University of Adelaide, I am keen to highlight the extraordinary work being done by the Adelaide Symphony

6 *Introduction*

Orchestra in reaching across the vast distances of regional and remote South Australia. Before moving to Adelaide, I worked in London as an orchestral musician and violin teacher for a Music Service, and it was here that my interest in orchestral education programmes was ignited. My London violin students engaged in a pilot scheme with the London Symphony Orchestra for their "Take A Bow" string education programme. I witnessed firsthand the inspiration that such a programme can provide to students at a pivotal stage of learning and development. This experience led to my PhD studies on the topic of Australian and British Orchestral Education programmes, which I researched between 2010 and 2015. I was fascinated then, and remain so today, by the similarities and connections between the wave of activity that had taken root in the United Kingdom in the 1980s, and which has since arrived in Australia. For *Opening Doors*, I have broadened the focus to include case studies from a wider range of countries, including Europe and the United States; I also broadened the focus to include opera companies alongside symphony orchestras.

The material presented here is the result of three key stages of research, each of which contributed to an overall understanding of the topic. Firstly, key relevant existing materials in the form of books, reports, theses, lecture transcripts, promotional materials, and journal articles were collated and analysed. This literature provided an overview and understanding of the development and current practice in orchestral and opera programmes. To establish the context for this period of development, the relevant literature on related topics such as music pedagogy, government policy, childhood development, El Sistema, music therapy, and tertiary music training was also consulted.

An analysis of this literature provided the basis for the second stage of the research process, in which new primary source material was generated in the form of detailed first-person interviews with leaders in the field internationally. These interviewees were carefully selected to provide maximum insight into best practice in the field of orchestral and opera education and community engagement today. Participants in the project included education managers past and present, who provided details of the day-to-day activities of their programmes, their goals, and their challenges. Managing directors and artistic directors were interviewed in order to gain insight into their role in guiding and directing the outreach activities at their organisations; they were also key to providing a clear picture of the positioning of outreach work within the overall strategic operation of their companies. Leading music educators and advocates were interviewed in order to help ascertain the impact of orchestral and opera education activities on the broader music education sphere. Musicians taking part in the programmes were interviewed to gain an understanding from their perspective of the impact of this work. I thank each and every one of the generous and inspirational interviewees: giving their work and their intentions a more prominent platform is foremost in my mind throughout the following chapters. During

Introduction   7

lengthy interviews they have shared their insight into their aims, goals, and challenges, their workplace practice and the philosophies underlying their work. Their generosity in sharing this insight, especially considering the extra challenges they were collectively facing due to COVID-19, was humbling and inspiring in equal measure.

The final stage of research involved further research on points of interest arising from the interview process. Early in the interview process, the decision was made to analyse the new primary source material through a qualitative, rather than a quantitative, method. It was apparent that it would not be beneficial to translate the information contained in the interview transcripts into statistical, numerical data. However, the information gained through the interviews underpins my work as a whole, with the interviews analysed for points of consensus in order to identify current industry-wide patterns.

The upheaval of the pandemic has significantly accelerated the rate of change in the industry. The stakes have never been higher for protecting and strengthening the future of the organisations that lie at the heart of the art form. Yet, through the interviews that inform this book, there has been a note of hopeful energy running alongside the expected stress and strain. There has been a feeling that this is a crucible of change for the industry, a possibly necessary period of rebirth, which will lead to orchestras and opera companies moving into the future with fresh purpose and relevance.

While these interviews provided the most immediate and clear insight into the field, examination of key sources have helped to cast light on a variety of areas. The following literature review gives an overview of the most relevant and informative sources consulted throughout the research.

Literature Review

The literature review for this study reveals a lack of academic research into orchestral and opera education programming, out of proportion with the importance of such work. This project aims to address this issue, being the first book to cover this area in detail. However, there are selected theses, journal articles, and books that are relevant to the study in either providing a social and educational context for education programmes, or in providing insight into the development stages of the orchestral and opera education field.

By far the most valuable resource available on the topic is Julia Winterson's doctoral thesis completed at the University of York, titled *The Community Education Work of Orchestras and Opera Companies: Principles, Practice and Problems*.[1] This study, completed in 1998, gives a comprehensive overview of the development of the British field of orchestral and opera education work to that date, as well as a frank and provocative examination of the issues hindering the field from achieving its maximum impact. Winterson's thesis also includes an illuminating set of interview transcripts

8   *Introduction*

with leading figures working in the field of British orchestral education at that date, including Gillian Moore, Richard McNicol, and Nigel Osborne. It is interesting to now ask, over two decades later, to what degree the issues highlighted by Winterson have now been overcome. Winterson was particularly concerned by the lack of attention being paid to evaluation by education managers. Winterson also noted the pressing need for tertiary training to mirror the evolving changes in professional orchestral activity: developments in these areas are discussed in this study in Chapters 7 and 10.

Winterson's article on the London Sinfonietta's groundbreaking, composer-driven, "workshop" model provides thoughtful insight into the development of a key British education department.[2] Insight into the early development of this programme was also provided by David Ruffer six years earlier in the same journal, in his article "The London Sinfonietta Education Programme: An Analysis of an Interface between the Professional Artist and Music in Education."[3] These articles, together with Winterson's interview with Gillian Moore, the first education manager of London Sinfonietta, help to establish an understanding of the aims and activities of this early, pivotal education programme, groundbreaking in many ways.

The main piece of academic writing on the topic of Australian orchestral education programmes is the 2002 honours dissertation by Emma Cochran through the University of Adelaide, titled *The Role of Symphony Orchestra Programs. Case Study: Adelaide Symphony Orchestra and Sydney Symphony Orchestra*.[4] While Cochran makes several insightful points, the short length of the dissertation curtails her ability to go into detail, and the study is restricted to only two of Australia's six state symphony orchestras. Cochran noted the need for a future intensive study on the topic to fill the gap in research.[5] Twelve years after Cochran's dissertation was submitted the same claim can be made, and it is this gap that the present study aims to fill. Another key point made in her dissertation was that as symphony orchestras receive part of their funding from the state, they have an obligation to be of service to their community.

Cochran's dissertation looks at the early development of the Sydney Symphony Orchestra (SSO) and the Adelaide Symphony Orchestra's (ASO) education departments and notes that in 1980 the SSO initiated a review of its programmes.[6] The measures taken by the SSO to overhaul their educational output transformed a lacklustre, underutilised arm of the orchestra into a vibrant and enriching part of the Australian music education landscape. Several sources were consulted in the examination of the formation of the SSO's education programme, including Richard Gill's autobiography, *Give Me Excess of It*, and *Play On! 60 Years of Music Making with the Sydney Symphony Orchestra* (Sametz, ABC Sydney, 1992).[7,8] Brett Johnson's speech, *The Development of an Orchestral Education Program – Sydney Symphony Orchestra 1987–1991*,[9] provides insight into a key turning point for the SSO's education department. It makes very valuable reading for anyone interested in creating a strong, relevant education programme.

Introduction 9

Stephen Boyle's 2007 PhD thesis, *Efficiency and Identity: The Transition of Australia's Symphony Orchestras from Government Departments to Corporate Entities*, gives insight into the process by which the Australian orchestras gained independence from the Australian Broadcasting Corporation (ABC).[10] His thesis gives a comprehensive overview of the early years of the symphony orchestra network of Australia, and insight into the process and impact of the devolution from ABC control. David Garrett's doctoral thesis through the University of Wollongong, *The Accidental Entrepreneur* (2012), provides a more recent analysis of the development of Australian orchestras.[11] In addition to Boyle and Garrett's theses, several reviews and reports central to the process of devolution were examined. These included the Dix Report (1981),[12] the Tribe Report (1985),[13] Federal Government's Creative Nation Policy (1994),[14] and the Strong Report (2005).[15]

To provide insight into the founding years of orchestral education work, a variety of sources were consulted, including biographies of Sir Bernard Heinze, Sir Malcolm Sargent, Walter Damrosch, and Sir Robert Meyer. For information about more recent developments, the annual reports of individual orchestras and opera companies were consulted in order to gain a year-by-year overview of activities and plans.

Understanding of the impact of government policy on British orchestral and opera education programming was established through study of various reports and government publications. These included the Music Manifesto *Building on Excellence: Orchestras for the 21st Century* (2007),[16] the *Henley Report* (2011),[17] the *National Plan for Music Education* (2011),[18] the Ofsted report *Music in Schools: What Hubs Must Do*,[19] and the response from the industry by the Musicians' Union: *Summary in Response to Ofsted*.[20] The 2014 King's College London report, *Step by Step: Arts Policy and Young People 1944–2014*, was also of great benefit in providing a detailed investigation of 60 years of British arts policy.[21]

The link between a nation's orchestral and opera education work and the music curricula delivered in its school system is of ongoing interest. To gain insight into the impact of the UK curriculum on orchestral and opera education work, a variety of sources were consulted. In addition to the curriculum document itself, the iconic work by John Payntor and Peter Aston, *Sound and Silence*, provided insight into the spirit of adventure and vigour with which a new focus on classroom composition was launched.[22] Murray Schafer's work, *Creative Music Education: A Handbook for the Modern Music Teacher*, provides valuable and thought-provoking discussions on the essence of music, alongside creative-based learning plans for use in classrooms.[23] Stephanie Pitts' work, *A Century of Change in Music Education: Historical Perspectives on Contemporary Practice in British Secondary Schools* (2000), also provided crucial insight into the key points that impacted on the development of school music education in the United Kingdom.[24]

10 *Introduction*

In order to understand the development of the music curriculum in the Australian national curriculum and its potential impact on both the orchestral and opera education field, alongside the wider music education networks, several sources were of key benefit. Personal interviews with a key member of the planning committee of the national curriculum provided vital insight into the development process of the curriculum, although this interviewee needs to remain anonymous for the purposes of this study. The views of Richard Gill, Australia's much beloved and recently deceased music education advocate, on the introduction of the national curriculum were incisive and thought-provoking. Additionally, the national curriculum document itself has been studied in detail, alongside related books and reports, including the *National Review of School Music Education: Augmenting the Diminished,*[25] *Bridging the Gap in School Achievement through the Arts,*[26] *Education and the Arts,*[27] *Transforming Education Through the Arts,*[28] and the *Victorian Parliamentary Inquiry into School Music Education Provision.*[29]

International literature relating to the importance of music and the arts for children and society was also of relevance to this topic. As noted in the introduction, two landmark reports were of chief importance here in addition to the Australian publications noted above. These were the flagship 1999 American report, *Champions of Change*, and the 2015 British publication, *The Power of Music.*[30,31]

A growing body of research is available on the history, processes, and impact of El Sistema in Venezuela, and its global impact is also receiving scholarly scrutiny. Personal interviews were conducted with leaders of Sistema programmes internationally, including with Elsje Kibler-Vermaas, vice president of learning at the Los Angeles Philharmonic, and with Peter Garden, executive director of performance and learning at the Royal Liverpool Philharmonic Orchestra. Further information was gained through detailed study of evaluative reports, journal articles, books, DVDs, and websites.

The Association of British Orchestras (ABO) has been key to the development of British orchestral education work. In order to gain insight into the ways in which the ABO facilitates networking and seeks to promote examples of best practice in the field of orchestral education, a personal interview was conducted with Fiona Harvey, the education and youth ensembles consultant at the ABO. During this interview, Harvey not only discussed her role at the ABO but also gave valuable insight into the development of the Music Hub model. In addition to this interview, extensive research has been conducted into all relevant ABO publications.

Insight into the links between the orchestral education work of Australia and the United Kingdom can also be gained by studying published reports and conference presentations by leaders in the field. Among the most relevant of these is Christopher Wainwright's Churchill Fellowship Report (2014), in which Wainwright, past director of the Adelaide Youth

Orchestras, discusses his international trip to study leading orchestral education programmes.[32] Also of interest to this study is the Churchill Fellowship Report by Nicholas Bochner (assistant principal cellist with the Melbourne Symphony Orchestra), which details his observation of the LSO Discovery Department and related training offered at London's Guildhall School of Music and Drama (GSMD).[33]

Insight into the early development of training for orchestral education work in the United Kingdom is chiefly provided through several articles by Peter Renshaw in the *British Journal of Music Education*, published between 1985 and 1992. These articles detail Renshaw's establishment of a new course in animateur skills at London's Guildhall School of Music and Drama, and his thoughts on the need for a fresh approach to the training of orchestral musicians at the tertiary level. The 2005 GSMD book, *The Reflective Conservatoire: Studies in Music Education Research Studies 4*, was also of particular interest. This work offers insight into developing trends in tertiary music education, as well as practical advice on leading workshops and teaching improvisation.[34] A further GSMD publication, *The Art of the Animateur*, helped to define and explain the aims and practice of "animateurs," a key role in British orchestral programming but one little known in Australia to date.[35] Interviews with Sean Gregory (executive director of innovation and engagement at the Barbican and Guildhall) and Eric Booth (author of the seminal work, *The Music Teaching Artists' Bible*[36]) provided insight into current trends and best practice in innovatory leadership in the tertiary music industry.

Alongside the question of training is the issue of the structure of the symphony orchestra and its place in society. Informative and provocative points have been made on these topics by several key figures over the past half-century. Ernest Fleischmann's "Community of Musicians" concept, previously discussed in the introduction, was first presented in a lecture at the Cleveland School of Music in 1987. This lecture was subsequently published as the article "The Orchestra is Dead."[37] Fleischmann reiterated his views on this topic in a subsequent speech in 2000 to the Royal Philharmonic Society.[38] His concept, while radical, was foreshadowed by the views of Boulez as expressed in *Orientations*,[39] and also validated by Leonard Slatkin in his book, *Conducting Business*.[40] Slatkin, writing in 2012, remarked: "Now, more than 20 years later, I think not only was he [Fleischmann] right but also very much ahead of his time."[41] This view is supported by many leaders in the classical music industry today. Looking close to home, Stephen Boyle identified the Adelaide Symphony Orchestra as one that was looking to potentially remodel its structure along Fleischmann's suggestions.[42] While this has not eventuated, it is a sign of the far-reaching impact of Fleischmann's ideas.

The Royal Philharmonic Society's annual lectures provide insight by leaders in the classical music profession. In addition to Fleischmann's address in 2000, the lectures presented by Nicola Benedetti (2019), Alan

12   Introduction

Gilbert (2014), Roger Wright (2013), Sir Peter Maxwell Davies (2005), and Graham Vick (2003) were of particular interest to this study in their often provocative and visionary commentary on aspects of the relationship between classical music and contemporary society.

Marshall McGuire (former executive manager of artistic planning, West Australian Symphony Orchestra) presented a speech titled *Australian Orchestras – The State of Play* at the Classical Music Summit 2010, which was also of relevance to this study. In this presentation, McGuire was critical of the models of outreach and education commonly used by Australian orchestras, claiming that much more participatory programmes needed to be developed.[43] The TED Talks by Richard Gill and Sir Ken Robinson also provided much food for thought on the importance of music education for children's development.

The report "Psychological Well-Being in Professional Orchestral Musicians in Australia" (2006)[44] provides insight into the various stresses and pressures under which Australian orchestral musicians are operating. The final report, *Sound Practice*, delivered in 2017 by Ackermann, Kenny, Driscoll, and O'Brian at the conclusion of the five-year research project is a landmark publication in the area of health and wellbeing for orchestral musicians. The report has had a national and international impact on understanding the workplace environment within classical music organisations.[45] It is the view of the author that participation in education work can help to alleviate many of these stresses and can provide a much more balanced and fulfilling career path for orchestral musicians. Further studies in this area, for example by Abeles and Hafeli (2014)[46] and Levine and Levine (1996),[47] point to the potential benefit of education and outreach participation for orchestral musicians themselves.

Several American theses were of value in providing an overview of the orchestral education and outreach in the United States and also offering examples of evaluation of such programmes. *The Contributions of Leonard Bernstein to Music Education: An Analysis of his 53 Young People's Concerts*, by Brian David Rozen,[48] discusses the approach taken by Bernstein in his "Young People's Concerts," which remain a landmark in orchestral music education today. Bernstein's education work is also a salient lesson in the impact that a celebrity figure can have: his education concerts were so popular that Americans were putting their children's names down before birth. *Lillian Baldwin and the Cleveland Plan for Educational Concerts* provided insight into another formative figure in American orchestral education work.[49]

A more current American thesis, *Conversations with Five Music Directors Regarding the Current State and Future of American Symphony Orchestras* (Harrison, 2009), was also consulted.[50] Prompted by the financial struggles of several American orchestras in the past decade, Harrison seeks to provide possible measures to rectify the fortunes of the American symphony orchestra through interviews with five chief conductors. The points of consensus

Introduction 13

in the interviews are of interest: for example, both Michael Christie and Robert Spano suggest that Fleischmann's Community of Musicians concept could be the best future model for their orchestras.[51] Additionally, all five music directors acknowledged the importance of the integration of symphony orchestras and their communities.[52]

Philip Hart's article "The Educational Role of the Symphony Orchestra," published in 1973, raised several points that have remained valid and relevant to the present date.[53] Hart was the orchestra and concert manager for the Seattle, Portland, and Chicago symphony orchestras, and director of planning and programmes at the Juilliard School, New York. Hart's key statements include that "to a distressingly great extent, symphony management and artistic directors know very little about education theory"[54] and "if funds and personnel are limited, it would be far better to plan multiple exposures for a smaller number of children."[55] The importance of understanding theories of music education, and the question of how to best use funding, were points echoed by several key figures interviewed for this study.

The 2006 American report, *The Search for Shining Eyes, Audiences, Leadership and Change in the Symphony Orchestra Field (the Knight Report)*, provides detailed quantitative data on the impact of orchestral education work.[56] These data are based on a survey of 25,000 American classical audience attendees, which remains to date the largest audience survey of its kind. Its key aim was to assess the impact created by orchestral education initiatives sponsored by the Knight Foundation. The report is of great relevance to orchestral education personnel and management staff both in the United States and internationally.

Eric Booth's seminal work, *The Music Teaching Artist's Bible* (2009), gives an American perspective on orchestral education programming and training for such work at tertiary institutions.[57] Booth began teaching education skills to performance students at the Juilliard School of Music in 1994, and has delivered professional development to the New York Philharmonic's teaching artist faculty for ten years. His experience in these roles and his own work as a leading music educator inform his writing with an illuminating and ultimately uplifting perspective on classical music in the 21st century. Booth is also the founding editor of the *Teaching Artist Journal*, which is a key resource of opinion and data for the developing "teaching artist" field.[58] Booth gave further insight into his views and experiences in a personal interview with the author.

Gillian Moore, currently director of classical music at the Southbank Centre, began her career as the first British Orchestra education manager in 1983, when appointed to the London Sinfonietta. Moore's views have been expressed in various formats, such as journal articles, interviews, articles, and lectures. Interestingly, although Moore was key to the early establishment of the orchestral education field, she has also been openly critical of certain aspects of practice in the field. Her views have, in turn, influenced the line of questioning taken in this research.

14   *Introduction*

Beyond Britten: The Composer and the Community, edited by Peter Wiegold and Ghislaine Kenyon, is a treasure trove of a book, compiling the perspectives of key composers on their experiences connecting with their communities. The work also shares best practice as delivered by leading facilitators of collaborative co-creation music programmes.[59] This work takes as its central focus the landmark speech delivered by Benjamin Britten on receiving the 1964 Aspen Award, which gave insight into his views on the relationship between composers and their communities. The book provides superb insight into Britten's work and legacy in this respect, as well as examining the ripple on effect of his concepts on composers, arts managers, and creative workshop leaders over the past 50 years.

Francois Matarasso's study of participatory art, *A Restless Art: How Participation Won, and Why it Matters*, was key in unpacking the activities delivered in the early decades of artists working in their communities with social or political motivation.[60] Chris Dromey and Julia Haferkorn, alongside Dawn Bennett, provided insight into the complex realities facing musicians entering into the classical music profession of the 21st century with their respective works, *The Classical Music Industry*[61] and *Understanding the Classical Music Profession: The Past, the Present and Strategies for the Future*.[62]

Pauline Tambling's excellent article "Opera, Education and the Role of Arts Organisations" gives a superb level of insight into the early years of her work with the Royal Opera House, Covent Garden.[63] *Education at the Met: Creating Original Opera Resource Guide* is a detailed handbook outlining the pioneering creative work of the Metropolitan Opera Company in the 1980s, work which had an international influence and remains a landmark in practice today.[64]

Alongside materials relating directly with orchestral and opera education programmes, a variety of other sources were also consulted in order to establish the social and educational context in which orchestras are operating. Articles on the benefits of music in hospitals, prisons, and nursing homes were consulted, alongside resources on the role of music in developing creative skills. Websites of relevant organisations were consulted regularly to obtain information about present activities, current data, and mission statements. Overall, study of these materials helped to form an understanding of the development of the field and shaped the line of questioning in the interview process.

Notes

1 Julia Winterson. *The Community Education Work of Orchestras and Opera Companies: Principles, Practice and Problems*. PhD thesis, University of York, 1998.
2 Julia Winterson. "The Evaluation of the Effects of London Sinfonietta Education Projects on their Participants," *British Journal of Music Education*, Vol. 11(2), July 1994, pp. 129–141.

Introduction 15

3 David Ruffer. "The London Sinfonietta Education Programme: An Analysis of an Interface between the Professional Artist and Music in Education," *British Journal of Music Education*, Vol. 5(1), March 1988, pp. 45–54.

4 Emma Cochran. *The Role of Symphony Orchestra Education Programs. Case Study: Adelaide Symphony Orchestra and Sydney Symphony Orchestra*. Music Education Honours Dissertation, University of Adelaide, 2002, p. 4.

5 Ibid., p. 4.

6 Ibid., p. 9.

7 Richard Gill. *Give Me Excess of It*. Sydney: Pan Macmillan Australia, 2012.

8 Phillip Sametz. *Play On! 60 Years of Music Making with the Sydney Symphony Orchestra*. Sydney: ABC Books, 1992.

9 Brett Johnson. *The Development of an Orchestral Education Program – Sydney Symphony Orchestra 1987–1991*. In Australian Society for Music Education. National Conference 8th, 1991, Melbourne, pp. 24–27, cited 22 Jan 2013.

10 Stephen Boyle. *Efficiency and Identity: The Transition of Australia's Symphony Orchestras from Government Departments to Corporate Entities*. PhD thesis, Macquarie University, 2007.

11 David Garrett. *The Accidental Entrepreneur*. PhD thesis, University of Wollongong, 2012.

12 *The ABC in Review: National Broadcasting in the 1980s. Report of the Australian Broadcasting Commission* (the Dix Report) Vol. 2. Commissioned by the Commonwealth of Australia. Canberra: Australian Government Publishing Service, 1981.

13 *Study into the Future Development of Orchestras in Australia* (the Tribe Report). Commissioned by the Commonwealth of Australia. Canberra: Australian Government Printing Services, 1985.

14 *Creative Nation: Commonwealth Cultural Policy*. Commissioned by the Australian Government. Canberra: National Capital Printing, 1994.

15 James Strong (chair). *A New Era: Orchestras Report*. Commissioned by the Department of Communications, Information Technology and the Arts, Canberra, 2005.

16 *Music Manifesto, Building on Excellence: Orchestras for the 21st Century*. Published by the UK's eight publicly funded orchestras, 2007. Retrieved from http://www.liverpoolphil.com/download.php?id=43, accessed 18 February 2014.

17 Darren Henley. *Music Education in England: A Review*. Commissioned by the Department for Education and the Department for Culture, Media and Sport, London, 2011.

18 *The Importance of Music: A National Plan for Music Education*. Commissioned by the Department for Education and Department for Culture, Media and Sport, London, 2011.

19 *Music in Schools: What Hubs Must Do*. The Office for Standards in Education, Children's Services and Skills (OFSTED), Manchester, 2013.

20 *Report Summary in Response to Ofsted*, Musicians Union, UK, 2014.

21 James Doeser. *Step by Step: Arts Policy and Young People 1944–2014*. Commissioned by Culture at King's, King's College London, 2014.

22 John Payntor and Peter Aston. *Sound and Silence: Classroom Projects in Creative Music*. Cambridge: Cambridge University Press, 1970.

23 R. Murray Schafer. *Creative Music Education: A Handbook for the Modern Music Teacher*. New York: Macmillan Publishing Company, 1976.

24 Stephanie Pitts. *A Century of Change in Music Education: Historical Perspectives on Contemporary Practice in British Secondary Schools*. Aldershot: Ashgate Publishing, 2000.

16 *Introduction*

25 *National Review of School Music Education: Augmenting the Diminished.* Commissioned by the Australian Government, Department of Education, Science and Training, Canberra, 2005.

26 Tanya Vaughan, J. Harris, and B. Caldwell. *Bridging the Gap in School Achievement through the Arts.* Commissioned by the Song Room, Melbourne, 2011.

27 Mary Ann Hunter. *Education and the Arts: Research Overview.* Commissioned by the Australia Council, 2005.

28 Brian Caldwell and Tanya Vaughan. *Transforming Education Through the Arts.* London: Routledge, 2012.

29 Jan Kronberg (chair). *Inquiry into the Benefits, Extents and Potential of Music Education in Victorian Schools.* Commissioned by the Education and Training Committee, 2013.

30 Edward B. Fiske (editor). *Champions of Change: The Impact of the Arts on Learning.* Co-commissioned by the Washington DC Arts Education Partnership and the President's Committee on the Arts and the Humanities, 1999.

31 Susan Hallam. *The Power of Music: A Research Synthesis of the Impact of Actively Making Music on the Intellectual, Social and Personal Development of Children and Young People.* Commissioned from the Music Education Council by the International Music Education Research Centre, Department of Culture, Communication and Media, London, 2015.

32 Christopher Wainwright. *To Learn from the World's Best Participatory Orchestral Programs to Aid the Development of Similar Programs in South Australia.* Churchill Fellowship Final Report, 2014.

33 Nicholas Bochner. *The Use of Improvisation in the Teaching of Classical Musicians.* Churchill Fellowship Final Report, 2010.

34 George Odam and Nicholas Bannan (editors). *The Reflective Conservatoire: Studies in Music Education Research Studies 4.* Co-published by The Guildhall School of Music and Drama and Ashgate Publishing Ltd, England, 2005.

35 Anna Ledgard and George Odam. *The Art of the Animateur.* Report by Animarts, Guildhall School of Music and Drama and London International Festival of Theatre [LIFT], 2003.

36 Eric Booth. *The Music Teaching Artist's Bible: Becoming a Virtuoso Educator.* Oxford: Oxford University Press, 2009.

37 Ernest Fleischmann. "The Orchestra is Dead," *Musical America*, Vol. 107(6), January 1988, pp. 14–16, 27.

38 Ernest Fleischmann. *Community of Musicians: Musicians for Community.* Royal Philharmonic Society Lecture, 2000.

39 Pierre Boulez. *Orientations.* London: Faber & Faber, 1986.

40 Leonard Slatkin. *Conducting Business: Unveiling the Mystery Behind the Maestro.* Milwaukee: Amadeus Press, 2012.

41 Ibid., p. 240.

42 Stephen Boyle. "Achieving Community Ownership: The Case of a Regional Symphony Orchestra," *International Journal of Arts Management*, Vol. 6(1), 2003, pp. 9–18.

43 Marshall McGuire. *Australian Orchestras – The State of Play.* Classical Music Summit, "Australian Musical Futures," 2010.

44 D. Kenny, T. Driscoll, and B. Ackermann. "Psychological Well-being in Professional Orchestral Musicians in Australia: A Descriptive Population Study," *Psychology of Music*, Vol. 42(2), 2014, pp. 210–232.

45 Bronwen Ackermann (editor and author), contributing authors D. Kenny, T. Driscoll, I. O'Brien. *Sound Practice.* Final Report, Sydney, 2017.

46 H. Abeles and M. Hafeli. "Seeking Professional Fulfilment: US Symphony Orchestra Members in Schools," *Psychology of Music*, Vol. 24(1), 2014, pp. 35–50.

Introduction 17

47 Seymour Levine and Robert Levine. "Why They're Not Smiling: Stress and Discontent in the Orchestra Workplace," *Harmony: Forum of the Symphony Orchestra Institute*, No. 2, April 1996, pp. 12–25.
48 Brian D. Rozen. *The Contributions of Leonard Bernstein to Music Education: An Analysis of his 53 Young People's Concerts*. PhD thesis, University of Rochester, 1997.
49 Richard Lee Massman. *Lillian Baldwin and the Cleveland Plan for Educational Concerts*. PhD thesis, University of Michigan, 1972.
50 Jacob Galloway Harrison. *Conversations with Five Music Directors Regarding the Current State and Future of American Symphony Orchestras*. PhD thesis, Arizona State University, 2009.
51 Ibid., p. 26.
52 Ibid., p. 11.
53 Phillip Hart. "The Educational Role of the Symphony Orchestra," *Music Educator's Journal*, Vol. 60(4), December 1973, pp. 26–29 and pp. 79–81.
54 Ibid., p. 28.
55 Ibid., p. 29.
56 Thomas Wolf. *The Search for Shining Eyes, Audiences, Leadership and Change in the Symphony Orchestra Field*. Knight Foundation, US, September 2006.
57 Booth, *The Music Teaching Artist's Bible*.
58 Eric Booth (founding editor). *The Teaching Artist Journal*, published quarterly. Routledge/Taylor and Francis. Chicago: Office of Academic Research Columbia College.
59 Peter Wiegold and Ghislaine Kenyon (editors). *Beyond Britten: The Composer and the Community*. Woodbridge: The Boydell Press, 2015.
60 Francois Matarasso. *A Restless Art: How Participation Won, and Why it Matters*. London: Calouste Gulbenkian Foundation, January 2019.
61 Chris Dromey and Julia Haferkorn (editors). *The Classical Music Industry*. New York: Routledge, 2018.
62 Dawn Bennett. *Understanding the Classical Music Profession: The Past, the Present and Strategies for the Future*. Abingdon: Ashgate, 2008.
63 Pauline Tambling. "Opera, Education and the Role of Arts Organisations," *British Journal of Music Education*, Vol. 16(2), 1999, pp. 139–156.
64 *Education at the Met: Creating Original Opera Resource Guide*. New York: Metropolitan Opera, 1989.

1 Musicians Offstage
An Overview of the Aims and Activities of Orchestral and Opera Education and Community Engagement Programmes

The daily activities of an orchestral musician or an opera singer in the 21st century are highly diverse. A weekly schedule may well include, alongside rehearsals of a Mahler symphony or a Puccini opera, involvement in highly participatory community outreach programmes. These could include creative workshops with a community health-care organisation, a visit to a school, a video-linked chamber performance, or a visit to a juvenile detention centre. While some organisations devote more of their time and resources to these outreach programmes than others, it is fair at this date to say that education and engagement activities are now a part of normal operations globally.

In order to better understand the context in which orchestral and opera outreach programming currently operates, it is useful to first understand the general background and philosophies underpinning the work. The latter half of the 20th century was a period of radical growth and change in the area of classical music education and community engagement. Until the 1970s, school concerts and radio broadcasts were the key focus of activity, primarily passive affairs with a lecture concert format. The 1980s and 1990s saw a major period of growth in the industry, with companies across the world appointing education officers and managers for the first time. While policy and funding were factors in this growth period, companies were also motivated by a desire to bolster music education in schools and to maintain their relevance in society.

Although outreach programming has steadily diversified from the 1980s to today, a key focal point has remained the desire to support music education for school-aged children. This work is of crucial importance for several reasons. Firstly, there is a growing body of evidence of the benefits of music education towards the cognitive and emotional development of children. Landmark publications on the value of music education have been released internationally, including *Transforming Education through the Arts* (Caldwell and Vaughan, 2012),[1] *Champions of Change* (ed. Fiske, 1999),[2] and *The Power of Music* (Hallam, 2015).[3] Each of these reports analyses substantial quantitative data to demonstrate the importance of music and arts education. Additional notable studies include data collected

DOI: 10.4324/9781003198512-2

on 112,916 school students in Canada, which clearly demonstrated that music participation – in particular instrumental music tuition – was linked to higher scores in English, maths, and science.[4]

The Australian philanthropic "Tony Foundation" commissioned a significant report into the current state of music education across Australia. Published in 2019 with research led by Dr Anita Collins, an internationally recognised expert in music education, the report is both a clear advocacy argument for the value of music education and a concerning highlight of the inadequate and inequitable provision of music education across Australia.[5] The report also stresses the value of a collaborative approach to improving the music education system:

> There is a shared desire within the sector to collaborate and work together on advancing music education in Australia. Professional associations and large non-profits acknowledge their limitations within the current system and recognise that desired changes cannot come from business as usual, or even from increased funding into their existing operations. There are also numerous smaller non-profits that are contributing to the provision of music education, although not always in a sustainable way, in regional and Indigenous communities. The case of South Australia and the leadership group, which included music industry, education department, philanthropists and philanthropic bodies, elected ministers and education experts, demonstrate that models of collaboration can have a large, material impact on the music education system.[6]

These findings are consistent with other research reports, including a survey taken in 2012 showing that 63% of Australian primary schools have no classroom music and that, in total, only 37.25% of schools (both primary and secondary) offer music.[7] This situation is by no means unique to Australia. Across the United Kingdom, the United States, Canada, and Europe, similar situations are documented where music educators battle against similar hurdles. A picture of the uneven provision of music to schools, training hours in the delivery of music in tertiary teaching degrees cut to ludicrously low levels, and cuts to government-sponsored music education programmes, is an international refrain.

The music industry, however, is nothing if not persistent, showing initiative and tenacity in its efforts to ensure that music education is available to all and that the value of this education is widely appreciated throughout society. Orchestral and opera education departments are an integral part of these efforts, utilising their platform and resources to achieve a more equitable system of school music education.

Orchestral and opera education programmes for school students aim to establish a positive connection between children and their local symphony orchestra and opera company. It is important for children to experience

20   *Musicians Offstage*

classical music during their formative school years in order to establish a personal connection with the art form. For many children, an education activity run by one of these organisations may be their first point of contact with classical music. This experience may also be a motivation for students to start, or persist with, learning to play an instrument or take vocal training themselves. Maximum involvement in music at the grassroots level is essential for a healthy music ecosystem as, while not all students will reach professional standards, an education in the arts has been shown to be a key indicator for lifelong engagement with the arts.

This link is evident in Figure 1.1, which is based on data collected from the Surveys of Public Participation in the Arts (SPPA), conducted for the National Endowment for the Arts in the United States between 1982 and 2008. The responses from these surveys were subsequently analysed in the 2011 report *Arts Education in America: What the Decline Means for Arts Participation*. A key finding of this report was that education in the arts is the strongest contributing factor to attending arts events as an adult, as demonstrated in the graphs in Figure 1.1.

Interestingly, the data demonstrate that adult arts education is a stronger motivator towards arts involvement than childhood arts education. While childhood arts education is, of course, important, this finding emphasises the importance of music education programmes for adults. This is an area increasingly explored over the past decade by orchestras and opera companies.

Programmes now provide opportunities for a wide age range, linking with a diverse array of community organisations and facilities, including schools, universities, local corporations, hospitals, prisons, nursing homes, housing estates, pre-schools, and even shopping centres. This development is demonstrated in changes to the title "education department." In recent years, many orchestras and opera companies have added "community engagement," "community outreach," or "learning and participation" to the department title, in recognition of the shift in focus to include the community as a whole.

Leading figures within the music industry advocated for this activity throughout the 20th century. Ernest Fleischmann (the prominent general manager of first the London Symphony Orchestra [LSO] and subsequently the Los Angeles Philharmonic) was outspoken and provocative in his advocacy for the need to restructure orchestral practice. In a landmark speech presented at the Cleveland Institute of Music in 1987, subsequently published in essay form, Fleischmann claimed that the traditional symphony orchestra was no longer viable and that a new, more flexible, and dynamic setup was urgently needed.[8] He suggested replacing the traditional symphony orchestra model with a "community of musicians." His concept was that orchestras should in effect merge, thereby not only increasing the number of players but also exponentially expanding the variety and scope of their work. He felt that the pool of players in the "community" should be

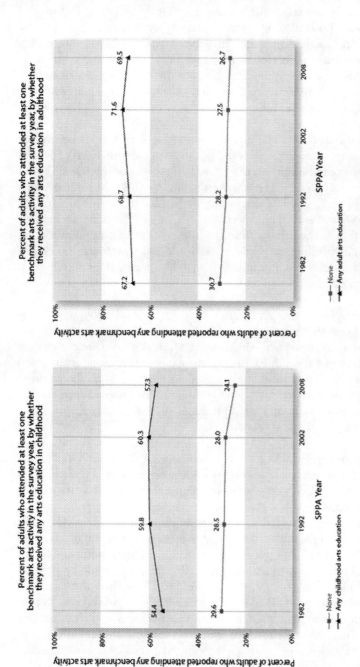

Figure 1.1 Nick Rabkin and E.C. Hedberg. *Arts Education in America: What the Decline Means for Arts Participation*. NORC at University of Chicago, National Endowment for the Arts, 2011, p. 14.

22 *Musicians Offstage*

able to turn their hand to classical music, new music, period music, and education work. In Fleischmann's words:

> What can we do to make a life in music more fulfilling, more stimulating for the talented musician in order to attract her or him to a symphony orchestra, and at the same time provide a more valuable, interesting, and exciting musical service to our audiences? I think there are ways of doing this – and they begin by altering the rather rigid structure of the traditional symphony orchestra and turning it into a more flexible Community of Musicians.[9]

Fleischmann felt that this new construct would be of particular benefit for education programming, as there would be different combinations of groups all able to make contributions according to their specialist interests.[10] These ideas were later revisited by Fleischmann in his 2000 Royal Philharmonic Society (RPS) lecture, titled "Community of Musicians: Musicians for the Community." While his original speech in 1987 noted the practical benefits of the concept, such as cutting administration costs and offering musicians more varied and fulfilling careers, the RPS address was more forceful in its message to musicians to strengthen their relevance to their community. Fleischmann stated:

> If we do not give urgent and serious thought to this problem (creating new audiences) there is a real danger that over the next decade or two the symphony audience will shrink to small pockets of elite enthusiasts found mainly in a few large cities … Musicians and musical institutions must be prepared to invest, to give their services freely to the community, and particularly to the young community in order to turn around the decline in the size and perceptiveness of audiences for symphony concerts in many parts of the world.[11]

Fleischmann's concern for creating the audience of the future was also a motivating factor of early orchestral education programmes, and the data presented in Figure 1.1 certainly point to a correlation between arts participation and arts education.

However, it is interesting to note that over the past decade a clear shift has emerged, with orchestral education managers now much more focused on the present impact of their work, rather than any potential future legacy. The creation of future audiences is today regarded as a possible by-product of orchestral education programmes: a desired outcome, but not a primary focus. The chief concern of all education managers interviewed was to provide high-quality, engaging experiences to all participants in their education programmes. Their aim is to help a wider sector of the general community, including children, to establish a point of personal connection and relevance with orchestral and opera performances. Through this sense of connection and relevance, it is hoped, will grow a greater understanding for and engagement with these art forms.

While Fleischmann's call for community engagement made a significant impact on the classical music profession, Pierre Boulez was also early to recognise the problems inherent in the traditional structure and operation of a symphony orchestra. In his essay "Composer and Audience: Where Are We Now?" Boulez makes the bold pronouncement that the symphony orchestra model was untenable in its traditional format and suggests a shift to more "polymorphous groupings."[12] Boulez also states:

> The fact that must now be faced is that it [the orchestra] will not continue unless a profound remedy is discovered – and how is that to be done? By organising either concert halls or actual concerts in a much more flexible way.[13]

Many leading orchestral education figures consulted in this study have made mention of concepts related to Fleischmann and Boulez's visions. Orchestras and opera companies are now reaching into their communities in ways undreamt of even a decade ago, and new research is pointing to the value of their work in the spheres of health, rehabilitation, cognitive development, and social cohesion.

Orchestral and opera education programmes are gradually shifting from the sidelines of an organisation's activity to take a central role, a point more fully discussed in Chapter 10. While there were initial concerns that education managers were marginalised in their organisations, their work is increasingly gaining central industry support. Over the past three decades, some of the early pioneers have progressed to take key roles in the music industry: leaders such as Kathryn McDowell, Gillian Moore, Stephen Langridge, Richard McNicol, and Katie Tearle all began their careers as adventurous groundbreakers in education and outreach work. Today, these pioneers are found in central roles in key music organisations, shaping the overall industry direction.

Leading performers in the classical field, including Alan Gilbert, chief conductor of the New York Philharmonic; Gustavo Dudamel, chief conductor of the Los Angeles Philharmonic; and Sir Simon Rattle, chief conductor of the London Symphony Orchestra, are all passionate advocates for the importance of education and outreach work. As Alan Gilbert recently commented, he and many other music leaders are now exploring anew:

> What it means to be an orchestra today. What is it that orchestras, and the musicians in them, do, and what can we mean for the societies for which we perform?[14]

Gilbert's comments were made in London in 2015, while presenting the Royal Philharmonic Society Annual Lecture. His chosen topic, "Orchestras

24 *Musicians Offstage*

in the 21st Century: A New Paradigm," provides illuminating insight into education and outreach work from the perspective of one of the music world's leading figures. Gilbert himself is clearly supportive of such work, stating:

> There are obviously as many explanations for why orchestras fail as there are orchestras that fail, but I am pretty sure that a common feature one can find in all such unfortunate situations is the sense, in some form, that there are simply not enough people in the community who care about what the orchestra provides.[15]

This point was reinforced by all interviewees consulted in this research: it is clear that the primary aim of current education work is to maintain the relevance and connection of an orchestra or opera company with its community. Gilbert feels that the field of education and outreach work will continue to grow and develop. He commented:

> The world of orchestras has reacted to external forces and embraced education and outreach. This shift away from merely presenting concerts to becoming organizations [*sic*] that think of education as central is fairly universal ... now virtually all orchestras have educational wings and have made access central to their very missions.[16]

Alongside increased efforts to widen points of access to the entire community, another key development has been a gradual shift in education programming from passive learning to highly participatory involvement. From the original, passive lecture concert model, orchestras and opera companies today focus on participatory education programmes that offer immediate engagement with making music. These may have a performance focus, such as events allowing students or community musicians to play and sing in side-by-side performances with the orchestra and opera company. Other models involve the audience in education performances through compositions that incorporate singing or body percussion. Some programmes, known as "creative workshops" or "jam sessions," focus on composition and improvisation skills, with participants working with musicians and a workshop leader to create a new piece of music.

Throughout this book, you will notice a strong focus on the outreach work of British orchestras and opera companies. The United Kingdom has been an acknowledged leader in this field now for four decades, stemming from its groundbreaking work in the 1980s and 1990s. This extra experience has allowed the United Kingdom to reach a strong level of both expertise and reflective evaluation of participatory orchestral and opera education programmes. Companies across the world are taking note of the work delivered by British leaders in the field in their efforts to develop a more dynamic approach to their education programming. For example, during its 2014

Australian tour, the LSO delivered a high-profile, creative-based education programme in Sydney involving 130 students from across the state of New South Wales.[17] The LSO, as discussed in the case study focusing on its work, has now identified its strength in outreach and education programming as a key area of interest when planning tours and international partnerships.

Leading orchestras and opera companies internationally have previously taken influence from the British approach with great success: notably the Berlin Philharmonic and the Los Angeles Philharmonic. In 2002, the Berlin Philharmonic engaged with the field of education and outreach under the direction of British conductor Sir Simon Rattle. To assist in the establishment of this programme, Rattle engaged leading British animateur Richard McNicol, working alongside Denise Mellion.[18] The Berlin Philharmonic education and outreach programme rapidly gained worldwide acclaim for the dynamic and creative ways in which it engages with the Berlin community. Australian-born Catherine Milliken was subsequently appointed director of education for the Berlin Philharmonic, and is now contributing to Australian orchestral programming.

Another British leader in the field, Gillian Moore, was instrumental in developing the Los Angeles Philharmonic's education department between 1993 and 1995, after its general manager observed a creative-based London Philharmonic Orchestra education concert in which students were mentored by Sir Harrison Birtwistle.[19] Moore explains that she, together with some of her British colleagues, mentored LA Philharmonic musicians, running projects and training sessions. Moore notes:

> The clear message from the orchestra was that, while their "Neighbourhood Concerts" in far-flung areas of the city were successful, they wanted to develop their outreach programmes in the direction of the hands-on British approach – and they consequently invested a lot of money in importing British expertise.[20]

The Los Angeles Philharmonic education programme is today a world leader in its own right, renowned for the work delivered by its flagship YOLA programme. However, strong collegiate links remain between its activities and those of key British institutions. For example, during its residency at the Barbican Centre the LA Phil has been closely involved in projects run by the Barbican's Creative Learning Department, an international leader in the area of creative music education. The impact on the LA Phil's outreach activities by its dynamic and charismatic chief conductor, Gustavo Dudamel (who was himself influenced by his roots in the El Sistema movement), is also discussed in the LA Phil case study in Chapter 4.

The British influence in orchestral education is revealed in the breadth of countries across which the leading animateurs work. Even as early as 1995, British orchestras had delivered community engagement projects in America, Japan, across Europe, and to the Nordic countries.[21] This

26 *Musicians Offstage*

international work continues: leading British animateur Paul Rissmann, for example, has recently worked with the New York Philharmonic, the Vienna Philharmonic, and with other orchestras in America, Europe, India, Malaysia, and the Middle East. Rissmann works on an ongoing basis with several Australian orchestras and has already made a significant impact on current practice in the field in Australia.

In order to fully understand the current activities of orchestral and opera education departments, the social, financial, and political context in which they operate needs to be understood. This book is written during a period of extreme social and economic turbulence, with the global impact of COVID and the financial impact of the Ukrainian–Russian conflict compounding the disruption of Brexit and, looking a little further back, the global financial crisis. In the 2022 UNESCO Report "Re-Shaping Policies for Creativity: Addressing Culture as a Global Public Good," Audrey Azoulay, director-general of UNESCO, notes:

> The COVID-19 pandemic has led to an unprecedented crisis in the cultural sector. All over the world, museums, cinemas, theatres and concert halls – places of creation and sharing – have closed their doors. In 2020, the income drawn by creators fell by more than 10%, or more than 1 billion euros. What was already a precarious situation for many artists has become unsustainable, threatening creative diversity. At the same time, we have realised how much we need culture, creativity and the diversity of cultural expressions protected by UNESCO's 2005 Convention on the Protection and Promotion of the Diversity of Cultural Expressions. We need the vitality of a sector which employs young people and nurtures innovation and sustainable development. As shown at the height of the crisis, we also need what culture and creation, in all the diversity of their expressions, can do to provide some personal respite and what they can do to unite our societies and forge the road ahead. Today, we must secure culture's rightful place in our recovery plans in order to overcome the crisis. But we also need long-term policies in order to respond to the structural challenges highlighted by the crisis.[22]

The performing arts sector, reliant not only on the whim of the paying public but also on the goodwill of government and corporate sponsorship, has felt the precariousness of its situation particularly keenly. Several American orchestras, for example, have had well-publicised financial troubles in recent years that have necessitated closures, bankruptcies, and pay cuts.

In Australia, the financial situation for symphony orchestras has been additionally complicated by divestment from their original central Australian Broadcasting Company administration, which left orchestras with a larger than foreseen bill. A series of government reports into the financial operations of Australian symphony orchestras revealed discouraging conclusions.

These reports culminated with the Strong Report, which recommended a reduction in player numbers and even possible disbandment of orchestras.[23]

Financial troubles are not the only challenge for orchestras and opera companies at present. They are also battling against an ongoing perception of elitism, with an increasing sense of urgency in their mission to maintain their relevance in today's society. Classical music has long had to battle against preconceptions that it is for the rich, white, and predominantly elderly sectors of society. This is evident in the common representation of orchestral or opera performances in box office cinema – a stuffy, black tie and pearls affair, frequently the recreation of choice for a psychopath or murderer. In order to tackle these image problems, significant efforts are clearly required. As Peter Renshaw, an early advocate for orchestral education programming, commented: "The point is simple. If orchestras fail to confront the future with vision and energy, if they fail to find a creative place within contemporary culture, they will become extinct."[24]

Of course, predictions of the imminent collapse of the symphony orchestra or opera company are not a new phenomenon and will hopefully be proven to be exaggerated and premature over the coming years. In the inimitable words of Charles Rosen: "The death of classical music is perhaps its oldest continuing tradition."[25] At present, however, these concerns are naturally uppermost in the minds of music managers and are an underlying motivation behind much education activity.

The success or failure of education projects in safeguarding the future of symphonic and operatic music will, of necessity, take decades to prove. In the meantime, however, every measure should be taken to evaluate the work being undertaken to ensure that the most effective approaches are being followed. The question of how to evaluate orchestral and opera education work and whether sufficient evaluation is being undertaken is at the forefront of planning within outreach departments.

Recent research has pointed to the value of music education for students from disadvantaged backgrounds, and this is increasingly a consideration for orchestras and opera companies when planning their community programming. For example, the *Champions of Change* report claimed: "learning in and through the arts can help 'level the playing field' for youngsters from disadvantaged circumstances."[26] *Champions of Change* notes the findings by James Cotterall, which he based on data collected from 25,000 students. Cotterall found that "Students with high levels of arts participation outperform 'arts-poor' students by virtually every measure."[27] *Champions of Change* notes that these findings have a clear implication for policy, stating: "If we now know that arts experiences help level the educational playing field for disadvantaged students, as revealed by James Cotterall, then we need to bring more proven arts learning resources to these students."[28]

Education managers interviewed in both Australia and the United Kingdom have revealed a deep commitment to this issue. Several of the case studies reveal a variety of ways that orchestras and opera companies

28 *Musicians Offstage*

are aiming to make a positive contribution to the social equity of their local community. Further significant and rigorous academic research is currently being undertaken on many such programmes, for example on the Sistema-inspired programmes in Melbourne, Los Angeles, Scotland, and Liverpool, as well as the Hallé Symphony's flagship "SHINE on Manchester" programme. This research will be of immense value upon its publication, adding to our understanding of the quantifiable impact of the industry.

During the writing of this book, it became apparent that this is still an industry in a dynamic growth phase, despite the challenges of COVID. As such, there remain several points on which consensus has not yet been reached. In many ways, these points of debate and dissension will drive the industry forward, and the research was undertaken with this in mind, in particular when interviewing key figures.

Notes

1 Caldwell and Vaughan, *Transforming Education through the Arts.*
2 Fiske, *Champions of Change.*
3 Hallam, *The Power of Music.*
4 M. Guhn, S. Emerson, and P. Gouzouasis. "A Population-Level Analysis of Associations Between School Music Participation and Academic Achievement," *Journal of Educational Psychology*, Vol. 112(2), 2020, pp. 308–328.
5 Anita Collins, Rachael Dwyer, and Aden Date. *Music Education: A Sound Investment.* Sydney: The Tony Foundation, 2019.
6 Ibid., p. 52.
7 Irina Petrova. *What Makes Good Music Programs in Schools?* PhD thesis, University of New South Wales, 2012, p. 422.
8 Ernest Fleischmann. "The Orchestra is Dead," *Musical America*, Vol. 107(6), January 1988, pp. 14–16, 27.
9 Ibid., p. 14.
10 Ibid., p. 16.
11 Ernest Fleischmann. *Community of Musicians: Musicians for the Community.* Royal Philharmonic Society Lecture, 2000.
12 Pierre Boulez. "Composer and Audience, Where Are We Now," in Pierre Boulez, *Orientations*. London: Faber & Faber, 1986, p. 467.
13 Ibid., p. 450.
14 Alan Gilbert. *Orchestras in the 21st Century: A New Paradigm.* Royal Philharmonic Society Lecture, 2015.
15 Ibid.
16 Ibid.
17 "LSO Discovery at 25," retrieved from www.lso.co.uk, accessed 15 August 2015.
18 An "animateur" is a British term commonly used to denote an orchestral education leader or presenter, often with additional skills in composition.
19 Gillian Moore. "Do Your Homework Next Time, Mr. Robinson," *The Times UK*, 22 October 1998, p. 47.
20 Ibid.
21 Ibid.
22 Audrey Azoulay, Foreword, *Re-Shaping Policies for Creativity: Addressing Culture as a Global Public Good*. Paris: UNESCO, 2022, p. 5.

Musicians Offstage 29

23 James Strong (chair). *A New Era: Orchestras Report*. Commissioned by the Department of Communications, Information Technology and the Arts, Canberra, 2005.
24 Peter Renshaw. "Orchestras and the Training Revolution," *British Journal of Music Education*, Vol. 9(1), March 1992, p. 70.
25 Charles Rosen. "The Irrelevance of Classical Music," in Charles Rosen, *Critical Entertainment: Music Old and New*. Cambridge, MA: Harvard University Press, 2001, p. 295.
26 Fiske, *Champions of Change*, p. viii.
27 Ibid.
28 Ibid., p. xi.

2 Origins and Development
Understanding the Early History of Orchestral and Opera Education and Community Engagement Programmes

From the early 1920s to the 1970s, the education programmes of orchestras and opera companies across the world developed along similar lines, primarily focused on lecture-format education concerts. The success of these early education activities often rested squarely on the shoulders of one dynamic, politically astute, and ambitious man. In Australia, for example, this figure was Sir Bernard Heinze (1894–1982); in Britain, Sir Robert Mayer (1880–1985); and in America, Walter Damrosch (1862–1950). Sir Mayer was a remarkable man by any standards, not least by the length of his life: he lived to the grand age of 105 years and was active to the end, indeed marrying his secretary when he was 101 and she 51. Mayer demonstrated significant musical ability as a child, learning the piano from the age of 6 at the Mannheim Conservatorium and playing for Johannes Brahms when aged 11.[1] Like many others, however, his parents did not wish him to have a career in the unstable world of music. In 1896, aged just 17, Mayer migrated to London to take up a banking position. He proved to be an astute businessman and made a significant fortune as a merchant of industrial metals, principally copper.[2] Fortunately for musical life in Britain, Mayer decided to use his wealth to become one of the world's leading music philanthropists, establishing the "Robert Mayer Children's Concerts" in 1923 and the "Youth and Music" organisation in 1954.[3]

Both Mayer and Heinze were inspired in their music education efforts by the education concerts led by Walter Damrosch in New York. Heinze was influenced by a meeting with Damrosch in London at Frank Bridge's house, while for Mayer the point of inspiration came in 1919 when he and his wife attended one of Damrosch's concerts during a trip to New York. Mayer later described this as "the experience that changed my life."[4] Mayer returned to London determined to create his own children's concerts season, and the first concert was held in the Central Hall in Westminster in 1923. Following a philosophy that he adhered to throughout his life, Mayer charged a nominal fee of a shilling because, as he later explained, "they wouldn't appreciate it otherwise."[5] The first three concerts were conducted by Adrian Boult, replaced by Malcolm Sargent in 1924, who then conducted all the London concerts until 1939, when they were interrupted by the war. The concerts

DOI: 10.4324/9781003198512-3

Origins and Development 31

grew to be an equal success to those of Damrosch and provided a musical education to generations of British children, including the late Queen and King Charles III.[6]

The ethos of the concerts was succinctly explained by Mayer: "You give children good music, well performed, and explain it, and they can't help but like it."[7] Sargent not only conducted the concerts, but he also acted as compere, and audience participation was used to keep the audience focused and involved. Sargent was criticised for allowing applause between movements, but to this he replied:

> With young children it's absolutely essential they should have a chance, after sitting still for ten minutes, to clap and relieve muscular tension. And why shouldn't they clap if the music's marvellously performed?[8]

The points made here by Sargent are still valid today. The need for young children to be actively involved with the music is at the core of present participatory programming for that age group – these days, of course, the activity has moved well beyond being merely allowed to clap! It must be noted here, however, that etiquette concerning applause during orchestral concerts continues to attract controversy even today. Many feel that the unspoken rule of not clapping between movements of long pieces has a negative effect, contributing to classical music's elitist reputation.

Whole symphonies and concertos were generally avoided in order to keep the children's attention, performing single movements instead. One notable exception to this was a performance by Schnabel, who gave several concerto performances for the Mayers (always without a fee), and said that he would "undertake to do a complete concerto, Mozart's G Major, without boring the children for a moment."[9] All went according to Schnabel's plan, showing the power of a truly great performer to hold the focus of children.

Two programmes at Westminster Central Hall focused on The Messiah, followed by a larger-scale concert at the Royal Albert Hall soon after World War II. For thousands in the audience, this was their first introduction to the piece, and Sargent later spoke of their positive reaction to the music as proof that "It isn't true that young people can't take the best things in life first time. They usually do."[10]

The school concert model established by Mayer and Sargent in the early 20th century was to continue without significant change for the next half century, and was planned along similar lines to those in Australia, Europe, and the United States. In the 1970s and 1980s, however, the next stage of orchestral education projects began to take hold in the United Kingdom, with orchestras becoming more actively involved in partnerships with schools and the community.

A shift in UK government policy concerning arts education was key to this development. In 1965, Jennie Lee, the first government minister for the arts, wrote *A Policy for the Arts: The First Steps*, the foundation document

32 Origins and Development

for many successive government papers concerning the arts and education.[11] Roy Shaw was another key figure in establishing support for arts education. Secretary-general of the Arts Council from 1978 through to 1983, Shaw was a passionate crusader for mass education and believed that the Arts Council's major role was to ensure that excellence was accessible by all.[12] In 1983, the first Arts Council education policy was created, which set clear education targets for all funded organisations.[13] Sue Robertson, former Arts Council education liaison officer, reflects on this development:

> The Arts Council stated that it would require all its funded organisations to engage in some form of education work and it also set a budget for education, which it used on a rolling basis with the art forms. That was a big change.[14]

The terms could hardly have been spelt out more clearly: if an organisation is seeking to apply for or retain funding, it must demonstrate that significant effort is being made in the field of community engagement and education. This was to set in motion the proliferation of orchestral education and community engagement work in the United Kingdom throughout the 1980s and into the 1990s, which effectively created a new area of employment for musicians and educators.

A further important development was marked in 1986 when the Arts Council appointed 14 animateurs to partnership posts.[15] While only three of these made it past the trial period, the role of the animateur has gone on to become a strong part of the UK's music education landscape and a viable career path for both composers and performers. An animateur's role in orchestral and opera education programmes is to present concerts; however, often they are also composers. A key skill for animateurs is the ability to guide students in improvisation or composition workshops, and their impact on orchestral and opera education work is a feature of this book.

Richard McNicol is one of the United Kingdom's most high-profile animateurs and has been pivotal to the development of current orchestral education practice. McNicol remains an international leader in the field, recently establishing the Berlin Philharmonic's Education Department at Sir Simon Rattle's invitation and now leading the education programmes for the Klavier-Festival Ruhr. McNicol's career has covered a diverse range of the activities available to a professional musician: he was a flautist in several leading London orchestras, after working as a school teacher. As a freelance London flautist, McNicol performed in several schools' concerts and became dissatisfied with the way in which they were operated and planned.[16]

One issue is that school concerts are often the first engagement offered by orchestras to young emerging conductors, and are frequently seen as a way of "trying out" a new conductor in what is regarded by management as a low-risk concert. Of course, to the conductor this concert is seen as their chance to showcase their skills, so it is only natural that their preoccupation

Origins and Development 33

is with showcasing their technical and interpretative abilities rather than on creating a concert with repertoire tailored to the age of the audience. The ideal scenario would entail using a conductor for school concerts who already has a regular role with the orchestra, or at least has been chosen for their skills as a presenter and educator. It is unfortunately rare to see a chief conductor in charge of an education concert, with Leonard Bernstein, Sir Simon Rattle, and Gustavo Dudamel being notable exceptions.

Another issue was that concerts were too passive, with children required to sit and listen with no interactive element. Today, most orchestras work to ensure that their education work has a highly participatory element in order to fully engage the children. It is generally recognised that if an orchestra is looking to create a meaningful and positive connection with a child then it is imperative that the work is both of the highest standard and engaging. However, in the early 20th century, a much more passive approach was common and McNicol was pivotal in achieving significant change in orchestral education practice. McNicol began organising and delivering a highly participatory, creative education programme which launched the child directly into the inner workings of a composition. McNicol was a true trail blazer at this stage, as he wryly comments: "I was the only orchestral player doing it, so I was the best in the world. I was also the worst in the world. I was the only one!"[17]

In 1976, McNicol approached John Stevens, then the chief inspector of the Inner London Education Authority, with the idea of radically reformatting school concerts to produce a highly interactive experience.[18] Like many at the time, McNicol was inspired by John Paynter's work *Sound and Silence*, with its emphasis on the importance of participation and composition.[19] The impact of groundbreaking music educationalists such as Paynter and Aston on the development of music education principles and practice is further investigated in Chapter 6.

In 1977, McNicol formed the Apollo Trust in partnership with Stevens, an organisation that facilitated participatory, creative education work between orchestras and schools. The groundbreaking activities of the Apollo Trust established a new, more interactive, and dynamic format of education concert. Many of its projects included a piece composed by the children and performed in the final concert, modelled on a piece in the orchestra's repertoire, a format still commonly used today in the United Kingdom and increasingly taking root internationally.[20]

In 1992, McNicol joined the London Symphony Orchestra (LSO) with its newly established Discovery Department, which remains arguably the most dynamic orchestral education department internationally. His philosophy at the LSO centred on partnerships, co-operation, and excellence in performance, as discussed further in the following case study.

While McNicol was pivotal to this period of development, other key players were emerging in the classical music outreach field in the United Kingdom. These included Gillian Moore, leading groundbreaking projects

34   Origins and Development

with the London Sinfonietta; Kathryn McDowell, education manager at the Scottish Chamber Orchestra in the 1980s and now the managing director of the London Symphony Orchestra; Katie Tearle and Stephen Langridge working together in community opera projects; and composers including Sir Peter Maxwell Davies, James MacMillan, and Jonathon Dove. Each of these figures has continued to shape the progress and direction of the classical music landscape in profound ways across the subsequent years. Their work is analysed and discussed in detail further throughout this book.

Here, McNicol acknowledges the sector-wide growth in the 1980s:

> During the 1980s the climate changed. Orchestras throughout Britain began to look critically at the educational provision they were offering. Simon Rattle, whilst principal conductor of the CBSO, became so convinced of the importance of education that he immersed himself in the educational activities of his orchestra. There were no bored expressions on the faces of those players, none of the shoddy ensemble and suspect tuning that comes from orchestras full of non-members for low-priority concerts. Most importantly of all, the repertoire was exciting.[21]

McNicol makes particular mention here of the impact of Sir Simon Rattle. Throughout his career, Rattle has continued to raise the profile of orchestral education programming, and has demonstrated the positive impact that a chief conductor can make in this area.

While, as McNicol acknowledges above, many orchestras have devoted their energy and ingenuity to their education work, the London Symphony Orchestra has been internationally acknowledged as a leader in the field since the 1990s. For this reason, we now analyse the key points in the development of the LSO Discovery Department.

Development of LSO Discovery

The LSO Discovery Department is an international leader in the field of orchestral education and outreach. In this chapter, the early development of this department is analysed; the current practice of LSO Discovery is discussed in Chapter 4. Firstly, the structure of the orchestra itself needs to be considered. As a self-governed orchestra since its origin in 1904, LSO musicians have always had the ability to manage their own careers and development to a greater degree than those in a contracted orchestra. Thus, the choice to pursue education and outreach work is one that has grown organically from within the players' committee and not a decision imposed from above. Kathryn McDowell CBE, the current general manager of the LSO, comments on this point:

> One clear example of how the LSO's structure has driven its success, particularly in recent years, is through the LSO's community and

Origins and Development 35

education programme LSO Discovery ... Every member of the LSO participates in one or more of LSO Discovery's projects and these are seen by the musicians as complementary to their role with the LSO ... It is unlikely that LSO Discovery would have grown to its current scale without this depth of commitment by the members of the Orchestra and it could easily have been no more than a minor ancillary activity rather than a core part of the LSO's work.[22]

While there is no doubt that the players' commitment has been key to Discovery's growth, the impact of key management personnel must also be acknowledged. Kathryn McDowell, as managing director of the orchestra since 2005, has had a major role in supporting and steering the orchestra's outreach activities. Indeed, McDowell had an impact on the LSO even before taking up her role with them, with her activities as education manager at the Scottish Chamber Orchestra influencing the interest in outreach by LSO musicians. While McDowell's impact is more fully discussed in the case study of the LSO in Chapter 4, the decisions made by two past managers have also left a lasting legacy for the orchestra. The first of these was Ernest Fleischmann, appointed as general manager in November 1959, a post he held for eight years before moving to the Los Angeles Philharmonic.[23] Fleischmann's provocative and influential ideas regarding the future of the symphony orchestra have been outlined in Chapter 1. In summary, his philosophy was that orchestral musicians need to be much more flexible in their skills and in the way they approach their work: that it is not sufficient to solely present concert performances, no matter how superb they may be. While this viewpoint is today widely accepted, it was quite radical in the mid-20th century. Having such a dynamic and forward-thinking manager in the 1960s clearly impacted on the development of the LSO.

Sir Clive Gillinson, general manager from 1984 to 2005, also made a lasting impact on the orchestra.[24] Gillinson's contribution to music in the United Kingdom through his work at the LSO was recognised with a knighthood in 2005 upon his departure for Carnegie Hall. Gillinson's 21 year tenure left two significant legacies to the education arm of the organisation. The first was the establishment of an education policy and the Discovery Department in 1988, setting in place the beginnings of today's organisation. The second was in pushing through the controversial and costly renovation of St Luke's church in Islington into an education and outreach centre, with building completed in 2003, two years prior to Gillinson's move to America. Norman Lebrecht has commented on the impact of both Fleischmann and Gillinson on the LSO in rethinking the role of the orchestral musicians and the organisation as a whole.[25] The LSO has the flexibility to form a variety of ensembles, from intimate chamber music groups to a full-scale symphony orchestra, and the musicians work together to engage with their community.

Gillinson certainly made a very wise choice with the initial animateur appointed to shape the programme, Richard McNicol. As previously

36   Origins and Development

discussed, McNicol was instrumental in introducing a participatory, creative element to orchestral education programming. Through his dynamic work, and his mentoring of younger animateurs including Paul Rissmann, Gareth Malone, Rachel Leach, and Hannah Conway, McNicol's impact on the industry has been immense. In the Association of British Orchestras' *The Workbook, Volume 2*, published in 2000, McNicol gives insightful detail into his methods of planning and delivering education concerts. Some key points made by McNicol are to choose music that is varied and demanding; to concentrate on one or two key aspects of the music; to prepare the audience in advance through teachers' sessions and workshops; and to choose a presenter who is part of the performance.[26]

In order to maintain the strength of its animateur tradition, the LSO established a training programme known as the Edward Heath Assistant Animateur Scheme. Paul Rissmann (1996), Rachel Leach (1998), and prominent choral director and media personality Gareth Malone (2001) are three animateurs who started their career through the scheme.[27] The assistant animateur scheme has enabled the Discovery team to build on the strong traditions set in place by McNicol. By getting the department off to a good start, development then followed on naturally, with funding attracted as the LSO education team's reputation continued to grow. Alongside the importance of laying down a strong foundation for a programme are the LSO's ability to forge and maintain strategic partnerships. Another major contributor to the success is the venues in which the Discovery team work.

Richard McNicol focused on providing a highly engaging and inspiring experience to the LSO education audiences. According to McNicol:

> First and foremost, our young guests must be riveted by the experience of coming to a concert and hearing a great orchestra performing live. We must offer them first-class music superbly played, and the way it is presented must fire the imagination of each individual listener. Each child must feel personally involved and must go away feeling that the concert was put on especially for him or her.[28]

Paul Rissmann has worked with the LSO for 20 years as an animateur and has thus witnessed the growth of the Discovery Department. Rissmann echoes the importance placed on quality by Ackrill and McNicol. However, he also credits the flexibility of the programme as key to its success:

> I think retaining artistic quality is the most important thing that an orchestral education programme can do. It needs to be delivered by the musicians in the orchestra and it is ok to start small but to do things that are outstanding, that are world class, rather than churn out a whole string of events that are underfunded or rehearsed. It should be about producing world-class work that stands alongside an orchestra's aspirations for an evening performance. I've watched the programme grow

Origins and Development 37

and seen the type of work that we do change as funding streams change and requirements for engagement have changed and the curriculum has changed. So the programme has had to adapt massively to reflect those things.[29]

As Rissmann notes, all orchestral education departments are inextricably linked to developments in policy and education philosophies. The keys to LSO Discovery's continued growth across successive decades are an unwavering commitment to quality alongside a willingness to adapt to changing circumstances.

The venues in which the LSO presents its education and community engagement programmes are also key to its success, and here both Fleischmann and Gillinson made pivotal decisions. The location of the LSO and the Guildhall School of Music and Drama (GSMD) in the same complex gives them a unique basis for their partnership. This relationship began in the late 1960s, when the LSO was selected to be the resident orchestra in the proposed Barbican complex, anecdotally outbidding the Philharmonia Orchestra at the last minute thanks to Fleischmann's backroom dealing.[30] When the centre was opened in 1982, the two organisations began to explore ways in which to connect with each other and the local east London community.

The LSO's other key venue is LSO St Luke's, the UBS, and LSO Music Education Centre, which opened in March 2003 in a church in Islington and is today the venue for most LSO Discovery programmes. Having a venue specifically tailored for education work allows the LSO to establish a strong connection with its community, and allows it to schedule regular activities and rehearsals without needing to hire a venue. Clive Gillinson gives an insight into the benefits that St Luke's brings to the LSO: "It is vital. Music education needs to be a special experience ... In St Luke's every aspect of the experience becomes a thrill for the children."[31]

Gillinson commented that St Luke's allows for stronger connections between the LSO and neighbouring Bangladeshi and Turkish communities, and expressed his hopes that St Luke's can become an "interface" between the orchestra and local people: more than simply a place where classes are held. Gillinson explains: "We have staked the stability of our organisation on our beliefs ... an orchestra has not only a responsibility to its art, but also to society."[32]

This is acknowledged on the LSO website, which speaks of its aim to work in partnership with local communities, and provide long-term opportunities for the local community to join in.[33] The decision to renovate the dilapidated old church and turn it into a state-of-the-art performance and education venue was, with the benefit of hindsight, visionary. When one considers that it came at a time when the LSO was not in a comfortable position financially, the bravery of the decision is even more striking. Originally budgeted at 17 million pounds, the costs grew to 18 million, creating significant

38   *Origins and Development*

financial stress on the LSO even with the support of funders, UBS. Gillinson reflects on the financial implications of the building project:

> We've had a really tough three or four years because in making the decision to create St Luke's, we put colossal demands on the orchestra. For an organisation that turns over 11m pounds as we do, to raise 17m pounds was a huge undertaking.[34]

This interview took place following Gillinson's departure from the LSO in 2005. Further in the interview, he observes that St Luke's was at that date breaking even and that the deficit was almost cleared. However, even before the financial impact of the build had been resolved, the benefits of the decision were clear. Public perception of the project was positive, with strong media coverage commenting that the venture marked the LSO as a leader in the orchestral field. The following is typical of British press coverage of the opening of St Luke's: "LSO St Luke's is a vision of the future for the symphony orchestra. It is the kind of move that makes most London orchestras look like stick-in-the-muds, adrift in the thinking of the last century."[35]

In the decade following the opening of St Luke's, the LSO Discovery Department has continued to grow, becoming a key element of the orchestra's identity. The current activity and practice of the LSO Discovery Department is discussed in detail throughout this book, revealing the legacy created by the pivotal early decisions discussed above.

Development of Opera Education Programmes

Two of the "big guns" of the opera world – London's Royal Opera House (ROH), Covent Garden and New York's Metropolitan Opera – have both been engaged in innovative education programming since the 1980s, with an interesting degree of cross-inspiration between the two through this period. However, the seeds of this high-profile work in fact rested on the groundbreaking work developed at the Seattle Opera Company by JoAnn Forman and Bruce Taylor in the 1970s. While working as education coordinator for the Seattle Opera Company in 1976, Forman and her colleague Taylor were approached by a local school principal with the request to make opera accessible for his students. He wanted his students to engage with opera, but found that watching an opera production was not holding their attention. At this stage, the primary mode of opera education in Seattle – and worldwide – involved exactly that; inviting school students to watch a production in the main auditorium. Forman and Taylor took up the challenge with gusto and, thanks to the support of an open-minded school, they took a radically immersive and creative approach. They created a new opera company – staffed entirely by students. As Forman recalls: "Initially, the reaction was one of scepticism and disbelief. Yet the school staff gradually

Origins and Development 39

became sufficiently curious to see whether their students could actually do what appeared to them to be the impossible."[36]

The performance, which involved 40 students aged between 10 and 11, was a resounding success.

> In only nine weeks these ten and eleven year old students had written an original libretto, composed a score, designed and built costumes, sets and lights, created and distributed publicity and press releases and auditioned, rehearsed and performed the production.[37]

The aims of the programme have been eloquently expressed:

> We want to create and nurture an atmosphere in which direct, firsthand involvement in the arts can take root and flourish. Opera is often alienating because it has no perceived relationship to students' experience. Yet when children put together original material about a subject of their own choosing and create their own performances from start to finish, they are better equipped to respond to, appreciate and understand opera in a professional context. In addition, they reap other personal rewards along the way. We now have persuasive evidence that early exposure through sustained and supervised participation in the creative process enables a child to identify with the arts experience and gives the arts a familiar, personal meaning that will in all likelihood endure.[38]

Following the success of the creative programme in Seattle, Forman and Taylor brought their pioneering ideas to New York's Metropolitan Opera Guild. Now known as "Creating Original Opera" (COO), their programme was given a strong platform, and by 1980 Forman was appointed education director for the Met. The programme was initially delivered in a small number of New York City schools, including the Harlem School for the Arts. The projects quickly began to receive significant media attention, with the *New York Times* publishing an article celebrating the work of the 30 students who collectively created an opera together in the Harlem School for the Arts' summer session. By 1985, a documentary film had been made on the programme by Gene Searchinger, titled "Young Wonders Incorporated," which tracked the creation of an opera by 45 fifth- and sixth-grade students in New York's PS.75. Their opera, created over eight weeks with the assistance of three staff from the Met Opera Guild and their school teachers, was titled "Decisions" and focused on how making decisions impacts children's lives.

After eight years of running the COO programme as an artist residency from the Met in schools, the programme broadened to include teacher training in the process and format. The teacher training module, first initiated in 1983, enabled further expansion and reach for the format, as well as enabling the programme to be linked more closely to the school curriculum.

40 Origins and Development

In addition to connecting with 50 states across the United States, the programme began to make an international impact at this point, with one particularly influential contact with the Royal Opera House, Covent Garden, London.

The ROH had been running dance and opera activities with young people since 1946; however, in the early 1980s there was a substantial upscaling of its education programming. From 1983, the company began running a year-round education programme of school performances, lecture demonstrations, special projects, and courses for teachers. In 1985, the lecture demonstration programme was piloted, exploring the theme of "What Is Opera?," delivering 60 sessions each year.

In 1985, a further significant moment occurred when the Royal Opera House Education Department facilitated a teacher professional development session delivered by Forman's team from the Metropolitan Opera Guild. The professional development sessions guided British teachers in the process of enabling school students to effectively run their own opera companies. Forman and Taylor's concept was intended to develop pupil ownership over the concept and delivery of the opera, including writing the script. The UK education scene was a fertile ground for creative-based immersion work, with its strong focus on creativity. In the United Kingdom, no fewer than 200 creative opera projects were delivered between 1985 and 1997 in primary schools following the six-day immersive course. Projects also took place between 1995 and 1997 in several other European countries as a result of developing the project for the European Union's Kaleidoscope programme.

In 1989, the Metropolitan Opera published the principles for undertaking the creative opera project in a comprehensive 346-page book titled *Creating Original Opera*.[39] Forman was the project director for this curriculum resource guide, which covered all stages of the ambitious programme. The resource guide provides the steps necessary for the children to develop the skills needed to facilitate all the varied roles required in an opera company. The children would act as set designers, costume designers, makeup artists, librettists, composers, performers, electricians, publicists, stage managers, and front of house. Each of these roles is taken seriously in the resource guide, with an outline of the simple set of steps required for the child to gain confidence and knowledge.

By 1992, the programme had connected with over 250,000 schoolchildren and 200 school teachers internationally. One particularly significant connection was made with Spain, through the work of educator Mary Ruth McGinn. During the intense nine-day session in which she learned the format of the creative opera programme, she found lasting inspiration in the work and the educational philosophies connected with it, of project-based learning and learning through experience. In 2006, McGinn developed a similar programme in Spain, which continues strongly today, with McGinn returning to Madrid on a bi-annual basis to train local educators

Origins and Development 41

in the format. More than 500 teachers and 14,000 students have now participated in the Spanish programme, known as LOVA ("La Opera, un Vehiculo de Aprendizaje," which translates as "Opera, A Vehicle for Learning").[40] Other similar programmes are the UK's "Write an Opera," Utah's "Opera by Children," and "Create and Produce" (Opera America). Across America, however, the programme has significantly diminished from its peak. This can be seen as a result of a shift in educational philosophies, the move towards standardised testing, and a less flexible approach to school timetabling.

Scottish Opera has been another leader in the education and outreach opera field since the 1970s. It was the earliest company in Europe to form an education and outreach department in 1971, under the leadership of the founder of the company, Sir Alexander Gibson. Gibson felt that it was hugely important for Scotland to have its own national opera company, and for it to serve the people. In 2021, Scottish Opera celebrated 50 years of outreach and education, retaining international attention for its continued innovation and excellence in the area. Jane Davidson, the current director of the Scottish Opera Outreach and Education Department, has worked with the department since 1984, bringing a unique level of experience and expertise to her role.

Davidson explains:

> Gibson wanted Scotland to have its own opera company, he felt it is incredibly important and is seen as a very, very important symbol of Scottish culture. From the beginning there was also a focus on accessibility, to get small scale work out into the islands and Highlands and all the remote parts of the country. So we've always toured, unlike a lot of European houses – we're serving the people of Scotland and a lot of them don't live in urban areas.[41]

In 2017, Davidson was awarded an MBE in honour of her work with the department and continued innovation and commitment to the Scottish community. In a wide-ranging interview with the author, Davidson gave an insight into the challenges that she and her colleagues had experienced through the early decades of her work. In comments frequently made by pioneers in the field, Davidson revealed that it was challenging to have the work taken seriously within the art form, to have access to the required resources, and that singers were often lacking in the skills the work required.

Nevertheless, Davidson has had a significant impact on the development of opera education and community engagement through her decades at Scottish Opera. An early strength of Scottish Opera was in its delivery of small-scale operas for primary school–aged children in schools across the country. Davidson has now commissioned over 30 of these works. There was always a participatory angle to these performances. Davidson explains:

42 Origins and Development

The original concept basically was a little miniature opera, a 25 to 30 minute long piece, and the children would learn the songs in advance. Then they were workshopped by a team of facilitators, singers and drama facilitators and it was all brought together in a day and costumed and performed for their friends and relatives.[42]

Davidson took the participatory and learning aspects of this style of programme a step further through developing learning activities matched to each commission based on the theme of the work. In this way, the opera project delivered strong musical outcomes for the children, in addition to developing their skills across a wide range of areas. Davidson explains:

Since the early 1990s I was looking at it, thinking it's a fantastic tool for integrated learning. At that point, one of the many changes in the Scottish education system that was manifesting itself was looking at the concept of integrated learning and how valuable that could be. That was just the very, very beginning of people realising that expressive arts could do so much in terms of connectivity, linking concepts and ideas and also providing children with discursive skills, being able to communicate their ideas. Engaging with that kind of work was helping that enormously. And so I began to develop associated education materials, so that when the children were learning the songs for the piece, they would also look at the theme of the piece. The theme, of course, could be anything – it could be science, technology, history, languages, folk stories. You could align a whole series of activities and tasks that could be done so that the whole experience was quite a holistic experience.[43]

Davidson gives an example of this cross-disciplinary education model, the "Big Bang Show," which featured three groups of characters representing nuclear, renewable, and fossil fuel. The grouping of characters into three groups was a design feature of the operas, so that three different classes of children could participate. Each group of characters was led by an opera singer playing the part of an "energy" star: Gaia, Einstein, and Scottish scientist Lord Kelvin. Davidson is surprised that this model has not been more widely adopted internationally. The Scottish Opera team has, however, had an international impact, with high-profile projects in Ireland and Finland providing examples of their cross-national collaborative skills.

The Finnish National Opera (FNO) has adopted the Scottish Opera interactive and interdisciplinary approach. Davidson has worked with the FNO several times; however, their most high-profile collaboration was in 2000 when they collaborated on a project "The Turn of the Tide." Not to be confused with the orchestral education commission of the same name, this project was co-commissioned between the Helsinki Department of Education and North Ayrshire Council. It had a focus on nationalistic epic tales, featuring the Finnish national epic the "Kalevala," and Scottish

Origins and Development 43

historical events such as the Viking Battle of Largs in 1263. This project was delivered in two very different formats: a nimble, 30-minute production with piano accompaniment that could tour schools in both Finland and Scotland, and a two-act opera, fully orchestrated, which was performed with a cast of over a thousand at the Irving Maritime Museum and at London's Millennium Dome.[44] While the Scottish Opera model was highly influential to the Finnish National Opera team, Davidson also explains that the Finnish National Opera influenced her work. The Finnish National Opera's first theme for its version of the Scottish Opera's interactive children's opera was based on the war with Russia – a much bleaker and more poignant choice of topic than the typical Scottish Opera theme at that time. This encouraged Davidson to explore more challenging topics with her commissions, in addition to more humorous topics.

The connection between Scottish Opera and Ireland also created a significant impact on community arts engagement in both countries. In the early 1990s, Scottish Opera was commissioned by the Northern Irish Arts Council to create a community opera project working with schools on both sides of the border, on the eve of the "Good Friday" Agreement. The project, named "Crossing Borders," was an artistic means to reconnect these fractured communities. Davidson recalls:

> We did a series of community operas in quite remote cross border communities in Ireland. We were developing stories that came from the community with a cast of people who came from both sides of the community, and using it literally as a means, a tool for social change, social interaction. We performed the pieces on both sides of the borders, and we did have people saying "this is the first time I've come on the roads since they were blocked in 1922". So that kind of work, I think, is really powerful. We've always had a massive social interaction strand in our work.[45]

Scottish Opera's early strength in community opera engagement owes a considerable amount to the energy of Davidson. However, Davidson, in turn, recognises the impact of the Craigmillar Festival, which developed in Edinburgh over the 1970s and 1980s in connection with the Edinburgh Festival and the Edinburgh Fringe. The Craigmillar Festival is recognised as a blueprint for community engagement, rising from grassroots energy. The origin of the Craigmillar Festival is explained here by Andrew Crummy, showing the power of the individual in shaping social and cultural change:

> One of the key starting points of the Craigmillar Festival Society and, therefore, of the Scottish Community Arts Movement was in the early 1960s after a mother, Helen Crummy, asked the headmaster of Peffermill School if her eldest son could learn to play the violin. The headmaster, Mr Lyall, refused her on the grounds that "it takes all our time to teach

44 *Origins and Development*

these children the three R's". Helen went back to the mothers' group, who were very angry at first and could have made the usual response and gone back to complain to Mr Lyall. Instead, over a period of time, they decided to take the unusual and bold step of organising their own festival to showcase the talent of local children ... "The Festival", as it became known locally, grew very quickly, showcasing not only the children of the area but anyone who had a creative talent. The violin story was in fact a historical step that would start an annual festival that has lasted up to the present day and also powerfully demonstrated an attitude of self-help that would start the regeneration of Craigmillar.[46]

Scottish Opera began to work with the Craigmillar Festival early in its development, a partnership that strengthened the social focus of the opera company and cemented its reputation as a groundbreaker in education and engagement.

Davidson tells of the formation of the networking collaboration, the European Network for Opera and Dance Education (RESEO), as a turning point for her and her colleagues in opera education and outreach. RESEO provided a sounding board, a supportive community for individuals working in silos in a challenging and uncharted field of work, and structure to their work and development. Glyndebourne Opera Company has also had a strong impact on the development of opera education in the United Kingdom, both through a strong relationship with RESEO and through the activities delivered since its education department was established in 1986. Glyndebourne's pioneering work in opera education and outreach, first led by Katie Tearle OBE, as well as the current programmes of Glyndebourne under the direction of Lucy Perry, head of learning and engagement, is discussed further in Chapter 4. Further programmes delivered by Scottish Opera are also discussed throughout the book, with particular reference to its work in the health field.

Early Orchestral Education Work in Australia

The early development of orchestral education in Australia is inextricably linked with the career of Australian conductor Sir Bernard Heinze. Such was the impact of Heinze (1894–1982) that his biographer, Therese Radic, declared:

> Heinze was responsible for the fact that we have state symphony orchestras, the ABC concert systems (in schools, youth, celebrity and subscription series), and organisations able to promote effectively the creation and practice of Australian music and to educate musically a new generation. Directly or indirectly nothing in Australian musical life has been untouched by his presence.[47]

In 1923, soon after his return home to Melbourne following a decade of study and war service in Europe, Heinze attended a performance of the

Origins and Development 45

Melbourne University Conservatorium's Symphony Orchestra. He found the concert poorly attended and to his ears the playing quite amateur. Heinze commented:

> When the orchestra came out to play a little before 8 o'clock there would have been enough people in the hall to fill two rows ... Then the orchestra played (remember the sound of the Berlin Philharmonic under that god of a man, Furtwangler, was ringing in my ears) and made a terrible, amateur sound. I could not believe my ears; it was so different from what I had expected to hear from something called a symphony orchestra. This was, of course, 1923. There was not one professional orchestra in Australia and there was not to be one for many years to come.[48]

Heinze then made it his firm intention to do what he could to improve the status and standard of music in Australia, aiming to achieve this through the establishment of children's concerts. While staying in London at Frank Bridge's house, he met the conductor of the New York Philharmonic Orchestra, Walter Damrosch, who had instigated a very successful programme of children's concerts in New York. Heinze later recalled this conversation with Damrosch:

> Damrosch said "New York is absolutely alight with interest in symphonic music and I've brought this about in a rather wonderful way – by giving children's concerts." Bridge asked what children's concerts were and Damrosch replied, "Just that – children's concerts: orchestral concerts especially for children in Carnegie Hall. The place is crowded every time we give one. The effect is showing up in audiences for our main public concerts by the New York Philharmonic. We are selling them out".[49]

Damrosch (1862–1950) was a German-born conductor and composer who migrated to America. He was greatly admired as a music educator, and was the conductor of the Symphony Society of New York Orchestra from 1903 to 1928 (this orchestra merged with the New York Philharmonic in 1928). In 1926, he inaugurated a series of radio broadcasts, which later aired as the "NBC Music Appreciation Hour" throughout the United States and Canada from 1928 to 1942. These were a very popular series of radio lectures on classical music aimed at students and broadcast during school hours. The radio network provided textbooks and workshops to school teachers, an initiative that would be taken up some decades later in both Australia and the United Kingdom.[50] He was also an innovator in terms of tailoring his concerts to the age group of the audience. While Walter Damrosch is the best-known musician in his family owing to these radio broadcasts, his brother, Frank Damrosch, also devoted his life to music

46 Origins and Development

education. Frank Damrosch was the superintendent of music in New York's public schools and also organised and conducted symphony concerts for children.

By late 1924, Heinze had secured 76 pounds sterling of funding from Sir James Barrett, chairman of the Finance Committee of the Melbourne Conservatorium, in order to stage his own children's concert, and the date was set for 11 October. This initial concert, however, was nearly a dismal failure. Two days before the concert, only 60 seats were sold, and Heinze discovered that the head teachers had been throwing out his information leaflets unread. Heinze borrowed Barrett's car and set off to visit every school he could get to in the time left. By the day of the concert he had found a full audience.[51] This story illustrates some of Heinze's most valuable character traits: his charm, his self-confidence, and his tenacity.

The following five years were a pivotal period both for Heinze's career and for the development of classical music in Australia. In 1925, he was appointed Ormond professor of music at Melbourne University and, in 1929, the director in general of music for the new broadcasting service. He campaigned for the Australian Broadcasting Corporation (ABC) to finance orchestras in each capital city, ostensibly to broadcast but also, Heinze intended, to perform in concert to local audiences. While the establishment of the ABC orchestras became the foundation of all symphonic music making in Australia, this inherent conflict between their role in a broadcasting organisation and their desire to deliver live concerts created a tension that grew until their eventual divestment from the ABC.

In the 1920s, however, all remained new, exciting, and dynamic. Others before had attempted to start a series of children's concerts, including Benno Scherek, Zelman, and Arundel Orchard, but Heinze was the first to make a success of the concept. In June 1925, Heinze partnered with the education department and from that date the concerts were well attended. The audiences were soon in their thousands, and by the early 1940s he had conducted more than 500 children's concerts and reached over 80,000 children. Throughout this period of growth, Heinze continued to promote his cause in the media, for instance in articles such as this, published in the *Sydney Morning Herald* in March 1930: "No educational institution is fulfilling its function unless it promotes the artistic development of the young minds under its care ... The plea in Australia, when one suggests these developments, is almost invariably that there is no money."[52]

Heinze makes the point that every school can, however, find the necessary funds to support the physical education of its students. These words are still relevant 85 years later, and indeed could believably have been spoken by a music education advocate of today such as Richard Gill.

Heinze's belief that children's concerts could build audiences was soon shown to be justified. In 1924, there were only 67 subscribers to Melbourne's University Symphony series. By 1937, however, the ABC's Annual Report to Parliament showed that subscribers were more numerous in Melbourne

Origins and Development 47

than in the other capital cities. In 1937, there were 2,094 subscribers in Melbourne, 923 in Sydney, 197 in Brisbane, 161 in Adelaide, and 176 in Perth.[53] In these early stages, education concerts unashamedly aimed to create audiences; today's orchestral education personnel prefer to see this as a potential benefit of their work but no longer the primary aim, as noted in the introduction.

Heinze's ability to promote his activities and views through the media, in both print and broadcast, was a key strength that helped him throughout his career. In 1942, with the children's concerts under threat of cancellation owing to war-related safety fears, Heinze proclaimed:

> The concerts for young people are in some ways of greater importance than the big symphonic concerts, for they are directed towards the future ... These young people are the audiences of the future, and they will come to concerts with a knowledge of music to back up what they want to hear.[54]

Making concert programmes relevant, exciting, and accessible to differing age groups has long been a chief preoccupation for orchestral education personnel. Heinze attempted to address this issue in the early 1940s, troubled by some signs of inattention in the audiences. He conducted one of the earliest orchestral education evaluation surveys, asking for letters from audience members in 1941 and again in 1942. Criticism included that the concerts were too programmatic and too thematic. The question of the extent to which concerts should be themed is still relevant today, and indeed is an issue that is still debated by current education managers. Clearly at this point, the concerts were not adjusted to different age groups, one complaint being that they had "to hear the same or similar talks on the orchestra and such topics time and time again."[55] Soon after these surveys, Heinze started to make age-differentiated programmes and by 1947 a series of "youth concerts," with a higher age limit of 25, were established. In a radio interview from this period, broadcast in 1946, Heinze spoke of his views on the relative benefits of educating children in music as opposed to adults, also speaking of his belief in their greater receptivity towards contemporary music:

> I have even come to believe that adult education in music, in the strict sense, can hope for only a partial success. The adult who is sufficiently interested in music to devote part of his time to it, usually knows what he wants and isn't inclined to listen to anything else. The intolerance of the average concert-goer for modern music is an example of this, and is in strange contrast with the eagerness with which my school audiences listen and write to me about the music of contemporary composers.[56]

In more recent times, the London Sinfonietta's education outreach has had particular success in helping young audiences understand and connect with

48 *Origins and Development*

contemporary music. Many orchestral education directors may, however, dispute Heinze's claim as to the lack of adult interest in discovering new genres of music. Several orchestras, including the Sydney Symphony and the London Symphony orchestras, have developed highly popular education programmes focused on adult learners.

In the same 1946 radio address, Heinze spoke of his wish for greater co-operation between the education department and the ABC, in order to maximise the benefits of the children's concerts:

> The children's orchestral concerts would gain in usefulness by a close co-operation between the Education Department and the Commission. With such a policy the programmes could be more progressive and instructive, particularly were it possible to ensure that the same group of children attended a series of successive concerts.[57]

The importance of effective co-operation between orchestras and the education department has been a constant focus throughout the development of the field. It is currently of particular relevance in Australia as the new national curriculum is established in schools across the country, presenting fresh ways for orchestras to link with school syllabus requirements.

Youth concerts, established in 1947, were extremely popular for over a decade. In his study of this period in the history of the Sydney Symphony Orchestra (SSO), Philip Sametz states:

> The popularity of the series was enormous, partly because the adult subscription concerts were becoming so hard to subscribe to, partly because the Youth Concerts were cheaper (sixteen shillings for a season ticket) and partly because the forward looking aura of Goossens' leadership gave the SSO an energy to which young people responded.[58]

The youth concert concept had clearly tapped into the young adult's search for the new, exciting, and slightly subversive. At the height of their popularity, the audience needed to queue overnight. For many, this only added to the glamour of the process, much in the same way that today's tennis fans willingly camp out in a soggy British summer to claim tickets to Wimbledon. The promotion of the concerts, largely from young people themselves, kept the freshness of the organisation. In recent years, some orchestras have similarly experimented with letting university students market youth concerts to their peers with positive results. Crucially, the soloists and conductors were kept at the same standard as those performing in the main series concerts, and programming was kept on the progressive side, featuring composers such as Bloch, Chausson, Arthur Bliss, and Schoenberg. The success of the youth concerts also helped to revitalise the mainstream audiences. In 1950, conductor Joseph Post declared: "I preach the gospel of these concerts [the youth concerts] very strongly ... I think

Origins and Development 49

they are mainly responsible for the big audiences Australian concerts get now."[59]

By the mid-1950s, the youth concerts were at their peak; however, the success of the format could not be sustained through another decade. They gradually lost their spirit of adventure and, as Roger Covell comments, "they became gradually more fusty, because the ABC had somehow developed the attitude 'this is good for you' rather than 'this is exciting.'"[60]

Of course, many factors influenced the youth demographic in the 1960s. The emergence of pop music mania, television, and mass marketing all competed for the attention of adolescents and young adults. Another possible factor was the controversial and abrupt departure of the charismatic Eugene Goossens from the Australian musical scene, effectively deported in May 1956 after being found in possession of pornographic items. Heinze's biographer, Therese Radic, regards the concert on 24 October 1967, which marked 20 years of youth concerts with the SSO, as "the end of an era." Heinze's health was also starting to fail him, and his youth concert performances in 1974 celebrating his jubilee as a conductor were the beginning of "a long series of farewells."[61] Following the 50th anniversary concert, Kenneth Hince wrote:

> In those 50 years Heinze has utterly reshaped our music. To call him the most influential figure in Australia music sounds like hyperbole. It is not; it is sober truth. Heinze realised that orchestras needed subscribers even more than people wanted orchestras. In 1924, his concerts began in Melbourne with fewer than 70 subscribers. When he resigned the Ormond Chair at the University in 1956 there were nearly 11,000.[62]

While the popularity of the youth concert scheme gradually faded, the 1960s saw another successful concert format appealing strongly to the youth market, in the shape of John Hopkins' SSO Proms. In 1963, Hopkins was appointed the ABC's director of music, combining this role with his conducting and educational activities. The concept of the Australian Proms (which began in Sydney in 1965, soon to be followed by Melbourne, Adelaide, Brisbane, and Perth) was modelled on that of the Henry Wood Promenade Concerts, presented at London's Royal Albert Hall. Hopkins' programming staff included Richard Meale and Nigel Butterley, and together they introduced an adventurous approach with a focus on contemporary and Australian content. By 1968, the Proms were offering a wide range of music, by composers such as Lutoslawski, Machaut, Baird, Ives, Sculthorpe, Schubert, Mozart, and Bach. Hopkins describes his collaboration with Meale and Butterley:

> These two were the ones with the ideas. We would each keep a list of pieces we wanted to do, including new pieces we'd heard from overseas radio tapes, and we would pool these ideas and turn them into

50 Origins and Development

> programs. We went through an incredible sifting process to keep the programs sharp.[63]

The Proms shared much of the same glamour and excitement as the youth concerts at their peak, with similar stories of queuing overnight, and capacity crowds. Hopkins believes that the Proms were as much a marketing exercise as a musical one, and that the queuing system was an important part of its success, later saying: "It helped create a camaraderie among the Prommers, a special sense of occasion."[64] The Proms shared many similarities with the youth concerts including, unfortunately, a short life span. In 1973, Hopkins left the ABC to become dean of music at the Victorian Arts College, and in 1976 his successor at the ABC, Harold Hort, wrote:

> When John Hopkins left you will remember my own view that we could no longer rely on him to run the whole of the Proms season; that, in any case, his inspiration and the type of programming he had advocated was wearing thin and there was no way in which this kind of Prom could be continued.[65]

In 1977, the year after Hort expressed these concerns, the Proms were discontinued in Sydney and were gradually phased out nationally.

The following case study looks at the challenges experienced by the Sydney Symphony Orchestra during the 1980s and 1990s, and the new educational initiatives introduced during this period. The SSO's approach to education in the 1990s established the foundations for the present successful SSO Education Department, and has also had a considerable influence on the development of Australian orchestral education programming.

The Development of the Sydney Symphony Orchestra Education Department

Today, the Sydney Symphony Orchestra operates one of the leading education departments in Australia. However, the present strength of the SSO's education programming rests on certain key decisions made over the past 40 years, decisions which are of interest to other orchestras looking to develop their programme and build stronger links with their community. Here, we look at the key points of development in the SSO Education Department, as well as establishing the motivation behind them.

In the 1960s and 1970s, the SSO's education programming began to move into new areas, having at this date already offered school concerts and youth concerts since the 1940s.[66] In 1960, Dean Dixon (SSO principal conductor from 1964 to 1967) introduced a successful series of "Toddler Proms" concerts, aimed at three to four year olds, which were more participatory in style than school concerts.[67] An historical newsreel of a 1964 Toddlers' Prom has recently been released by British Pathé, providing a rare glimpse into this period of the SSO's history.[68]

Origins and Development 51

This period also saw the establishment of a National Training Orchestra, formed by the ABC in Sydney in 1967, with the aim of preparing young players for professional playing. This was essentially an early precursor of the current training model offered by Sydney Sinfonia and Fellowship, and several players made the transition from the training orchestra to the SSO.[69] In 1973, the Sydney Opera House was opened, and the glamour of this venue, situated on the sparkling harbour, became a valuable factor in attracting audiences to SSO concerts. The years immediately following the opening of the opera house were a honeymoon period, with generally full houses.

However, the following decade saw the SSO presented with significant challenges, and the years from 1980 to 1985 were perhaps the most critical in the history of the Sydney Symphony. In a paper presented in 1991, Brett Johnson (former Sydney Symphony education manager) gives an insight into the role the education department played in turning the tide. Johnson comments:

> A complex mix of factors in the years 1980 to 1985 led to a dramatic erosion of the subscriber base in all areas ... of great concern was the fact that the early evening series traditionally attended by large numbers of high school student and young people (for many years known as the Youth Concerts, but by the 80s renamed the 630 Meet the Music series) was nearly at the point of complete abandonment, such was the falling off of subscriptions.[70]

A common response by orchestras to the problem of falling audience numbers is to redouble their efforts in education and community engagement. The Sydney Symphony Orchestra did exactly this in the 1980s. The turning point for the SSO, in Johnson's view, began with identifying the issues contributing to the fall in audience numbers for the Meet the Music concerts. To achieve this, the SSO initiated a better communication process with teachers, to ensure their needs were being met. In 1986, a working party was established between the SSO and New South Wales (NSW) teachers. The first meeting of this working party directed strong criticism towards the SSO and made a number of recommendations:

1. That the orchestra play better.
2. That repertoire reflect syllabus requirements.
3. That the conductor and soloist roster be at the same artistic level as the adult evening series.
4. That all education programmes be supported by teaching materials.[71]

This critical feedback proved to be the catalyst for the SSO's present successful education department. In his paper, Johnson documents the reaction of the SSO to the meeting and its response to the recommendations of the

52   Origins and Development

working party. The first crucial step was the allocation of more sponsorship funds to the education department, which financed the deployment of a school music teacher to work full time for the SSO. Johnson explains:

> The position's duties would be to co-ordinate schools concert planning and marketing, channel advice from the education community to SSO and ABC Concert Music managers, and write resources kits consisting of booklets and cassettes along the lines of the successful Musica Viva resources.[72]

This position, together with the extra funding allocated, made it possible for the orchestra to immediately address points 2 and 4 from the meeting. According to Johnson, "The demand regarding repertoire made the programmers aware of the need to keep in touch with developments in syllabuses, such as the new senior syllabus requiring the study of post 1965 music with emphasis on the Australian scene."[73]

This request was immediately met during 1987 and 1988, when the orchestra devoted many days to recording excerpts and complete scores for inclusion in teaching material packs. Johnson comments:

> the first performance of a number of Australian scores ... have not been their concert premieres by one or other of the six ABC orchestras, but studio recording by the SSO for use in education kits supporting performance in Meet the Music series or other Education Program events.[74]

The prominence of Australian contemporary music continues to be a key characteristic of the SSO's programming to date and it is to be hoped that the introduction of the national curriculum does not impact on such an important commitment to Australian composition. The SSO's support of Australian composers has helped to build a public platform for their work and has developed a greater connection between students and contemporary music.

In addition to increasing the Australian content in programming and recording key works, the SSO also turned its attention to improving resources aimed at Kindergarten to Grade 8 students in 1988 and 1989. According to Johnson, the 1989 K-8 teaching kit was the first truly co-operative SSO/departmental venture, with the costs of production shared by the orchestra and the Department of Education.[75] The comprehensive kits included 40–50 pages of lesson plans and activities alongside a recording of core repertoire, and were free of charge. A similar format is still used today by the SSO for its teaching kits, which lead the field in terms of their detail and curriculum support.

Johnson acknowledges that the early SSO resource kits were influenced by those already provided by Musica Viva. Musica Viva, founded in 1945, is the world's largest chamber music provider. Since 1981, Musica Viva has

Origins and Development 53

made a significant contribution to school music education through a combination of school performances and teacher resources. Its activity lies beyond the scope of this research, being related to chamber rather than orchestral or opera music, but is worthy of a separate study in its own right.[76]

The first and third points from the August 1986 meeting, regarding the standard of performance, were also addressed by the SSO. Johnson remarks: "it was an opportune moment to establish loudly and clearly that second-best, whether in playing or skill of conductors and soloists, was not going to be tolerated by teachers or students."[77]

The importance of keeping the standard of playing at education concerts at a high level cannot be underestimated. While the aim of such concerts is to provide a positive, and hopefully inspiring, first experience of classical orchestral music, if the concert is not planned or performed at a high level then it is all too easy for the opposite effect to occur and for students to leave with a negative impression. This is a point which must be kept in mind by any orchestra offering education concerts.

By the 1990s, the SSO's Meet the Music school concerts were performed to a high standard and were warmly received by both teachers and students. The programming for the concerts gradually developed a formula: each concert would include repertoire representing three key categories. These were, broadly speaking, a piece from the classical canon, a modern work with interesting instrumentation or approach to tonality, and a work by a contemporary Australian composer. This combination of repertoire choices allows for a balanced concert experience to extend students.

The SSO also made improvements to its tailoring of concerts for different age groups in 1989, with attention paid to individual grade syllabuses. Concerts for students in Kindergarten to Year 2 (for approximately 5–7 year olds) were introduced in 1990. In 1997, these concerts were the subject of research by Louie Suthers at the Institute of Early Childhood, Macquarie University. Suthers praised the participatory approach taken by the SSO, which has increasingly been recognised as a key element of concerts for children, and noted that the programming reflected research on early childhood development.[78]

In 1992, Richard Gill was appointed artistic director of the Sydney Symphony Education programme, a position he held for over 20 years, alongside education managers Margaret Moore and, more recently, Kim Waldock. During this period, several new elements were introduced to the education department, including the flagship orchestral training programmes "Sydney Sinfonia" and "Sydney Fellowship."

Notes

1 Stanley Sadie. "Sir Robert Mayer at 100," *Musical Times*, Vol. 120 (1636), June 1979, pp. 457 and 474–475.
2 Ibid., p. 474.
3 Ibid.

54 Origins and Development

4 William G. Blair. "Sir Robert Mayer Obituary," *New York Times*, 20 January 1985.
5 Ibid.
6 Ibid.
7 Ibid.
8 Charles Reid. *Malcolm Sargent*. London: Hamish Hamilton, 1968, p. 180.
9 Ibid., p. 181.
10 Ibid., p. 182.
11 Doeser, *Step by Step*, p. 4.
12 Ibid.
13 Ibid., p. 13.
14 Sue Robertson, quoted in Doeser, *Step by Step*, p. 13.
15 Winterson, *The Community Education Work of Orchestras and Opera Companies*, p. 49.
16 Ibid. Appendix 3, p. 9.
17 McNicol, interview with the author.
18 Winterson, "The Evaluation of the Effects of London Sinfonietta Education Projects on their Participants," p. 54.
19 Paynter and Aston. *Sound and Silence*.
20 Winterson, *The Community Education Work of Orchestras and Opera Companies*, p. 57.
21 Richard McNicol. "Planning and Presenting Orchestral Concerts for Young Audiences," in Fiona Penny (editor), *The Workbook, Volume 2*. London: Association of British Orchestras, 2000, p. 8.
22 Caroline Julian (editor). *Making it Mutual: The Ownership Revolution that Britain Needs*, published by ResPublica, Case Study 23, 2013. Retrieved from www.respublica.org.uk/our-work/publications/making-mutual-ownership-revolution-britain-needs/.
23 http://lso.co.uk/orchestra/history, accessed 1 July 2015.
24 Ibid.
25 Norman Lebrecht. *La Scena Musicale*, 7 January 2004, retrieved from www.scena.org/columns/lebrechtweekly.asp, accessed 10 August 2013.
26 McNicol, *The Workbook, Volume 2*, p. 10.
27 "LSO Discovery at 25."
28 McNicol, *The Workbook, Volume 2*, p. 8.
29 Paul Rissmann, interview with author.
30 "Obituary of Ernest Fleischmann," *The Telegraph*, 16 June 2010.
31 Charlotte Higgins. "The Trumpets are Sounding for the LSO's Centenary Year, but Financial Problems Could Spoil the Party," *The Guardian*, 15 January 2004, p. 17.
32 Ibid.
33 www.lso.co.uk/aboutlsodiscovery, accessed 1 June 2014.
34 Stephen Moss. "It's Been Fantastic," *The Guardian London*, 13 May 2005, p. 11.
35 Martin Kettle. "Leader of the Pack," *The Guardian London*, 28 February 2003.
36 *Education at the Met*, p. 4.
37 Ibid.
38 Ibid.
39 Ibid.
40 www.learningforreal.org/about/ accessed 20 February 2022.
41 Davidson, interview with the author.
42 Ibid.
43 Ibid.

Origins and Development 55

44 https://operawire.com/60-50-scottish-operas-jane-davidson-karen-maciver-allan -dunn-on-the-companys-anniversary-education-outreach/ accessed 2 April 2022.

45 Davidson, interview with the author.

46 Andrew Crummy. "Craigmillar Festival, the Scottish Community Arts Movement of the 1970s and 1980s and its Impact: A View from Scotland," in Alison Jeffers and Gerri Moriarty (editor), *Culture, Democracy and the Right to Make Art: The British Community Arts Movement.* Bloomsbury Publishing Plc, 2017, https://doi.org/10.5040/9781474258395.

47 Therese Radic. *Bernard Heinze, A Biography.* Melbourne: Macmillan, 1986, Preface, p. xx.

48 Charles Buttrose. *Playing for Australia: A Story about ABC Orchestras and Music in Australia.* Sydney: Macmillan, 1982, p. 10.

49 Ibid., pp. 11–12.

50 Walter Damrosch. *My Musical Life.* New York: Charles Scribner and Sons, 1926.

51 Buttrose, *Playing for Australia*, p. 12.

52 Bernard Heinze. *Sydney Morning Herald*, 15 March 1930, as cited in Therese Radic. *Bernard Heinze, A Biography.* Melbourne: Macmillan, 1986, p. 45.

53 Buttrose, *Playing for Australia*, p. 13.

54 Radic, *Bernard Heinze, A Biography*, p. 136.

55 Ibid.

56 Ibid., p. 138.

57 Ibid.

58 Sametz, *Play On! 60 Years of Music Making with the Sydney Symphony Orchestra*, p. 143.

59 Ibid., p. 146.

60 Ibid., p. 212.

61 Ibid., p. 203.

62 Ibid., p. 204.

63 Ibid., p. 257.

64 Ibid., p. 261.

65 Ibid., pp. 264–265.

66 Retrieved from www.sydneysymphony.com/education/about-the-program.aspx, accessed 4 July 2014.

67 Ibid.

68 Retrieved from www.britishpathe.com/video/sydney-symphony-orchestra -invaded-by-children/query/Symphony, accessed 6 September 2015.

69 Robert Miller. "A.B.C. Training Orchestra" [online] in David Symons (editor), *Report of Proceedings of the First National Conference: Music in General Education.* Nedlands, WA: Australian Society for Music Education, 1969, pp. 179–186. Retrieved from http://search.informit.com.au/documentSummary;dn =665488922480902;res=IELHSS, accessed 8 September 2014.

70 Johnson, *The Development of an Orchestral Education Program*, p. 25.

71 Ibid.

72 Ibid.

73 Ibid.

74 Ibid., p. 26.

75 Ibid., p. 27.

76 www.musicaviva.com.au/education/about, accessed 1 June 2015.

77 Johnson, *The Development of an Orchestral Education Program*, p. 25.

78 Louie Suthers. "Introducing Young Children to Live Orchestral Performance," in Wendy Schiller (editor), *Issues in Expressive Arts Curriculum for Early Childhood.* London: Taylor and Francis, 1997, pp. 55–64.

3 Working Together
Models of Partnership Delivery of Music Education

While the music industry is undeniably under extreme pressure at the current time, there is a strong undercurrent of partnership and collaboration that is bringing together previously disparate strands of the profession. This collaboration is essential on many levels: for children to be provided with a rich, sequential, and stimulating musical education through their formative years, and for all professionals across the ecosystem to have an understanding of how their roles are interconnected. This collaboration occurs, of course, at the "micro" and "macro" level. In this chapter, we focus more on the "macro" – on the development of a systemised collaborative delivery of music education at the organisational or even the national level. We look at the aims of these collaborations, explore case studies of existing and developing models, and consider the impact that they are achieving through their activities.

Eric Booth, the acknowledged leader in the teaching artist field, has both shaped and closely observed the evolution of the field over the past three decades. Booth observes that there has been a much needed meeting of minds between performers and educators that is now resulting in a more impactful delivery of orchestral and opera education programmes. Booth reveals that at the early stages of the teaching artist movement in the United States there was often an air of arrogance around the visits of an artist to a school: "In the first generation of teaching artistry in the US, there was this little sense of the specialness of the artist who is now blessing you with their presence."[1] However, Booth feels that through the evolution of the industry a true partnership has developed between the goals and needs of the artists, the schools, and the students. Booth explains:

> Partnering with teachers became essential, and really listening to teachers, not just accommodating what teachers need to do and like to do, but actually *listening* to what's important in the community of a classroom, what that teacher needs to accomplish. Beginning to think about how a true partnership can accomplish the multiple necessities of a school – of which artistic engagement is one if you have a teaching artist there. As we got more mature in partnering, additional responsibilities came in

DOI: 10.4324/9781003198512-4

Working Together 57

with funding; things like assessment for example, we had to learn how to build in assessment. So, the field has gained sophistication in areas like learning, professional development of educators within schools, how to become a good partner for a teaching artist, how to extend the work of a teaching artist, how to maximise the glorious opportunity of a single trip to the symphony hall to see a performance, how much ripple effect can come from the scarce allocation of a live performance like that. And then developing, I would say, some facility with assessment methodology.[2]

Peter Garden, executive director of performance and learning at the Royal Liverpool Philharmonic Orchestra, shares the view that orchestras have developed a new level of true collaboration in their interaction with schools and their communities. Garden reflects:

So it's not "we are here to helicopter in do something good for six weeks and pretend that we've changed everyone's lives and disappear to the next one". Communities are fed up with that, and they see straight through that. We've heard that so clearly around the need for genuine authentic long-term partnerships where there can be space and honesty, and both meaning and relevance to all in the partnership. You've got to have the solid partnership structures, relationships and trust in place in order to be able to identify and celebrate your successes together, and be okay when things go wrong – you then learn from that, you refine and improve from that together.[3]

Sean Gregory, vice president and director of innovation and engagement at the Guildhall, has placed partnership working at the core of his activities. Gregory leads collaborative projects between the Barbican, the Guildhall, and the London Symphony Orchestra (LSO), and sees collaborative co-creation as being the centre of his work with local communities. Here, Gregory gives an insight into the collaborative partnership model of the Barbican, the Guildhall, and the LSO:

A significant aspect of more recent history for the Barbican, the Guildhall and indeed the LSO has essentially been about building relationships in East London. Looking back to the 80s and 90s East London was pretty rundown in places, pre-Olympics, pre-regeneration, so there was a real calling to get out there and work in those areas. By 2012 and beyond of course, there'd been the Olympics, and all the regeneration that comes with that and so we were starting to shift our relationship.

The way that we develop partnership working with other organisations is not just about what we offer, as the Barbican or the Guildhall, it's what's needed out in the community, which we learn through talking and co-creating projects and ideas with partners, be they schools, local

58 *Working Together*

community settings, other venues etc. And that's been a major shift over the last few years: co-creation, listening, collaborating, and jointly running things and setting things up.[4]

While, as we have seen, orchestral education departments have interacted closely with schools since the 1980s, there has been a more significant collaborative trend in recent years with orchestras forming schools or taking up residence in schools. The Deutsche Kammerphilharmonie Bremen was the first orchestra in Europe to gain international attention for this intense collaboration. In 2007, the orchestra moved its rehearsal venue to a building on the site of Bremen East comprehensive school – at the time a purely practical consideration of a suitable space available at the right time. This practical collaboration has proven to have remarkable benefits for both parties. From the school's point of view, they share that having the orchestra on site has improved morale for both students and teachers. They are also attributing improved academic success and a lower dropout rate to the positive impact of having the professional musicians on site. From the orchestra's perspective there have been equal benefits. For example, one of the musicians has shared that the experience has improved the morale within the orchestra:

> The experience has actually improved us as an orchestra … When the children sit between us at rehearsals, our concentration is better. We can actually see their eyes grow wide with excitement when we play certain chords or play quickly. It reminds us of the reason we make music.[5]

In the United Kingdom, three orchestras are, at the time of writing, following this precedent. The first is the Orchestra of the Age of Enlightenment, which in late 2020 moved into a large north London comprehensive school, Acland Burghley School. The motivation for this move is remarkably similar to Bremen – the orchestra's rehearsal and office space arrangements were coming to an end at King's Place, and the school realised the symbiotic benefits for them in sharing resources and facilities. At the launch of the new partnership Nicholas John, Acland Burghley's headteacher, stated that the partnership would connect not only with the school's music education, but also across other curricula areas, including mathematics and physics.[6]

At the time of writing, the City of Birmingham Symphony Orchestra (CBSO) and Manchester's Hallé Orchestra are both planning to create new schools in partnership with local education authorities. The CBSO is further advanced in these plans at the time of writing. The CBSO is partnering with the Shireland Collegiate Academy Trust to form the Shireland CBSO School, while the Hallé is looking to open a new school in Stoke-on-Trent, also working with an academy trust. The intention behind these partnerships is to make music a significant focus across the entire school, in a fight back against the downgrading of music in school curricula across the United

Kingdom. The CBSO was partly spurred into action by the low numbers of students taking music in schools across Birmingham, with only 38 students studying music at GCSE level in 2019. Once established, the plan is to research the activities and outcomes of the schools, in acknowledgement that there will be sizeable international interest on the impact of this new partnership system.

One of the most high-profile partnerships in the delivery of music education at present is the "Benedetti Foundation," led by charismatic concert violinist Nicola Benedetti and music educator Laura Gardner. This foundation, launched in the midst of the pandemic, has had collegiality and community at the centre of operations since its inception. This sense of community is present within the student body, highlighted in particular by the multilevel "Benedetti Sessions" in which string musicians of all levels play together in newly commissioned arrangements. However, the community spreads wider, towards inclusive support of music teachers across the United Kingdom and internationally. For example, the resource booklet compiled for teachers attending the first "Benedetti Sessions" gathering has a strong focus on the importance of teachers – of their value, their role in the ecosystem, their impact on their students. Benedetti gathered a diverse array of musicians, both performers and educators, to contribute to this resource, ranging from Sir Simon Rattle to jazz icon Wynton Marsalis, through to Jo Bradley, a Kodály expert. In her foreword, Benedetti states:

> Although I teach all the time, I have never been solely responsible for the development of a young person's playing, or their relationship to music. This responsibility is huge, and precious, and your work must be nurtured, valued, empowered and supported …We do not value teaching enough in this country [England] and we certainly do not value music teaching enough.[7]

Richard Morrison, chief music critic for *The Times*, writes:

> Whatever branch of music you work in, the potential for feeling not just isolated, lonely and unappreciated but sometimes even persecuted and redundant is very real … What I love about the Benedetti Foundation is that it provides an opportunity for the musical world to come together and make things better together.[8]

While the Benedetti Foundation is a new initiative, founded in late 2019 and scheduling its first events in January 2020, it has been outstandingly successful and impactful. The first session – weekend gatherings that provide a high impact stimulus for students and teachers alike – was delivered in January 2020 in Glasgow. This event was a model of collaboration, delivered in partnership with the Royal Scottish National Orchestra, Glasgow Royal Concert Hall, Glasgow Life, and UNESCO City of Music. Taking part were

60   *Working Together*

650 young string players in massed multilevel orchestras, with a further 1,400 primary schoolchildren participating in workshops. Teachers were at the heart of the event, with 150 string teachers and 70 classroom teachers receiving professional development.

The Benedetti Foundation is now part of a new project that has recently gained international attention – the plan to create a new National Centre for Music for Scotland, based in an historic site in Edinburgh. On 8 October 2021, Benedetti released a statement on this project: "The National Centre for Music presents us with an unprecedented opportunity to enrich the cultural life of Scotland and to serve as a beacon of true 21st century music education for the world to see." With Benedetti awarded the 2021 RPS Award for Instrumentalist of the Year, and the Benedetti Foundation awarded the RPS Inspiration Award, the future impact of this dynamic musical star and her passion for collaborative music education is sure to continue to build.

The partnerships between British orchestras and education organisations have attracted international attention over the past decade, and the role of UK government policy has had a significant impact in this respect. The *National Curriculum and Education Reform Act* (1988),[9] *All Our Futures* (1999),[10] *Creative Partnerships* (2002),[11] and the *Music Manifesto* (2005)[12] each mark a fresh attempt to establish an equitable and efficient arts education system. While there are current concerns about a reduction in the funding to arts education in the United Kingdom, the government has supported arts education in various key ways over past decades. On 21 November 2007, for example, the government made a funding commitment to music education of 332 million pounds, some of which was to be used to further develop orchestral and opera education programmes and the links between orchestras, opera companies, and their communities.[13] Two key programmes were developed from this funding, both of which have impacted on education programming: Sing Up, a nationwide singing programme, and Wider Opportunities, a programme for large-group instrumental teaching within schools. The "Music Hub" model is the current government-sponsored system in the United Kingdom, aiming to foster partnerships between arts and education organisations. While not without its detractors, the Music Hub model is nevertheless attracting international attention. This chapter charts the development of the Music Hub model, alongside an analysis of its early practice.

In 2010, the UK government commissioned a review of music education in England. Darren Henley was commissioned to chair the review and collated evidence on the current state of music education across England. Fiona Harvey represented the Association of British Orchestras in this process, alongside several orchestral education managers and chief executives.[14] The report was released in February 2011, with the over-riding message of the need for better partnership working between arts and educational organisations.[15] Henley also found that music education across England was not uniformly excellent and that areas of less wealth were proportionally offered less music education opportunities. The *Henley Report* rapidly led to the development of the *National Plan for Music Education*, published by the government on 22 November 2011.[16] The *National Plan* aimed to bring Henley's vision of fairness, collaboration, and partnership to fruition via a scheme of national music education hubs. In the Foreword to the *National Plan for Music Education*, Michael Gove (secretary of state for education) and Ed Vaizey (minister for culture, communications and creative industries) stated:

> Funds for music education hubs will be awarded following an open application process run by Arts Council England which will focus on outcomes for pupils, partnership working and economies of scale ... this is the first time that a National Plan for Music Education has set out a central vision for schools, arts and education organisations to drive excellence for music education. The National Plan is clear about the importance of music: it will ensure not just that more children have access to the greatest of arts forms, but that they do better as a result in every other subject.[17]

In an interview with the author, Fiona Harvey comments on the Music Hub model:

> It is about partnership working, it is about putting the child and young people at the centre and seeing what their needs are in each local area, and how can we provide this in the most effective way ... with probably less funding, because there is less funding to go around.[18]

The reduction in funding is acknowledged in the *National Plan*, although it is camouflaged by positive soundbites and hopeful predictions. The funding dropped from 77 million pounds in 2012 to 65 million pounds in 2013, then 60 million pounds in 2014.[19] So, the reality of the figures is that this new spirit of collegiality and partnership, while laudable, is also intended to help less money go further by streamlining operations. The rationale behind the new funding system is population based, as Fiona Harvey explains:

> Before the Hubs system there was no parity throughout the country in terms of how different music services were funded. As part of the Henley Review they decided that Hubs would be funded per capita of pupil in their area – they had to know what the school population was. So some Hubs (that were Music Services) got more funding while others got a massive decrease to start with.[20]

To fully understand the shift in England's music education system, it is necessary to understand the historical system for the provision of music education. In recent decades, England's music education has been provided

62 *Working Together*

to a large degree by Music Services as well as, of course, through classroom teaching. Music Services facilitate peripatetic teaching of singing and instruments in schools and specialised private tuition in after-school classes at music centres. Some Music Services were already working in partnership with symphony orchestras, opera companies, and their education programmes prior to the Henley Review, and the Music Hub system hopes to encourage further partnership along these lines.

Following a restructuring period, 123 music hubs were established in September 2012, with Music Services joining in partnership with symphony orchestra education departments, youth orchestras, and other relevant organisations.[21] However, in November 2013, after little more than a year in operation, a government report was released which made several negative comments on the progress made. Over visits to 31 schools from February to July 2013, Ofsted inspectors reported only "few examples" of good practice, criticising hubs for not evaluating their activities. The report claimed: "None of the hubs visited could provide a telling, qualitative, overall evaluation of the quality of the music education in schools in their areas."[22] It found that provision of activities by the music hubs was still patchy and not consistent across all post codes, and asked for both schools and hubs to respectively hold each other to account. The report made various recommendations for school music teachers, including that they should teach the fundamentals of classical music, in particular notation, more rigorously. For hubs, the Ofsted Report requested that they each make a school music education plan that would enable them to improve by April 2014. More positively, the report did note that "the hubs … brought new energy, collaborative approaches and vitality to working musically with young people."[23] However, this praise was balanced by the criticism that "while this work is essential it reaches only a minority of pupils."[24]

There was significant backlash to the critical Ofsted Report. The UK Musicians Union (MU) released an official statement stating that the report was "undermining and demoralising," and claimed that it did not, in fact, capture a correct view of activity.[25] The MU Report commented that Ofsted inspections were only made to a small sample of schools, and that visits began too soon after hubs were established, not allowing them time to settle into their new roles. The MU also criticised the government's funding cuts, saying that they had created a sense of deep instability. The emphasis on the importance of notation teaching in the Ofsted Report was also criticised by the MU. It is important to note that there has been debate over the place of notation in classroom music education since the 1960s. The MU's argument to Ofsted was that the emphasis on notation "undermines pedagogical developments based on encouraging creativity and the diverse approaches to music which are relevant to young people."[26] This is clearly an unresolved debate, although ideally a school music education would allocate sufficient time to allow a place for both creative projects and music theory.

Working Together   63

The MU did acknowledge room for improvement in certain aspects of the hub system, such as the need for greater funding security for hubs and for clearer accountability. The MU also noted that while professional organisations were increasingly working with hubs, some hubs were not behaving in a collaborative way. The importance of the spirit of teamwork was one of Henley's key points, so in order for the hub system to be fully realised it is imperative for Music Services to make effective links with arts organisations. As Fiona Harvey states:

> With examples of good practice it is about them recognising how they can make better use of each other's skills and expertise and how they can work better together, and some of them are doing it really well. In Greater Manchester Hub the Hallé, Manchester Camerata Royal Northern and BBC Philharmonic are all partners in the Hub, sitting around the strategic table. They're actually influencing strategy so that's the way forward for me and I think if you put the child at the centre then everything else revolves around them. That's how it should actually work – better than lots of different people competing for funds and competing for space etc.[27]

At this point, certain examples of best practice have emerged. These include the Tri-Borough Hub in London and the Greater Manchester Hub. Both are notable for not only the number of organisations involved, but also the quality. The Strategic Partnership for the Tri-Borough Hub, for instance, includes the Royal Albert Hall, the Royal College of Music, and the Aurora Orchestra, alongside the Music Services of Westminster, Kensington and Chelsea, and Hammersmith and Fulham. This partnership provides students of the 150 schools in the tri-borough with access to elite music venues and experiences.[28] Students from the Royal College of Music mentor younger children in the district, and the hub has staged multilevel performance opportunities. One of the more ambitious projects planned by the Tri-Borough Hub is the "Seven Seeds" project, a new commission inspired by the Greek myth of Persephone which premiered in June 2015. Children from across the tri-borough have contributed to the creation of the piece, which is scored for a large choir of 1,200 young singers alongside an orchestra that combines professional musicians from the Aurora Orchestra, Albert's Band, and the Southbank Sinfonia with students from the Royal College of Music and the Royal Academy of Music.

The Greater Manchester Hub (gmmusichub) includes the Hallé, Manchester Camerata, BBC Philharmonic, Royal Northern College of Music, the Bridgewater Hall, Chetham's School of Music, and nine Music Services.[29] These partners have the resources to work together to offer sequential learning and opportunities to students in the Greater Manchester region. The hub's mission statement is to develop partnerships that enable all children equitable access to high-quality music education.[30]

64 Working Together

One of the strengths of the Greater Manchester Music Hub is that all the delivery and strategic partners are working together to ensure that there are sequential steps in place in terms of both education and performance opportunities for students along their learning path. For instance, the Hallé set up its youth orchestra to ensure that there was a high-quality youth orchestra in the area available to students who were not enrolled at Chetham's School of Music or the Royal Northern College of Music. While this was initially perceived as a possible threat by the Music Services to their own ensembles and youth orchestras, they have now come to see that the extra opportunity in fact motivates students and acts as a necessary link towards National Youth Orchestra training. The Hallé plays a key role in the Greater Manchester Music Hub, and its chief executive, John Summers, sits on the strategic group.

The similarities between the construct of the Tri-Borough and Greater Manchester Music Hubs are of interest to those looking to establish similar partnership models. Firstly, the partnerships are strengthened by the chief executives of the Hallé and Aurora Orchestra, who sit on the strategic boards of their respective hubs. Secondly, leading personnel of both hubs stress the importance of laying out clear "musical pathways" for students, and of "sign-posting" them to the next sequential opportunity. This is at the heart of the spirit of partnership and involves a clear acknowledgement of both the strengths and the limitations of each member of the organisation. The key principle is to always keep the benefit for the recipient as the key motivation, and to strive to put aside selfish concerns.

While these hubs have a particular advantage in that they each have access to an unusual concentration of world-class arts bodies, their basic strategic framework can, in fact, be analysed and replicated in other cities and countries. The key elements to each hub are a delivery service for music tuition in schools, a professional orchestra or opera company, a tertiary music college or conservatorium, a youth orchestra, and a large performance venue. Most developed cities in the world today can provide these organisations, and together they can provide an entire community with lifelong support and training in music, at all levels.

The Music Hub models analysed above reveal the benefits when every element in this partnership works together, co-ordinating and aligning their activities. For instance, students from the music conservatorium can be inspirational mentors for developing instrumentalists, providing a relatable model of achievement in the field. This relationship may also introduce the concept of a career path in music to a young beginner for the first time. The symphony orchestra and opera company offer a point of inspiration to all other organisations in the partnership in various forms, from a first experience of live classical music for young children and their families, to support and inspiration for beginner students, a bridge to the profession for tertiary music students, and participatory music experiences for the community as a whole. The importance of the venue in the partnership can be seen in two

Working Together 65

important ways. Firstly, by widening access to a concert hall and thereby encouraging a wider sector of the community to establish a sense of ease and "ownership" with what can be for some an intimidating venue. Secondly, the experience of performing on stage at a prestigious venue adds considerably to the sense of excitement and achievement for participants in any music performance project.

While the Music Hub model is still evolving, the ways in which various hubs are establishing partnerships and working together are of interest internationally. We will see how the system continues to evolve over the coming years, and the international music community will continue to look to the model for new innovations, as well as learning from the less successful aspects of the system. Key to future progress in this area is a mutual respect and an emphasis on partnership and co-creation.

Notes

1 Eric Booth, interview with the author.
2 Ibid.
3 Peter Garden, interview with the author.
4 Sean Gregory, interview with the author.
5 Matt Pickles. "The Orchestra Fine-tuning the Performance of School Students," 22 April 2015, www.bbc.com/news/business-32381815.
6 https://oae.co.uk/abs/, accessed 1 January 2022.
7 Benedetti Sessions, Notes for Teachers. 2020.
8 Ibid.
9 *Education Reform Act*, UK Parliament, 1988.
10 Sir Ken Robinson (chair). *All Our Futures: Creativity, Culture and Education*. Co-commissioned by the Department for Education and Employment and the Department for Culture, Media and Sport. London: National Advisory Committee on Creative and Cultural Education, 1999.
11 *Creative Partnerships*. Commissioned by the Department for Culture, Media and Sport, UK, 2002.
12 *Music Manifesto*. Co-commissioned by the Department for Education and Skills and Department for Culture, Media and Sport, 2006.
13 http://webarchive.nationalarchives.gov.uk/20100612001226/; http://www .musicmanifesto.co.uk/about-the-manifesto, accessed 21 July 2015.
14 Fiona Harvey, interview by author.
15 Henley, *Music Education in England*.
16 *The Importance of Music*.
17 *National Plan for Music Education*, Foreword.
18 Fiona Harvey, interview.
19 Ibid.
20 Ibid.
21 www.artscouncil.org.uk/funding/apply-funding/funding-programmes/music -education-hubs/, accessed 12 July 2015.
22 *Music in Schools: What Hubs Must Do*, p. 18.
23 Ibid., p. 4.
24 Ibid.
25 *Report Summary in Response to Ofsted*, Musicians Union, UK, 2014. Retrieved from www.musiciansunion.org.uk/Home/News/2014/Feb/MU-calls-for-Government-to -do-more-for-music-education, accessed 3 January 2015.

66 *Working Together*

26 Ibid., p. 3.
27 Fiona Harvey, interview.
28 www.triboroughmusichub.org, accessed 12 July 2015.
29 www.gmmusichub.co.uk/about_gmmh.
30 Ibid.

4 Leading the Way

Case Studies of Orchestral and Opera Education and Community Engagement Programmes

The London Symphony Orchestra

The London Symphony Orchestra (LSO) has developed its education and community engagement to such an exceptional level that the LSO Discovery Department is now a major part of the identity of the orchestra, a useful edge to have in London's highly competitive classical market. Operating for 32 years, the Discovery Department now reaches over 60,000 participants annually, at a cost to the LSO of 1.3 million pounds per annum.[1] While the development years of the Discovery Department were covered in Chapter 2, the current status of the LSO's community engagement work is explored in this case study. The continuing strength of the LSO's education and community engagement programming owes much to the commitment and support of its managing director since 2005, Kathryn McDowell CBE.

To those who are only aware of McDowell's role as a world leader in arts management, her first step after completing music and teaching degrees may come as a surprise. McDowell, fresh from teacher training college, chose to volunteer to lead activities for political refugees at a United Nations refugee camp outside Vienna. McDowell explains that this decision was linked to her childhood growing up in Belfast:

> I was passionate about how children learn and how education can change the course of events for people from very different backgrounds. I'd grown up in the '70s near Belfast in Northern Ireland and education was the way out of many challenges for many people there.
>
> It was a very seminal experience for me, and I came away with an absolute conviction that you could build much greater understanding, and that you could encourage young people to learn in all subjects through musical experience.[2]

Upon returning to the United Kingdom after this experience, McDowell took a position with Welsh National Opera that combined marketing with education and community work. It was at this stage that she was inspired by her firsthand experience of the impact of opera and orchestral education

DOI: 10.4324/9781003198512-5

68   *Leading the Way*

and community engagement work. It was also her first connection with Richard McNicol, whose pioneering work in orchestral education programming would remain intertwined with both McDowell and the LSO for decades to come. From here, McDowell moved to a role with Scottish Chamber Orchestra (SCO) as development manager, another formative period, followed by a role as project officer with the Association of British Orchestras leading a flagship education programme, "The Turn of the Tide."

> I was Project Manager for a significant education project with the Association of the British Orchestras, "The Turn of the Tide", a commissioned work by Sir Peter Maxwell Davies. The idea was to involve more orchestras in education work, with Richard McNicol engaged as the animateur, and sixteen orchestras across the UK were involved. If an orchestra wanted to be part of the project they had to commit to setting up a dedicated post of Education or Community Manager, and they had to train their players. I think that there were nine or ten orchestras who were at that time completely new to it. For the ABO to lead a project like that was really significant – it also marked the point of the National Curriculum being introduced. So, having effectively driven that project in a freelance capacity from my job in Belfast and then through my work in the Arts Council in London, it did lead to a change in mindset where orchestras realised that they need to have education work within the mix, and that their public funding was going to be dependent on it. As the Music Department of the Arts Council evolved and I was appointed Music Director, we agreed with the large-scale music organisations that education and community work must be integral to what you do.[3]

On taking up her role with the LSO, McDowell brought a broad range of skills and understanding related to education and engagement work to her leadership of the organisation. This has provided a firm basis for the Discovery Department to continue to expand and deepen its activities and connections with the community under her support and leadership.

The LSO Discovery Department has a central focus on the population of its direct community in East London, but its impact is evident both nationally and, increasingly, internationally. The Discovery Department boasts the largest number of education and community engagement personnel of any orchestra internationally: 16 at the time of writing.[4] This large team oversees a wide range of activities, which can be broadly defined within three main groups: firstly a focus on access and equity; secondly a focus on lifelong learning and engagement; and thirdly a focus on the next generation of musicians, including performers, conductors, and composers. The following case study examines each of these areas in detail.

Regular activities focusing on access and equity are offered to people of all ages, and are intended to be a welcoming introduction to the world of the LSO. For young children and their families, there are music sessions for

Leading the Way 69

under-fives and their carers, themed as "Shake, Rattle and Roll" and "Musical Storytelling." For older children, the LSO offers a series of sequential school concerts, linked to the curriculum and with teacher support. Additionally, there are opportunities for students to join the LSO Discovery Choir, the Digital Technology Group, or to attend LSO Discovery Friday Lunchtime concerts. The LSO also reaches out to those who have difficulties accessing education programmes through its Children's Hospital Programme, for children aged 0–18 with acute or life-threatening illness, and LSO Create programmes, for adults and children with learning difficulties.[5]

Programmes in support of lifelong learning and engagement include the un-auditioned LSO Community Choir, which has over 100 members, and the LSO Community Gamelan Group, which teaches Balinese music to adults. The LSO has also run the successful format of "Discovery Days," which offer a whole day of activities aimed at increasing understanding of a particular composer to be featured in a main stage concert. These activities include an informative talk, a chamber music presentation, attendance at an open rehearsal, and finally the evening concert.[6]

While Discovery Days and the choirs are clearly linked with the core performance activity of the orchestra, the same link cannot be so easily perceived with many of the other programmes. However, the common theme is bringing the community into direct contact with the orchestra and its performance and rehearsal spaces, literally "opening the doors." One of the benefits of bringing a new sector of the community into LSO venues through these musical activities is that it offers an un-intimidating entry point into classical music. This allows people to become familiar with the space and with the musicians hosting sessions and rehearsals. The formal atmosphere of a large concert hall, while providing a certain glamour and sense of occasion, can also appear a daunting and unwelcoming prospect to those who have not had early experiences of them through family or school. Having gained familiarity with the venues and personal links with musicians, it is then easier to take the further step of attending LSO recitals and concerts.

A growth area for participation with the LSO, and across the United Kingdom in general, is choral singing. The LSO Singing programme, led since 2012 by Simon Halsey (director of the London Symphony Chorus) and David Lawrence (LSO Community Choir director), encompasses not only the prestigious, auditioned London Symphony Chorus but also the Community Choir and the Discovery Choir, which are un-auditioned but have weekly rehearsals at St Luke's. There are also regular "Singing Days" when repertoire is workshopped alongside LSO musicians.[7]

The increased interest in singing in the United Kingdom can, to an extent, be credited to another LSO choral director and animateur, Gareth Malone. Appointed the Edward Heath Assistant Animateur in 2001,[8] Malone went on to direct the Community and Discovery choirs for the LSO. While in this role, he was selected to present the highly popular BBC2 TV show "The Choir," which was released in 2006.[9] The Choir was succeeded by

70 *Leading the Way*

TV projects in which Malone worked on awaking a love of choral singing with different sectors of society, including adolescent boys and workplace choirs. As well as proving that choral singing, in the hands of an enthusiastic animateur, can connect with all sectors of society, the success of Malone also paved the way for orchestras to tap into the new-found popularity of choral singing.

A number of orchestras now have associated community and youth choirs, and it remains a growth field for the industry. There are also logistical reasons why orchestras are increasingly offering choral community activities, singing being the most accessible entry point into music and negating the need for instruments and equipment. The UK government has supported several school choral initiatives, such as the "Sing Up" Campaign, launched in 2007 as part of the Music Manifesto. This was a four-year programme aimed at raising the status of singing and increasing opportunities for children to sing every day. In April 2012, Sing Up became a not-for-profit membership organisation, which offers members access to resources that include 600 songs, backing tracks, and teaching activities.[10] Over 95% of British primary schools joined the Sing Up programme, which is still supported by Music Hubs. Thus, there are strong opportunities for orchestras to link with school choral projects.

In addition to the programmes discussed above, the LSO also offers a number of initiatives that aim to develop the next generation of musicians. These include LSO On Track; LSO Academies; LSO East London Academy, LSO String Experience; the Orchestral Artistry master's degree (in partnership with the Guildhall School of Music and Drama); Panufnik Composers Scheme; conducting masterclasses; and the Donatella Flick LSO Conducting Competition.[11]

The LSO was an early proponent of mixed-ability performances, where students perform alongside the symphony orchestra in concert. The LSO On Track programme is an example of this model, initiated in 2008 in line with the Olympic movement. Young musicians from ten East London boroughs have played alongside the LSO in high-profile performances, most notably at the opening ceremony of the 2012 London Olympic Games at which 80 On Track musicians performed Elgar's Nimrod, arranged by Welsh composer Gareth Glyn.[12] On Track students have also been included in the BMW Open Air Classics concert series staged annually in Trafalgar Square, performing arrangements by Glyn of Berlioz's Symphonie Fantastique (2013), Prokofiev's Lieutenant Kije (2014), and Shostakovich's Jazz Suites.[13] Glyn is a leader internationally in this style of arranging, and has to date arranged 48 popular classical works for multilevel orchestral performance.[14]

The value of performing such repertoire is that it offers an immediate point of inspiration for young musicians right from the start of their instrumental studies, often the most daunting stage of learning. By performing alongside an elite-level orchestra, young players can experience the power and beauty of instrumental music at the highest level. As the programme

Leading the Way 71

targets the boroughs of East London in particular, which have a very multicultural population, it also provides a familiarity with the LSO musicians and venues for many migrant families who may not have otherwise made the connection. The repertoire choices made by the LSO are an important aspect of the On Track model. By arranging such powerful and colourful symphonic works, students are able to experience the full range and colour of a symphony orchestra, alongside making their own contribution. While the original On Track programme was aimed towards the Olympic Games, it has been decided to carry the concept of instrumental participation into the future.

The next growth area for the LSO in terms of the development of young talent is the East London Academy. Growing out of the On Track programme and launching in 2019, the East London Academy is focused on students aged between 11 and 18 who are learning orchestral instruments, with an initial focus on string players. The goal of the programme is to rectify the under-representation of diversity (ethnical, economic, and geographical) in the cohort of students progressing to advanced-level study of orchestral instruments. The stated goals of the programme are to represent East London in all its diversity, assisting young musicians from backgrounds that are currently under-represented in professional symphony orchestras to advance their learning and potentially to make the step to a professional career.[15] The current activities of LSO East London Academy are further discussed in Chapter 8.

Previous activities aiming to support young talent have been delivered through programmes such as "Take a Bow" and "Rites of Passage." The "Take A Bow" programme has a similar philosophy to the "On Track" model, with students performing alongside the LSO. The repertoire includes arrangements of classical repertoire such as the Bach Double Violin Concerto, alongside new works commissioned for a multilevel orchestra. These works have the advantage of being designed from the beginning to fit with instrumental pedagogy, as well as having engaging themes and stories designed to spark the young players' imaginations. An example is "The Gypsy Violin," by Jeff Moore, which is based on a Transylvanian gypsy folk tale of a violin built by the devil. The Gypsy Violin was originally commissioned by Wiltshire-based charity Superstrings, but was also performed by the LSO Take A Bow group, conducted by Sir John Eliot Gardiner, in London and Paris. The LSO has commissioned similar works from Moore, including *The Sea and the Sky* (2011) and *River Journey* (premiered at the Barbican in June 2012).[16] The "Rites of Passage" concert, held at the Barbican each summer, integrates some of the On Track work with other projects.

While the East London Academy, On Track, and the earlier programme Take A Bow are each designed to support students in the early stages of learning on their instruments, a number of other LSO programmes are provided for the emerging generation of professional musicians and composers. The LSO and the Guildhall School of Music and Drama have close

72 Leading the Way

ties, strengthened by their shared residence of London's Barbican Centre. Students in the Guildhall's postgraduate orchestral artistry course are coached in elite-level orchestral skills by LSO musicians, alongside master-classes by orchestras visiting the Barbican, including the Concertgebouw, Leipzig Gewandhaus, the Los Angeles Philharmonic (LA Phil), and the New York Philharmonic. The course offers elite-level students not only the benefits of the Barbican location, but also training in the versatility that characterises the LSO. As stated in the course synopsis, the course aims to develop the skills needed to be a multi-versatile professional ensemble musician. They are aiming to create musicians who are able to play in orchestras, chamber ensembles, as soloists, who are confident with public speaking and delivering community and education projects.[17]

In addition to the orchestral artistry master's degree, the LSO has also offered recital opportunities for selected Guildhall students at the Barbican through the LSO Platforms programme. Opportunities for students at other London music colleges are provided through the String Experience, which has, at the time of writing, successfully transitioned 14 students into membership of the LSO and a further 19 as extra list players. Twenty-two past LSO String Experience graduates have positions with other leading UK orchestras.[18] Support is also provided to six young composers a year through the Panufnik Composers Scheme and LSO Soundhub, and to conductors through the Donatella Flick LSO Conducting Competition, with the winner appointed the LSO assistant conductor.

The strength of the LSO's education and community engagement work was given fresh publicity in March 2015, upon the announcement that Sir Simon Rattle would be their next chief conductor. Official press releases by both Rattle and the LSO stressed their shared belief in the importance of developing community links, with a goal of merging performing, teaching, and learning together in the orchestra's activities.[19]

In June 2015, a further announcement was made that Rattle would take on the role of artist-in-association with the Barbican Centre and the Guildhall School of Music and Drama, which increased the LSO's scope for collaboration and community engagement.[20] Specific initiatives delivered over Rattle's tenure have included a series of commissions by the Barbican for the LSO; an annual series of operas mounted jointly by the LSO and the Barbican; a regular series of side-by-side projects for the LSO and Guildhall students; and support for new postgraduate courses in conducting and choral training.

Rattle has a long history of supporting music education, raising the profile of education at the City of Birmingham Symphony Orchestra (CBSO) considerably during his tenure there, and advocating for the place of music in the national curriculum. Rattle showed that his allegiance lies with musicians over the government when he signed a petition for the Redbridge Music Service, one of London's leading instrumental music teaching providers, in protest against a threatened funding cut.[21] Upon his appointment as chief conductor in Berlin, Rattle again illustrated his commitment to education by establishing education programmes with the illustrious orchestra, which had not previously ventured into such territory. While Rattle changed the culture of the Berlin Philharmonic by introducing an education and community engagement department, when he moved to the LSO he was working with an orchestra which has been at the forefront of such work since the 1980s. It has proven to be a strong partnership that has delivered strong benefits for both the LSO and the community it serves.

A concrete indication of Rattle's vision for the LSO, and his commitment to community music making, is the commissioning of several works designed for community involvement. The first of these, a choral work for young people, the community, and the LSO by Jonathon Dove, titled "The Monster in the Maze," was premiered by Rattle and the LSO on 5 July 2015.[22] This was the first of a trilogy of community operas delivered by the LSO and conducted by Rattle. The second in the trio marked the last major work by Sir Peter Maxwell Davies with his opera "The Hogboon." Premiered on 28 June 2016, "The Hogboon" was poignantly completed only six months before Maxwell Davies passed away. With both score and libretto written by Maxwell Davies, the plot is based on an Orkney folk tale, inspired by his home community of 40 years. This work was critically acclaimed upon its premiere, with critics remarking on both the quality of Davies' compositional skill and the contribution he had made towards music education and community participation. As one reviewer stated:

> It's a measure of the man that his final work, The Hogboon, should fill a stage with hundreds of children, professional singers beside students and amateurs, a world-class orchestra – and Sir Simon Rattle; that it should be as rich and complex as it needed to be, with no concessions to its younger performers. Max lived out his belief that his art was genuinely to be made for everyone, and that children "must get their hands dirty in the music."[23]

The final in the trilogy is the 2017 "A Trip to the Moon" by Andrew Norman, a co-commission between the Berlin Philharmonic, the London Symphony Orchestra, and the Los Angeles Philharmonic. This whimsical work was inspired by the 1902 silent film of the same name, and has received several performances following its premiere in June 2017. Director of LSO Discovery Andra East explains the LSO's commitment to opera and choral works:

> Singing is one of the most accessible ways for people to engage with a musical experience. The choral programme focuses on people who live, study or work in the local area. That is very much about how we make sure that the people who are on our doorstep are engaged with the orchestra's activity and can take part, even if they don't play an

74 *Leading the Way*

> instrument. So singing is one of the ways that we've been able to do that.[24]

Each of the community operas involves a "monster" theme; however, East explains that this was a coincidence rather than a content brief to the composers:

> That was complete coincidence, but what they all had in common was they were all tales that could be told by a community, told by a large group of people. So that's why they were landing on these stories – whether they're existing stories or new stories, they were about how the community deals with a challenge. It obviously has to be family friendly because some of our youngest singers were as young as eight, so we had to make sure it was something that was accessible on that front. The other key elements are that it's on the Barbican stage; it's really closely aligned with the overall LSO programming, conducted by Sir Simon Rattle. The orchestra on stage was a mixture of professionals as well as our students from the Guildhall School; we also involved a lot of singers from the Guildhall School as well. We had several layers of ability and experience, which again was really important because you had young people looking up at the Guildhall students. Then we have professional soloists as well so it's mixed ability in the fullest sense of the word.[25]

The managing director of the LSO, Kathryn McDowell, has a long-standing connection with Sir Peter Maxwell Davies; indeed, in many ways the Hogboon commission marked a cyclical link to the early stages of McDowell's career in orchestral management. In the 1980s, McDowell worked as development manager for the Scottish Chamber Orchestra, which at that time was managed by Ian Ritchie. In this role, McDowell worked alongside Maxwell Davies on a large-scale commissioning project, the Strathclyde Concerti, in which Davies composed ten new concerti for soloists from the SCO in the lead up to Glasgow's City of Culture in 1990. McDowell project managed an education programme linked with this commission, in which emerging composers devised activities that linked with each new concerto. This event made a substantial and ongoing impact, as it proved to be a career launching pad for several composers who have themselves gone on to establish career paths merging composition with community engagement, most notably James MacMillan. McDowell's connection with Maxwell Davies, or "Max" as he is affectionately known within the music world, continued through her time with the Arts Council where she was project leader for Davies' large-scale education commission "The Turn of the Tide." Throughout her career, McDowell has kept a focus on supporting composers and promoting opportunities for them to link with orchestral education programming. In an interview with the author, McDowell explains:

Leading the Way 75

I would make a plea for the role of composers: that's something which is very strong in the LSO programme. If we're talking about the future, then we must always have the composers alongside us and involved in this work.

For the composers, working in orchestral education and community programmes develops their skills and opportunities as well. If you talk to a composer like James MacMillan for instance, you'll hear how important that work has been all throughout his career as a complement to his own writing.[26]

With McDowell's strong, community-minded leadership at the helm and Rattle's support, the LSO Discovery Department remains at the forefront of international best practice in orchestral education, community engagement, and partnership working. It has been a potent combination: an orchestra with a leading reputation in education and community engagement work, a managing director who was one of the pioneers of education and community engagement, and a chief conductor who matches rhetoric with action in his advocacy for such work. However, this relationship is entering a new stage, with Rattle announcing his departure from the LSO in 2023 to take the helm of the Bavarian Radio Symphony Orchestra in Munich. While classical music observers immediately made connections between Rattle's departure and the stagnation of plans to build a new concert hall in London, Rattle states that the decision was a personal one, made to enable him to be closer to his family. While this will be a period of transition for the LSO, with new Chief Conductor Antonio Pappano taking over the reins in 2024, the Discovery Department remains firmly prioritised by McDowell.

While the principal focus of LSO Discovery is on making connections with its local East London community and strengthening music making in the capital, it has an increasing international presence. This is due in part to the inclusion of Discovery projects in LSO international tours, including projects in Paris, Tokyo, and New York. During their tour of Australia, the LSO offered a Discovery project in which 130 students from across the state of New South Wales rehearsed, collaborated, and performed with the LSO. The LSO has also influenced the development of a community engagement programme at the Aix-en-Provence Festival through an ongoing residency partnership. The LSO's increasing digital presence has also broadened its access both nationally and internationally, an area of future growth for the orchestra, as discussed further in Chapter 8.

BBC Orchestras: "Ten Pieces"

While the BBC orchestras each individually deliver strong education and community engagement programmes, it is the joint BBC flagship programme, "Ten Pieces," that is gaining most attention at present. Launched

76 Leading the Way

Figure 4.1 LSO Create, 2019. Credit: Kevin Leighton.

in June 2014, the BBC "Ten Pieces" Project is a national campaign intended to raise the profile of classical music and encourage students to engage in creative responses to music.[27]

The first project was targeted towards primary school–aged students, with a subsequent three iterations delivering resources for early years, secondary students, and students with special needs and disabilities. The starting point for each project is a selection of ten orchestral pieces covering a wide historical span. For the initial project, the works chosen were Short Ride in a Fast Machine (John Adams), Symphony No 5 (Beethoven), "Storm" from "Peter Grimes" (Britten), "Mars" from "The Planets" (Holst), Zadok the Priest (Handel), In the Hall of the Mountain King (Grieg), Connect It (Anna Meredith), Horn Concerto No 4 (Mozart), A Night on the Bare Mountain (Mussorgsky), and The Firebird (Stravinsky).

The project has commissioned a new high-profile composition each year, adding to the body of orchestral and choral compositions with pedagogical appeal. Each of these compositions is linked to a set of inspirational creative activities in the free teaching resource packs provided by BBC Ten Pieces, in addition to highly participatory performance resources. In 2019, the featured commission was film composer Hans Zimmer's "Earth," inspired by visions of Earth from space and drawing on Zimmer's previous scores for Blue Planet II and Planet Earth II. This beautiful, shimmering work was designed with the core goal of igniting children's creativity.[28]

Figure 4.2 LSO On Track Next Generation 2018. Credit: Doug Peters.

While this work encourages students to tap into their inner film score composition skills, Anna Clyne's work "Night Ferry" provides inspiration on the use of graphic scores and poetry. Clyne explains that her initial inspiration for "Night Ferry" was a concept of a stormy ocean crossing, with the music based on moody paintings that she created and used as a graphic score, as well as Samuel Taylor Coleridge's poem "The Rime of the Ancient Mariner." The learning activities matched to this work help students to use these creative cross-arts processes themselves, as well as providing links to further compositions based on graphic scores, including John Cage's "Aria" and Ligeti's "Artikulation." Anna Meredith's new work "Connect It," commissioned for the project in 2014, includes body percussion, enabling an easy participatory entry point to the work for students without instrumental training. Kerry Andrews' "No Place Like" is a vocal score for a capella choir. This work is perhaps the most integrated with student creativity, as the sparking point for the work was a literacy project for Ten Pieces students in which they gave a written response to the theme of home and place.

78 Leading the Way

Figure 4.3 LSO On Track Next Generation 2018. Credit: Doug Peters.

Figure 4.4 Michael Tilson Thomas Workshop with LSO and Guildhall School of Music and Drama 2019. Credit: Clive Totman.

Leading the Way 79

Figure 4.5 Michael Tilson Thomas Workshop with LSO and Guildhall School of Music and Drama, 2019. Credit: Clive Totman.

Figure 4.6 Floods of Fire, Adelaide Symphony Orchestra. Credit: Matt Turner.

These words were then formed into a "long poem," which provided the basis for Andrews' composition.[29] The piece also features a soundscape of layered sounds from daily life, inspiring children to create their own soundscapes by recording the sounds of their day.

Many of the works have clear extra-musical themes, again clearly chosen to easily enable children an access point to engage with the piece imaginatively. The choice of repertoire for such a high-profile music education campaign was always going to attract scrutiny and no small degree of criticism. On the whole, however, there is strong support for the project across the United Kingdom. Some 260 organisations including Music Hubs, Music Services, orchestras, conservatoires, and other specialists in music, dance, and the arts have become "Ten Pieces Champions."[30] In some cases, this role entails performing some of the Ten Pieces in concerts, while other organisations are offering workshops to assist students with the skills required to make their creative responses. The creative response element is central to the project, and the website has a wealth of extra resources available to students and teachers, including teacher's notes and specialist videos to support students in their creative skills. In particular, the project is looking for original creative responses from students in three key art forms: composition, dance, and art/digital art, and students and schools have been encouraged to upload their completed projects to the BBC for potential inclusion in Ten Pieces Proms concerts.

Figure 4.7 Floods of Fire, ASO. Credit: Claudio Raschella.

Figure 4.8 Glyndebourne Opera Production of "Agreed" © Glyndebourne Productions Ltd. Photo: Robert Workman

The pieces have been recorded by several BBC orchestras, including the BBC Scottish Symphony Orchestra, the BBC National Orchestra of Wales, the BBC Philharmonic Orchestra, and the BBC Symphony Orchestra. Accompanying films have been released, making full use of the BBC's strength in film and digital technology. A strength of the programme is that there are many free arrangements of repertoire, created for the project, available on the website to suit players of differing abilities. This is an invaluable resource for schools and community music organisations, saving them from the logistical challenges of making such arrangements themselves.[31] Aiming to be a truly national programme, participation is well spread across the entire United Kingdom, including schools in Northern Ireland, Wales, and even remote islands in the Outer Hebrides. One of the obvious benefits of a project with a strong digital and online element is that its reach can be easily spread into remote geographical locations. While it remains to be seen what the longevity and full impact of the programme will be, it has certainly achieved its first aim: to raise the profile of orchestral music.

Adelaide Symphony Orchestra

The Adelaide Symphony Orchestra (ASO), founded in 1936, is the largest performing arts company in the state of South Australia. While Adelaide is

Figure 4.9 Glyndebourne Opera Production of "Belongings" © Glyndebourne Productions Ltd. Photo: Robert Workman.

a mid-size city by Australian and international standards, its musical contribution stands tall as Australia's only UNESCO City of Music, awarded in December 2015. This designation was founded on both the historical leadership of Adelaide in music – the Elder Conservatorium of Music, for example, is the oldest tertiary training institute of music in Australia – as well as the current vibrancy of the music education and performance ecosystem that the city enjoys. The ASO, a world-class orchestra with an ambitious education and community engagement programme, is integral to the network of both music education and performance across the state. It has some challenges to grapple with: the state of South Australia includes some of the most remote communities of Australia, including coastal communities along the Limestone Coast and the Eyre and York peninsulas, as well as rugged inland communities in the Flinders Ranges and the APY Lands. With the state including the famous wilderness of Kangaroo Island, a key challenge for any community-focused organisation is how to maintain connections with the entirety of the state, maximising inclusivity and participation and minimising inequity of provision. These issues are at the heart of the community engagement and education programmes of the Adelaide Symphony Orchestra, led by Learning and Community Projects Manager Elizabeth McCall. Despite the challenges of the pandemic, a number of new learning and community programmes have been developed by the ASO over

Leading the Way 83

the past three years, and the orchestra is now achieving new levels of participation and community engagement.

At the time of writing, the most high-profile programme delivered by the ASO's learning and community engagement team is "Floods of Fire," a community co-creation project that links the ASO with arts and community organisations across the state. This is a highly inclusive project with key partners including Tutti Arts, an Adelaide-based disability arts organisation, and Nexus Arts, an arts organisation with a multicultural inclusivity focus. The programme also links with the University of Adelaide's music access programme, the Open Music Academy, as well as Brink Productions, and the Country Fire Service and State Emergency Service. The theme was designed to allow the South Australian community to cathartically process and reflect on the fires and floods of 2019–2020, which had a large impact on the state. This project is directed by Airan Berg, an international theatre maker and artistic director who specialises in large-scale participatory inclusive projects. In addition to leading this project, Berg is also currently artistic director of Festival der Regionen in Austria and the *Orfeo and Majnun* collaborative opera project.

The Floods of Fire project is notable on several levels. It is a leading example of inclusivity, with people living with disabilities at the heart of the creative process and the performance of the project. It is also inclusive geographically, connecting students from remote Port Augusta's Carlton School through the entire process, from creative workshops that provided the foundations of a composition through to the high-profile performances in Adelaide. These students were connected to the project through the University of Adelaide's "Open Music Academy" access programme. The students, and their teacher, have told of how impactful the experience was for them. To give one example, from having no previous experience with orchestral music, one of the students now wants to be a professional musician.

The project has co-creation at its heart; in the words of McCall:

> It was originally conceived by Airan Berg, who is experienced in large scale participatory creative projects. The ASO came on board when Vince [Ciccarello, ASO Managing Director] met Airan, and looked at how the ASO could engage more deeply with its community. It's really about telling people's stories through music, and creating music to communicate those stories. It explores the themes of floods and fires – climate change and its impact on our earth, people's experiences of floods of fire, whether that is the creation story, biblical stories, cultural stories that they have. The original idea is that the themes can be created in many contexts, not just through orchestral music – it can be told through drama, dance … the ASO is trying to encourage this creativity across the city with many different partners. The partners come from many different walks of life and different cultural institutions. We're

84   *Leading the Way*

working with Tutti Arts, who have a number of professional and community artists with a disability; we're working with Nexus Arts who focus on culturally diverse and intercultural projects; we've worked with the University, with students from the Elder Conservatorium, with professional composers and First Nations artists.[32]

The ASO has a strong connection with the Elder Conservatorium of Music, the tertiary music department of the University of Adelaide. This connection is evident through the Floods of Fire project: in addition to the connection with the Open Music Academy, the project included the deputy director of the conservatorium conducting the ASO, the head of classical performance as concertmaster of the orchestra, three composers on the project are staff members of the conservatorium, and the ASO's string section was joined by tertiary string students from the conservatorium.

This level of collaboration and partnership is a strength of Adelaide. The Elder Conservatorium and ASO connection has been formalised by a memorandum of understanding with the two organisations delivering key training opportunities both to emerging orchestral musicians and, in a first for Australia, to conductors. Students in honours and master of music degree programmes at the Elder Conservatorium receive several opportunities to conduct the Adelaide Symphony Orchestra throughout each year of their training. Developed by senior lecturer in conducting at the Elder Conservatorium, Dr Luke Dollman, the conducting programmes are intended to develop more "home-grown" Australian conductors. This has been an ongoing issue in Australia, with only two orchestras featuring an Australian-born chief conductor over the past 100 years: the Sydney Symphony Orchestra with Sir Charles Mackerras, Stuart Challender, and current chief Simone Young, and the Adelaide Symphony Orchestra with Nicholas Carter.

"Silos and Symphonies" is a further flagship programme for the Adelaide Symphony Orchestra's learning and community engagement department. This programme was also launched in the middle of the pandemic, in 2020. The programme connects with school children at some of South Australia's most remote schools. Initially planned to include face-to-face activity, the pandemic required a rethink which resulted in the entire programme being delivered online. Like Floods of Fire, this programme centres on the co-creation of new musical works. The students work together with South Australian composers Julian Ferraretto, Adam Page, Hilary Kleinig, and Belinda Gehlert in creative workshops to devise and develop new musical works. Students develop improvisation skills, skills in arranging for multiple instruments, and songwriting skills through the sessions, supported and inspired by their composer-facilitator. The resulting works are then performed and streamed live by the Adelaide Symphony Orchestra from its home base, connecting the students to the heart of the orchestra's activity. Elizabeth McCall explains that the project, emerging from a pragmatic

Leading the Way 85

response to the pandemic, has evolved into a significant ongoing part of their programme:

> Silos and Symphonies was born in the year that the pandemic really started to impact Australia and we had to cancel our Festival of Learning, which meant that all our live performance initiatives going into schools had to be cancelled. So we were wondering how we could engage with schools when we didn't even know if people would be in classrooms at that point. We thought how do we use the internet, how do we make sure that it is still linked to the orchestra? So we came up with the idea of using composition via Zoom, whether that was going to be with a class or with students at home, to collaborate with a composer to create music for the orchestra. Since then it's evolved into composers working with classrooms both in person and via online platforms using a variety of collaborative composition techniques to create a new work, then the composer goes away and orchestrates that, building on the ideas that the students had contributed, whether that's melodic ideas, the shape of the composition. There is still input from the students through the orchestra's rehearsal process through a live stream, enabling regional students to access the rehearsal and contribute. They can ask to hear more of the harp for example, or ask for a decrescendo. They really contribute in the way a composer does in the room. Then we have a performance where either the students come in person or watch over the live stream. Themes that have been covered are personal to each school, students love to tell the story of their home or their place. Some are about the pandemic and its impact on them. Our upcoming project this year is working with a first nations artist to create a new piece for Reconciliation week. This format can be flexible and adaptable to each classroom, we can tie it in to whatever teachers are focusing on. For example, if they are working on a particular compositional technique we can tie that in to the workshops.[33]

Several of the ASO's projects feature the workshop leading skills of Australian jazz violinist, composer, and creative music education specialist, Julian Ferraretto. Originally from Adelaide, Ferraretto moved to the United Kingdom in 2002 where he built his career for 11 years. Alongside his performing career as a leading jazz violinist, composer, and director, Ferraretto also developed an interest in the creative, improvisation-based music education work for which the United Kingdom is particularly known. His workshop skills were developed with two key ensembles in London: the Wigmore Hall's resident creative ensemble, "Ignite," and the London Music Masters' (LMM) Bridge Project.[34] Ferraretto led the London Music Masters in several improvisation workshops that culminated in a performance alongside London Philharmonic Orchestra members and Ferraretto's jazz quartet at the Royal Festival Hall.[35] The influence of the UK workshop

86 *Leading the Way*

style is evident in the way Ferraretto works creatively with students, including his use of warm-up games, literacy links, and graphic-notated scores that create a sense of ease while improvising. Ferraretto also lectures with the Elder Conservatorium and delivers creative workshops for the Open Music Academy – he is making a significant impact on the development of creative-based music education in Adelaide.

Alongside creative workshop–based programmes, the Adelaide Symphony Orchestra also highlights opportunities for students and community musicians to play alongside the ASO, first introduced in 2014. The "Big Rehearsal" is an annual opportunity for students to play with the ASO, which immerses students playing orchestral instruments in the atmosphere and powerful sound-world of the professional symphony orchestra. The Big Rehearsal aims to solidify engagement and development for the emerging generation of young symphonists.

The "Festival of Learning and Participation" is a further new initiative for the ASO, first introduced in 2015. The festival is led by British animateur Paul Rissmann, who has also worked with several of Australia's other symphony orchestras. During the ASO Festival, Rissmann facilitates creative education workshops for secondary students and presents concerts with a participatory element for junior school, middle school, and family audiences.[36] Rissmann can potentially create a lasting impact on the practice of music education in Adelaide through his visits, as alongside his public performances and workshops he also offers training sessions for both classroom teachers and ASO musicians. While the exemplary quality of Rissmann's work has added substantially to the development of the ASO's learning department, there has also been over the past seven years an upsurge of involvement in creative music education by local South Australian musicians. From an initial point of UK influence on the ASO's development of a creative music focus, Adelaide's creative programming is now creating its own international influence.

An example of this is Paul Rissmann's recent commission by the ASO's learning department, at that time under the direction of Emily Gann, "What Do You Do With An Idea." Based on the enchanting children's book by Kobi Yamada, illustrated by Mae Besom, the commission brings the book's theme of the power of creativity, dreams, and ideas to musical fruition. The initial commission was premiered by the ASO at its Festival of Learning in 2018 in a performance produced by Emily Gann. The performance linked the ASO with Adelaide's flagship youth choral organisation, Young Adelaide Voices, in addition to linking across arts through a featured dancer and a multimedia focus on the book's words and images. In 2019, the work was given its northern hemisphere premiere in a performance by the London Symphony Orchestra and the LSO Discovery Junior Choir, conducted by the 2018 winner of the LSO's Donatella Flick Conducting competition. Now working independently as director of the organisation "Connecting the Dots in Music," Gann continues to develop the "Idea" project; in 2021,

Leading the Way 87

the Adelaide Symphony Orchestra recorded the work and the recording is to be launched alongside education resources in 2023.

Another recent initiative for the ASO, also led by Gann, was the commission of a new school concert project, "The Bush Concert." Composed by head of jazz at the Elder Conservatorium, Mark Simeon Ferguson, in 2015 and based on an Australian picture book by Helda Visser, this work tells the story of a group of birds that are experiencing a drought. With this programme the ASO musicians are on familiar ground, as the orchestra has for some time offered schools projects based on books, most notably "Edward and Edwina." A new, and very positive step, taken by "The Bush Concert" is that it places the focus firmly on the ASO musicians. The "Edward and Edwina" project, while very popular, was a joint performance by ASO musicians and puppeteers who acted out the story. As always in such a scenario, it is easy for children to lose focus from the musicians and become absorbed in the visuals of the puppetry. With the "Bush Concert" format, the eight musicians tell the story, supported by a singer/presenter.

The project is highly participatory, with students encouraged to learn songs and dances that are included in the performance. Schools are also given the opportunity to include a creative music workshop before the performance. During this workshop, students develop original music, which is then incorporated into the performance. The show is a delightful way for students to engage with music, and also offers substantial cross-curricula learning. The story and music closely connect with the Australian landscape and wildlife: for example, over 35 Australian bird calls are included in the music, and a tongue-twisting song lists a bewildering number of gum trees. The preparatory activities cover all five areas of the new Australian Curriculum for the Arts and are supported by a teacher professional development workshop.[37]

While there are clearly many positive developments underway at the ASO at the present time, their long-term planning can sometimes be hindered by the lack of a permanent venue. From an examination of best practice internationally, it has become clear that the availability of venues has a strong influence on education and community programming. Orchestras with a permanent space available to them are able to make significant developments to their programmes, with the venue providing a regular and ongoing point of community engagement. Looking to the future for this vibrant musical city, a new venue would allow the music performance and education organisations of South Australia to collectively create an even stronger impact.

There are further signs that the ASO management is keen to invest and develop its learning department. In 2013, the ASO undertook a strategic review, supported by the Australia Council and Arts SA, and arrived at several key recommendations to help them move forward. One of these recommendations was to form a comprehensive community engagement plan, with a learning programme central to that plan. Alongside this was

88   *Leading the Way*

a commitment to commission new works each year, and to develop a digital strategy for an online learning programme.[38] The ASO's learning and community engagement has subsequently grown considerably, and they have followed through with the commitment to commission new works. Currently, however, there remains an opportunity to continue to increase their digital engagement. The state of South Australia has many isolated communities, which would benefit from further investment in this area.

Los Angeles Philharmonic

Music and Artistic Director Gustavo Dudamel is integral to the programmes delivered by the learning department of the Los Angeles Philharmonic. Dudamel himself famously developed his skills through the Venezuelan El Sistema, coming to the world's attention as the curly-haired, charismatic conductor of the Simón Bolívar Symphony Orchestra taking the world by storm with its exuberance and electrically charged musical performances. While political circumstances have subsequently changed the context around El Sistema in Venezuela, Dudamel has deeply held convictions on the right of all children to access music education, and on the life-enhancing properties that music brings to all. Since his arrival at the Los Angeles Philharmonic, Dudamel has been hands-on and fully committed to developing and enhancing their delivery of learning and community engagement programmes across the entirety of the city – as well as creating connections nationally and internationally. Dudamel was strongly supported through the early period of his tenure by Deborah Borda, president and chief executive officer of the LA Phil from 2000 through to 2017. Borda, struck by the obvious talent and potential of the young conductor, also found his commitment to social engagement and his Sistema links highly appealing. Borda visited El Sistema in Venezuela with Dudamel in 2006, part of the courting period after his debut the previous year. A year later, the LA Phil launched its Youth Orchestra Los Angeles (better known as "YOLA") programme – a youth orchestra programme inspired by El Sistema that has now gained its own, independent acclaim.

In 2009, the wooing paid off as Dudamel joined the orchestra as music director. The YOLA programme was now firmly entrenched at the initial site, the EXPO Centre in South LA. The programme grew steadily across the years: the second programme, YOLA at HOLA (Heart of Los Angeles) was launched in 2010, followed by YOLA at Torres in East LA in 2014 and YOLA at Camino Nuevo in 2017, and finally the Judith and Thomas L. Beckmen YOLA Centre at Inglewood in 2021. The Beckmen Centre marks a new stage for the programme with the investment in its first permanent, purpose-built facility. Designed pro bono by Frank Gehry, the centre provides a focal point for the programmes. The centre features a space for collaborative ensemble rehearsals as well as possessing the digital capabilities to connect musicians and teachers, as discussed further in Chapter 8.

Leading the Way 89

While the YOLA programme stands firmly in its own right, it is grounded in the principles of the original Venezuelan Sistema. The programme connects with students in their own communities, providing them with free instruments, intensive music instruction, academic tutoring, and frequent performance opportunities. The YOLA programme shares the same expectation of commitment and dedication as El Sistema, with students required to attend between 12 and 15 hours of programmed activity each week. In return, they are provided with an opportunity that aims to provide access to the power of music, to boost their learning through school, and to support them through a safe, structured, and focused learning community. The opportunities provided have included some clear highlights – the YOLA students hit the limelight in 2016 with their performance at the half-time break of the Superbowl, performing for an audience of millions alongside superstars Coldplay, Beyoncé, and Bruno Mars. YOLA musicians are also provided with strong links to the LA Philharmonic, ranging from tutoring from LA Phil musicians for talented and advanced players, opportunities to observe rehearsals in the Walt Disney Concert Hall, through to invitations to join the LA Phil on international tours.

Elsje Kibler-Vermaas, vice president of learning at the Los Angeles Philharmonic, says that the experiences on tour have been highly enriching for the YOLA students, and have also influenced the growth of the programme. The tours included regular visits to the Barbican, where the LA Phil was the international orchestra-in-residence for several years, in addition to tours to South Korea and the Edinburgh International Festival. Kibler-Vermaas explains:

> The collaboration with the Barbican was a really interesting influence in our work. We always really try to connect with our partners and see how we can bring our young people from YOLA together with young people from the programmes who we partner with. At the Barbican we worked with their Creative Learning Department and with everybody there for a couple of years. We did a project that started here in LA, we had young people working in London, and we brought them together. It was very focused on who they are as artists: they made a statement about what the arts mean for them and what they think it should look like. It was very impactful just hearing it from young people's voices. We also worked with Guildhall through the Barbican and went into schools and that was very new to our young musicians to let go of their repertoire and do creative music making and those sorts of things.[39]

Elsje Kibler-Vermaas has been in her present role with the LA Philharmonic since 2017. She had previously worked with the orchestra as education director from 2006 to 2009, before taking up roles with the Concertgebouw Orchestra and spending six years as director of the master of arts in teaching programme at the Longy School of Music of Bard College, a flagship

90 *Leading the Way*

programme developing teaching artistry. Kibler-Vermaas feels that the YOLA programme, together with the LA Phil's other learning and engagement programmes, are now a part of the orchestra's DNA – core to their essential work. While it takes commitment from the entire organisation for this level of programme ownership, she believes that Dudamel's impact has been substantial. She explains:

> The connection really is the fact that Gustavo grew up in in El Sistema and came out of that with a high passion for music education and working with young people, and is very community driven. Those are all priorities for him, and that's a big part of who we've become too. We've also definitely learned a lot from the programmes in Venezuela and in other places but I think after having been around for 15 years now, YOLA is a programme of its own. It's really developed based on what the needs are here in our city and what's right for the young people here within our city and within our country.
>
> The fact that we have a Music and Artistic Director as our leader here for the LA Philharmonic who's so passionate about the importance of working with young people and including them and offering them access to the beauty of art and music making – I think, obviously that has to be one of the reasons that we are where we are today. He's been hugely inspirational to the young people within our programmes too. It was really important to him to work with an organisation that also had a shared interest in establishing programmes, not like his programmes in Venezuela per se, but that had that type of commitment to young people.[40]

The Beckmen Centre was constructed to celebrate the orchestra's centenary year, creating a statement about the future directions of the orchestra. The centre benefited from the expert contribution of Frank Gehry, who donated his time to help transform the site into a state-of-the-art performance and education venue, while maintaining a sense of inclusion and community. The centre is welcoming, light, and airy, and deliberately fosters connections and helps the wider YOLA community to feel at home. Kibler-Vermaas shares:

> What's important is that Frank knows the programme really well through Gustavo and he knows that a big part of our programme is not just about music making but also spending time together. So you'll see in the space that there's a lot of little nooks, for instance, with benches. There's a family lounge where you can spend time, where siblings do homework for instance, and there's a kitchenette for parents. So there is very much a take your time, spend time here together feel, while very much focused on learning. Then you step into the performance space and that is a high quality, beautiful, *beautiful* space. It has similar

Leading the Way 91

acoustics to those we have at Walt Disney Concert Hall, which is very glamorous for a music school obviously, and we have retractable seating that allows us to have a very open floor plan. We have the same footprint as Walt Disney Concert Hall on the stage. So what I love the most is that for the seven year old student who starts here at YOLA at Inglewood, this is what they know. This is how they roll, this is where you get your music lessons and that's what we wanted.[41]

These points echo the views of many experts interviewed for this book – the importance of a venue, of a place for connection for programming. The opportunity to enhance the performance experience of students through access to a beautiful concert hall adds immeasurably to the impact of a programme. While great work can, of course, be achieved anywhere through the magic of a good music teacher – El Sistema famously began in a garage – the ability to connect children to a space that is designed to elevate their learning and performance is an important factor in their growth. The orchestra is clearly very proud to have the Beckmen Centre as the physical embodiment of their centennial celebrations. Kibler-Vermaas explains the planning:

It was really important for us to not just look back to the past and celebrate what's happened over those 100 years. It was a really important moment for us to look at the next 100 years of who we are as an organisation, as an orchestra, what our role is within our community. What was really prioritised was investing in the future of our young musicians, those who are currently in our programme, but also those of coming years and the building is evidence of that.[42]

Kibler-Vermaas feels that the programme is now moving into a new stage of its growth. She explains that they are not focusing on growth of the number of students in the programme, but rather on growth for impact. During the pandemic, the ties with the local community became in many ways stronger. Their community was hit hard by the economic as well as the health blows of the pandemic, and the YOLA programmes stepped in as food banks as well as striving to maintain teaching programmes digitally. With the YOLA programme now established for 15 years, Kibler-Vermaas has members of her team who originally began as students. This is a key focus for her plans for development – she is thinking of career development, workforce development for the student body. There is also growth in the national impact of the programme, and growth into teacher training. The orchestra has strong links with the Longy School of Music of Bard College with its master of arts in teaching degree. The development of the "Take a Stand" conference in 2012, in collaboration with Longy, has been pivotal in establishing a mentoring and industry hub role for the orchestra in the training of teaching artists and for organisations who are running similar programmes. This conference has established an international profile in

92 Leading the Way

providing a networking platform that elevates and supports the work of teaching artists and education personnel.

Another area of growth for the future is in opening up pathways to professional orchestral work for typically under-represented demographics of the Los Angeles community. As with many programmes discussed in this book, it is to be hoped that the pathways established by orchestral education and engagement programmes help to rectify this imbalance. Perhaps in another 10–20 years, as a result of YOLA and the East London Academy for example, we will see a very different demographic of players in the LA Phil and the London Symphony Orchestra.

In addition to the YOLA programmes, the LA Philharmonic offers several other learning and engagement programmes that have caught national and international attention. From 2012 to 2015, Dudamel conducted three projects that united the Simón Bolívar Symphony Orchestra with the LA Philharmonic. The first of these, in 2012, was the "Mahler Project." Ambitious by any measure, this project involved the performance of all nine of Mahler's symphonies, as well as the Adagio of the incomplete Tenth, with performances shared by the LA Philharmonic and the Simón Bolívar. The orchestras united for the mammoth Eighth – Symphony of a Thousand. Not content with doing the Mahler cycle once in Los Angeles, the entire cycle was repeated in Caracas with an even larger body of musicians (1,600) performing the Eighth. Following the acclaim and international platform of this event, two further similar projects were scheduled in subsequent years: in 2014 the "TchaikovskyFest" and in 2015 "Immortal Beethoven."

In addition to the programmes linking with and supporting young orchestral musicians, the LA Phil also has a focus on the development of young composers. The Nancy and Barry Sanders Composer Fellowship Programme, designed by Steven Stucky, offers young composers a rich multiyear experience that combines tuition in composition with performance and recording opportunities for their works with musicians from the LA Phil and other professional musicians. The fellows are also offered a unique level of access to the LA Phil's performance schedule, with tickets to 20 concerts annually and access to rehearsals. Visiting composers give talks and presentations to the composers, including some of the leading composers of the 21st century, such as John Corigliano, John Adams, Esa-Pekka Salonen, and Kaija Saariaho.

Although the LA Philharmonic has undeniably had its challenges over the past years – Los Angeles was particularly hard hit with the pandemic – it is clear that their commitment to their education programmes remains undimmed. Research projects have been undertaken on the work of YOLA by both Stanford University's SPARQ Centre and the University of Southern California's Brain and Creativity Institute. Findings from the longitudinal studies include that auditory processing shows increased development through YOLA training, in addition to changes in working memory. These findings, the researchers believe, will have transferable benefits to the

Leading the Way 93

development of literacy skills and social interaction. In their 2016 publication of their key findings, the researchers state:

> Our findings provide evidence, for the first time, that experience with music training in younger children interacts with development and is associated with accelerated cortical maturation necessary for general auditory processes such as language, speech and social interaction. This finding is especially important since we showed an equal baseline among the children in the music group and the two comparison groups on these measures prior to training ... Our findings demonstrate that music education has an important role to play in childhood development and add to the converging evidence that music training is capable of shaping skills that are ingredients of success in social and academic development. It is of particular importance that we show these effects in children from disadvantaged backgrounds.[43]

With the "Take a Stand" annual symposium of El Sistema practitioners and teaching artists from around the world now firmly consolidated, the Los Angeles Philharmonic is clearly going to be taking a leadership role in both the practice and advocacy of the value of music education through the coming decades.

Glyndebourne Opera

Glyndebourne Opera is a name that conjures visions of ultimate sybaritic pleasures for music lovers, a treasure box of an opera house nestled in the bucolic folds of the South Downs countryside. The location and story of the opera company's creation by landowner John Christie in 1934, alongside his operatic soprano wife Audrey Milmay, are both swooningly romantic. To modern audiences, the layers of escapism that surround a visit to Glyndebourne – the gardens, the candle-lit suppers – rival the sheer wonder of hearing some of the world's finest opera in a remote country setting.

However, alongside the idyllic location and elite musical standards there is another, very different, story to be told of Glyndebourne Opera. One that is rooted in a strong commitment to inclusion, to diversity, to local community life. One that sees the main stage shared by schoolchildren, that in 1956 staged Fidelio at the local prison, that sees John Christie's ethos "The best that can be done anywhere" applied to the development of one of the world's most innovatory opera education and engagement programmes.

For 25 years, fired by the determined innovation of Katie Tearle MBE, and now under the strong leadership of the current learning and engagement manager, Lucy Perry, Glyndebourne's education department has consistently delivered programmes of radical purpose since 1986. These programmes are underpinned by the same commitment to musical excellence that is brought to the main stage opera programming. The company is now led by renowned

94 *Leading the Way*

director Stephen Langridge, who brings a wealth of experience and insight to his role as artistic director of Glyndebourne. Having developed an illustrious international career, Langridge's roots with Glyndebourne are deep. His first engagements with the company were in the 1980s, working alongside Katie Tearle on projects with the education department. Langridge shares his perspective on his work in opera education and community engagement:

> It shaped me as a creative artist, definitely. Working in the way that I have in community operas and having the opportunity in that sphere – which I would not have had had I stayed just in the area of producing opera – means that I've worked with people I would never have worked with otherwise and would not have understood their processes. So it's taken me some extraordinary places – artistically places and unlikely physical spaces – which have definitely shaped who I am and how I work.[44]

The current programme combines several main streams of activity including education operas, which feature community and youth participation in both the performance and creation stages of the projects; programmes which focus on music and health; and programmes focused on talent development and diversity.

The 2013 Economic Impact Report by Glyndebourne provides evidence of its positive impact on the local area.[45] In a comprehensive research study funded by Arts Council England, East Sussex County Council, Glyndebourne, and the East Sussex Arts Partnership, the report established that Glyndebourne contributes 16 million pounds to the local East Sussex economy each year. With an annual turnover (pre-COVID) of 25 million pounds, Glyndebourne employs 150 full-time staff (many of whom live in local villages) and 1,500 visiting artists and seasonal staff. Glyndebourne's audiences of 150,000 per year, who tend to be on the well-heeled side, spend on average 11 million pounds per year in local hotels, restaurants, shops, and attractions. In terms of the non-economic impact, staff of Glyndebourne also act as governors at three local schools, as well as contributing to local arts and council organisations. The report established, however, that there remained the potential to further develop the company's local impact – lessons for Glyndebourne and other similar companies to learn from. For example, there was further room to develop partnerships and connections between Glyndebourne and other local attractions. A link between Glyndebourne and the Bloomsbury icon Charleston House, for example, would seem a very natural fit. The report also established that there was an appetite from local residents for greater access to Glyndebourne – perhaps in the form of year-round, behind the scenes tours, or the opportunity for local residents to have weddings there.

Katie Tearle has shared valuable insight into the aims, goals, and the process of instigating and developing Glyndebourne's education and community

Leading the Way   95

programmes. In her recent book, *Beyond Britten*, which investigates the role of the composer in the UK community, Tearle explains her goals in creating the pioneering main stage youth operas:

> To create a new work that will build on Glyndebourne's reputation for presenting innovative and ground-breaking work; to meet an over-arching audience development aim by creating an "entry point" work that will attract a diverse audience, many new to opera; to achieve local engagement with national significance that will raise the profile of Glyndebourne – an opera house that is very much part of its community. It should have a strong educational reach, with participants drawn from local and partner schools and our local community, especially young people from disadvantaged areas, provide vocational learning and be linked to the creation of a documentary film and website presence to ensure that the project has greater reach than the four performances at Glyndebourne.[46]

In her first piece of work with the company, Tearle worked with Peter Sellars on Nigel Osborne's work "The Electrification of the Soviet Union." Her goal here was to create education work that linked participants to the essential message and themes of the opera:

> My role was to look at the opera, really interrogate it, and draw out where I thought practical exploration would be useful. I was very clear at the beginning that I wanted young people to get up and sing, impro-vise, understand the story and the music through living it.[47]

This project was followed by further projects connecting Glyndebourne with the local community; there were return projects from 1989 onwards in Lewes Prison, inspired by the 1956 Fidelio Prison project, as well as operas co-created and delivered with community groups. In facilitating these pro-grammes, Tearle established close relationships with composers and direc-tors, several of whom have gone on to forge careers at the highest level. These figures include Langridge, Osborne, and Sellars. Langridge speaks of this early, pioneering stage of community engagement work:

> I was on the front of that really and did an enormous amount of par-ticipation work which I found hugely exciting, and genuinely experi-mental and edgy and risky, and, back then every time we wanted to do something we somehow managed to. We were taking huge risks – artis-tic risks. There was much less formality and there wasn't any kind of orthodoxy really; it was emerging through practice. At Guildhall School of Music and Drama, a systematic approach to training was emerging but the rest of us were making it up as we went along. I cared very much about the work from an artistic and political perspective. If it's a

96 *Leading the Way*

genuine meeting then, like a chemical reaction, both parties have been changed by it.[48]

Tearle also established a close working relationship with Jonathon Dove at Glyndebourne, and in 1990 they worked together on their first community opera, *Hastings Spring*. For this project, Tearle and Dove went into the community and asked them their stories, which were then woven into the story of the opera. Dove linked with the groups and musicians who were already in the community to contribute to the new opera – for example, he found that there were recorder groups and brass bands, so he wrote music for those groups. After hosting an open audition day (anyone over the age of nine could come and take part), they ended up with a cast of 300, which were then rehearsed following the Glyndebourne model.

Hastings Spring was followed by two similar projects based in county communities. Firstly, *Dreamdragons* in Ashford in 1993, about the building of the Channel Tunnel, which was also scored for specific local musical groups (in this case guitars, beginner strings, and recorders). This was then followed by a three-year project called *Walking the Downs*, completed in 1996, working with communities over all of East and West Sussex with funding by the Paul Hamlyn Foundation, again with composer Jonathon Dove. Despite the success and impact of these community works, Tearle reveals that she thought:

> We've got to do things nearer to Glyndebourne, we're a bit too far away from the mothership. I felt that we were a bit divorced from the company and we needed to be more integrated to the values and operation of the company as a whole, but doing this brought its own challenges as we advocated for the work.[49]

This was, however, the inception for the youth and community operas being performed on the Glyndebourne main stage, another pioneering step. The first youth opera on the main stage was *Misper* (1997), a commission with Stephen Plaice and composer John Lunn with 5 professional singers and 73 young people, accompanied by a youth orchestra. This was followed by *Zoe* (2000), with the same partnership of composer John Lunn and librettist Stephen Plaice, again accompanied by Brighton Youth Orchestra. For this work, students were involved in the creative process with workshops in Brighton and Hove schools, as well as the performance. The next project was *School 4 Lovers* (hip hop Cosi fan Tutte) in 2006.

In 2010, the company delivered *Knight Crew*, based on a book by Nicky Singer. This urban retelling of King Arthur was a large-scale community opera, commissioned specifically for the main stage. The production involved every department of Glyndebourne, and was created by Glyndebourne Composer-In-Residence Julian Phillips. Gareth Malone was the chorus master, also featuring in the high-profile BBC TV series "Gareth Goes to

Leading the Way 97

Glyndebourne," which won an Emmy Award in 2011. The programme was launched with a series of 20 skills workshops to support interested participants leading up to the auditions, which were of particular benefit to members of the community with low levels of previous experience. The project also linked with the delivery of a new work-related qualification, the "creative and media diploma," which was made available to young people aged between 14 and 18 years of age, living in the local community.[50]

The 2014 community opera *Imago*, composed by Orlando Gough, again featured Stephen Plaice as librettist (Plaice also wrote *Misper*, *Zoe*, and *School 4 Lovers*). This opera production built on the high profile established by previous works, winning the Royal Philharmonic Society Learning and Participation Award. The cast included professional singers and performers from the local community, accompanied by the high energy Aurora Orchestra joined by young instrumentalists, conducted by Nicholas Collon.

Glyndebourne's youth and community operas do not shy away from controversial or hard-hitting topics; several feature impactful themes linked to current affairs. *Belongings*, composed by Lewis Murphy and premiered in 2017, has twin points of inspiration. It draws on the history of Glyndebourne in World War II, when 300 children were evacuated from London in 1939 and sheltered at Glyndebourne during the Blitz. Entwined alongside this theme, the opera also references the evacuees sheltering across the channel at Calais in the makeshift refugee camp of 2016. *Agreed*, premiered in 2019 and composed by Howard Moody, features a multi-genre score merging classical, world, and jazz music. This opera featured 80 local auditioned singers, local young instrumentalists, 5 professional singers, and the Orchestra of the Age of Enlightenment. The opera was given a spectacular staging at Glyndebourne.

The Place Beyond Tomorrow focuses on ideas for a better future. Despite the challenges of COVID experienced across 2020 and 2021, this work led to a groundbreaking collaboration between Glyndebourne and Minnesota Opera with online sessions. There is a previous connection between Glyndebourne and Minnesota Opera – Minnesota gave the first international performance of *Belongings*.

While the progression of Glyndebourne's community and education programmes may look effortless from the outside, their development was built on the hard work and determination of Katie Tearle. During her 25 years leading the engagement and education work of Glyndebourne, Tearle evolved from a youthful pioneer to a leader in the field; her appointments included chair of RESEO and the regional council member of Arts Council England for the South East. Now working as the manager for New Works, Peters Edition, Tearle has given valuable insight into her years at Glyndebourne in an interview with the author. Tearle explains:

> Luckily I think I've always had a very strong political feeling about democratising opera, democratising the arts and making sure it's for

98 *Leading the Way*

everybody. And that came from my childhood. So I would challenge the status quo as there were many people in the organisation who weren't of the same opinion. I think they were lucky that they had someone who would fight ... I also had support from other education organisers from around the country who were having the same challenges. At the time another Head of Education said to me "you've just got to keep chipping away," so that was my little mantra – just keep chipping, chipping away. And of course, by the time I left, it was central. The role was part of the strategic team setting the direction of the company. There was funding available from a fund that was set up especially. At the beginning I saw a big job that needed doing, and a beautiful place to do it. I was so lucky, it was amazing, apart from the very hard times, but I often thought keep your "iron knickers" on and with a wonderful supporting family, the amazing artists and participants and the champions within the organisation we made it happen.[51]

While the process of bringing the community engagement work to the centre of the organisation was extremely challenging at times for Tearle, she speaks of the support and encouragement she was given by key figures, such as Peter Sellars:

Peter Sellers would always come and talk to the young people. He said working in places like Salzburg and Glyndebourne was good because he knew the movers and shakers came and he could hopefully create some change. Peter makes people think about what they're doing, why they're doing it. He said to me in the 90s: you are the most important person, you do the most important work. It really boosted me, he was very empowering.[52]

At the time of writing, under the strong leadership of Stephen Langridge and Lucy Perry, the community engagement work of Glyndebourne looks set to continue to develop and grow, despite the challenges of COVID and Brexit. Langridge explains:

Fundamentally, my hope is that this kind of engagement and these opportunities for deep learning and artistic development, come closer to the centre. I mean to make the link between the, let's call it the elite output, and the engagement work, which is elite in a different way. We need each other to function. It's one thing, hopefully.

We've also really tried to dig into the challenges of making opera – this Western art, music-theatre form – accessible and diverse in its accessibility and also in its output. That's really important, and of course that means that we need to be looking at how we expand the diversity of people who are participating at all levels, because we want

Leading the Way   99

to be fully inclusive in our work, and we want to broaden the talent pipeline.[53]

Glyndebourne is currently undergoing a strategic review, and the learning and engagement department is central to the forward vision. Even the recent name change, from "education" to "learning and engagement" is a part of this vision, with collaboration and engagement at the heart of programmes. Another change is in the annual touring programme, which is now going to have more of a residency model in the tour venues with learning programmes attached. The touring programme has been a part of Glyndebourne's core annual activity for 50 years, an indication of the company's commitment to accessibility and equity. In the next stage of tour development, they are planning to have a deeper connection with the regional communities with more of a year-round presence. Each venue will be connecting with the company, with a bespoke approach, tailoring projects to match. With a focus on co-creation, on collaboration and inclusivity, it will be interesting over the coming years to see how this approach creates impact and growth in regional venues.

In addition to their celebrated youth and community operas, Glyndebourne has several other flagship programmes with which they connect with their community. "Raise Your Voice" is a programme for local people living with dementia and their carers, delivered in collaboration with the Royal Academy of Music's Open Academy programme. For the past 12 years, the programme has been managed by Glyndebourne's learning and engagement (formerly education) department; however, as of 2021, it has been given the status of a registered charity. Remarkably, the programme managed to continue throughout the pandemic with garden visits by a small team from Glyndebourne and Open Academy, working on a project themed on *L'Elisir D'Amour*. Inspiration for musical creativity was provided by love letters on the theme of Tristan and Isolde, as well as cuttings from the Glyndebourne garden, providing musical, spiritual, and physical connections for the project's participants through a period of isolation and anxiety.

The Glyndebourne Academy, also discussed in Chapter 7, delivers intensive training to promising young singers who would not typically follow pathways to opera training. This could be for financial reasons, lack of opportunity, lack of career guidance, or personal circumstances. Given the current – and very necessary – focus within opera companies and orchestras on increasing diversity and inclusion in their workforce and activities, this programme is fulfilling a very important role. Launched in 2012, the programme has already paved the way for several students to progress on to tertiary opera studies at music college, and also to the profession – one participant from 2015, for example, has returned as a member of the Glyndebourne Chorus. Through their existing programmes and plans for future development, Glyndebourne Opera is certainly making significant contributions towards social equity in accessing the power of their art form.

100 *Leading the Way*

La Monnaie de Munt

La Monnaie de Munt, known as "Europe's opera house," has most recently made a significant impact through its co-leadership of the groundbreaking "*Majnun and Orfeo*" project. This was a large-scale international collaboration, fusing cultures, community organisations, professionals, and art forms into vibrantly creative outputs. The core of the project, which was led by Brussels' La Monnaie de Munt, was a contemporary exploration of two of the great myths and stories of the world: the Greek myth *Orpheus and Eurydice*, and the Arab tale of *Layla and Majnun*. With co-funding from the Creative Europe Programme of the European Union, the work was collaborative at all levels, from the organisations leading and co-producing the work through to the incorporation of community workshops in multiple European cities. International co-producers of the project included the Festival d'Aix-en-Provence, KBF (Krakow Festival Office), Operadagen Rotterdam, Santa Maria de Feira, Valleta 2018 Foundation, and Wiener Konzerthaus. This impressive array allowed the project to be truly international, working with community groups across Europe. The cultural collaboration extended through the artists engaged to lead the project: Airan Berg was overall artistic director and Martina Winkel the librettist and shadow puppeteer. Three composers from richly varied backgrounds worked on the creative output, combining their expertise in a true marriage of musical styles. The composers were Dick van der Harst from the Netherlands, who was responsible for the overall shape and orchestration; Moneim Adwan, a Palestinian from the Gaza Strip, who is an expert lutenist and singer; and Howard Moody from the United Kingdom, who was responsible for the community creative workshop components of the project. Conductor Bassem Akiki conducted musicians from the Mediterranean Youth Orchestra, which is itself a multicultural body with musicians from over 20 different countries.

The *Orfeo and Majnun* project was structured in two phases or parts. Part One was designated "Parcours," which took a different format in each host city. This freedom of form and emphasis on community input is a trademark of Artistic Director Airan Berg. In an interesting connection that reveals the international influence in the field of classical engagement work, Berg is also the artistic director of the Floods of Fire project currently being delivered by the Adelaide Symphony Orchestra, also featured in this chapter. Berg's other key projects have included his work for Linz's celebration as European Capital of Culture, as well as the Festival der Regionen in Upper Austria. Berg's projects focus on large-scale community collaborations that begin with significant community consultation and take their shape from the input of local professional and amateur performers and artists. This process, while needing to allow time for the input to "gel," ensures that there is true co-creation and a community voice in the final product, and that the performance will truly reflect the community who create it, perform in it, and watch it.

Leading the Way 101

For *Orfeo and Majnun*, the "Parcours" stage included workshops focused on singing, music, gesture, theatre, masks, puppets, shadow theatre, and videos. In Vienna, for example, sessions included an eclectic range of events connecting with over 3,000 people. These included a joint improvisation on Arabic composition with Ud player Marwan Abado, a beatboxing workshop, and a cultural symposium on culture and society at the Vienna Konzerthaus. In Krakow, workshops included thoughtful sessions linking together blind and sighted participants through sight, touch, and sound. Multicultural guided walks gave concrete expression to the themes of connection and intercultural understanding of the project, and the project even emerged at a Fashion Week parade with the puppets and masks inspiring a fashion collection. Rotterdam hosted a joyous city parade, with events across the city, as did Aix-en-Provence and Brussels.

Musically, the work achieved its intention of unifying cultural voices and bringing together community and professional voices. In reviews, the Arabic writing for the love story of *Layla and Majnun* was particularly praised, as was the choral writing which merged the two stylistic genres.[54]

La Monnaie has a rich tradition of delivering community operas, including the highly impactful "*Push*," composed by Howard Moody, who has a strong connection with the company. "Push" was performed at La Monnaie in 2019, telling the true story of holocaust survivor Simon Gronowski. Gronowski was literally saved by a push – his mother pushed him off the train from Mechelne to Auschwitz in 1943. The 2019 production of "Push" was remarkably cyclical, as the initial inspiration for the work was the result of a meeting between Moody and Gronowski at La Monnaie in 2014, following the performance of Moody's opera "*Sinbad – A Journey through Living Flames.*"

La Monnaie's community focus owes much to the work of Bernard Foccroulle, who was general manager from 1992 to 2007, at which point he took up the leadership of the Festival Aix en-Provence. In both Brussels and Aix, Foccroulle has demonstrated a deep commitment to broadening and deepening community engagement with opera. In Brussels, in addition to supporting initiatives with local schools, Foccroulle instigated the highly inclusive programme "A Bridge Between Two Worlds" at La Monnaie. This programme delivers programmes to vulnerable people, partnering with organisations including the Public Centre for Social Welfare, assisted living centres, centres for literacy, and mental health services. In 1995, Foccroulle was a founding member of RESEO, the European Network for Education Departments in opera and dance. He has been a strong advocate for the role of arts and culture in society for several decades, forming the Belgian organisation "Culture et Democratie" in 1993 and maintaining his commitment through his years in Aix.

Notes

1 http://lso.co.uk/lso-discovery/about-lso-discovery, accessed 3 March 2022.

102 Leading the Way

2 McDowell, interview with the author.

3 Ibid.

4 Ibid.

5 http://lso.co.uk/lso-discovery/about-lso-discovery.

6 Ibid.

7 http://lso.co.uk/lso-discovery/about-lso-discovery.

8 Ibid.

9 www.garethmalone.com/programmes/the-choir.

10 www.singup.org, accessed 20 June 2015.

11 http://lso.co.uk/lso-discovery/about-lso-discovery.

12 Ibid.

13 http://lso.co.uk/lso-discovery/schools-young-people/lso-on-track.

14 http://garethglyn.info/eng/cyfansoddiadau.html, accessed 1 June 2015.

15 https://lso.co.uk/lso-discovery/lso-east-london-academy.html.

16 www.jeffnicity.com, accessed 12 June 2015.

17 http://lso.co.uk/lso-discovery/the-next-generation/orchestral-artistry,   accessed 29 July 2015.

18 http://lso.co.uk/lso-discovery/about-lso-discovery.

19 London Symphony Orchestra Press release, 3 March 2015, retrieved from http://lso.co.uk.

20 http://slippedisc.com/2015/06/just-in-simon-rattle-adds-two-new-city-jobs.

21 www.slippedisc.com/2015/02/simon-rattle-signs-cuts-petition/.

22 www.lso.co.uk, accessed 1 July 2015.

23 www.theartsdesk.com/classical-music/hogboon-lso-rattle-barbican.

24 East, interview with the author.

25 Ibid.

26 McDowell, interview with the author.

27 www.bbc.co.uk/programmes/articles/5clQVzSPv8nPJvVQNdCW0rq/the-ten-pieces-champions, accessed 20 June 2015.

28 www.bbc.co.uk/teach/ten-pieces/classical-music-hans-zimmer-earth/zh4k382.

29 http://downloads.bbc.co.uk/tv/tenpieces/arrangements/kerryandrew/NoPlaceLikelongpoem.pdf.

30 www.bbc.co.uk/programmes/p01vs08w, accessed 20 July 2015.

31 www.bbc.co.uk/programmes/articles/3xWSYQhHfM9dZYfmRmTwVqN/key-stage-2-music-resources, accessed 2 July 2015.

32 McCall, interview with the author.

33 Ibid.

34 https://julianjazzviolin.tumblr.com/biog, accessed 10 March 2022.

35 Ibid.

36 ASO website.

37 www.aso.com.au/products/schools/the-bush-concert, accessed 2 July 2015.

38 ASO 2013 Annual Report, pp. 11–12.

39 Kibler-Vermaas, interview with the author.

40 Ibid.

41 Ibid.

42 Ibid.

43 Assal Habibi, B. Rael Cahn, Antonio Damasio, and Hanna Damasio. "Neural Correlates of Accelerated Auditory Processing in Children Engaged in Music Training," *Developmental Cognitive Neuroscience*, Vol. 21, October 2016, pp. 1–14.

44 Langridge, interview with the author.

45 http://s3-eu-west-1.amazonaws.com/glyndebourne-prod-assets/wp-content/uploads/2019/02/19171941/Economic-Impact-Report.pdf, 2013.

46 *Beyond Britten*, p. 140.

47 Tearle, interview with the author.
48 Langridge, interview with the author.
49 Tearle, interview with the author.
50 www.glyndebourne.com/opera-archive/explore-our-operas/explore-knight-crew/knight-crew-about-the-project/, accessed 31 August 2021.
51 Tearle, interview with the author.
52 Ibid.
53 Langridge, interview with the author.
54 OPERA NEWS – Seven Stones, Orfeo et Majnun (metguild.org), accessed 10 March 2022.

5 Orchestras Building Communities
The El Sistema Model and Its Global Influence

The *Fundacion del Estado para el Sistema Nacional de las Orquestas Juveniles e Infantiles de Venezuela,*[1] better known as "El Sistema," is one of the greatest music education success stories of recent history. El Sistema was established in Venezuela in 1975 by the economist, politician, and keen amateur musician Dr Juan Antonio Abreu. From humble beginnings teaching a handful of children in a garage, there are now over 1 million students who have studied across Venezuela via a network of 443 orchestra centres, known as nucleos.[2] Alongside impressive musical standards, El Sistema also has a well-publicised extra motive, namely to improve the quality of life and prospects for children from low socio-economic neighbourhoods. El Sistema is credited with saving generations of Venezuelan children from involvement in crime or drugs by offering an alternative to negative peer influences and the dangers of street life. This has been achieved through a system of highly intensive music tuition, of up to 4 hours per day, chiefly focusing on learning orchestral instruments through group lessons and ensemble rehearsals.

The flagship orchestra, the Orquesta Sinfónica Simón Bolívar (also known as the Simón Bolívar Symphony Orchestra), has gained a strong international profile through DVDs, documentaries, and frequent international tours. Gustavo Dudamel, who first came to the world's notice conducting the Simón Bolívar, is arguably the system's greatest success story. Currently the music director of the Los Angeles Philharmonic, Dudamel regularly conducts the world's leading orchestras, including the Berlin Philharmonic and the Vienna Philharmonic. Largely due to Dudamel's influence there is now a thriving Sistema-inspired programme operating in Los Angeles, linked with the Los Angeles Philharmonic (known as YOLA).[3] This programme was discussed in the Los Angeles Philharmonic case study in Chapter 4.

The technical finesse and infectious joie-de-vivre of the Simón Bolívar musicians have won them worldwide attention; this international profile has, in turn, been a significant factor in the global proliferation of El Sistema–inspired programmes. In August 2007, for example, the Simón Bolívar's celebrated performance in the UK's Proms series raised their international profile to a new level. In recent years, changes to the political system in Venezuela and controversies regarding misconduct within the programme

DOI: 10.4324/9781003198512-6

Orchestras Building Communities   105

have clouded its initial positivity; however, internationally the "Sistema dream" remains alive and well, with its impact having already been indelibly marked on the world's music education ecosystem.

Currently, programmes modelled on the Sistema ideals and practice can be found in more than 60 countries, although the original Venezuelan approach is generally adapted to fit with differing cultural and social factors.[4] Marshall Marcus is well placed to give insight into both the early development of the Venezuelan Sistema and the global spread of the model. In the 1970s, Marcus, a British-born and educated violinist, was appointed concertmaster of Venezuela's Orquesta Filarmonica de Caracas. At this point, Marcus also became involved with El Sistema for the first time, teaching within the system in Caracas. Currently the chief executive officer (CEO) of the European Union Youth Orchestra, Marcus has remained committed to Sistema projects throughout his subsequent career. He is founder and chairman of Sistema Europe, a director and trustee of Sistema England, founder of Sistema Africa, and a member of Sistema Global's advisory board. In his online writings, as well as his numerous speeches given at conferences and council meetings internationally, Marcus has made insightful and perceptive comments on the international spread of Sistema. He remarks that the Sistema inspiration rightly takes different forms in different countries – although cautions against an overly flexible approach here that runs the risk of people slapping the tag "Sistema" on to a programme when it is really only paying lip service to the original structure and ideals. Marcus has been astute in predicting, and contributing to, the core phases of the international spread of the Sistema movement.

From the first wave of enthusiasm and associated new Sistema programmes, the second phase was intentional networking, providing a structure at both the national and global level. The "Take a Stand" conference hosted in February 2012 by the Los Angeles Philharmonic and the Longy School of Music of Bard college facilitated meetings and discussions that naturally led to the establishment of the required networks. From this conference sprang the Sistema Europe network (established in 2012) and the seeds for the Sistema Africa network, founded by Marshall Marcus and Gabriel Prokofiev. Sistema Global is the ambitious worldwide website interface for Sistema programmes, the result of Glen Thomas' work. *Ensemble* magazine is devoted to sharing news of Sistema programmes to a global readership, initially published by Eric Booth and Tricia Tunstall, now delivered by the Longy School of Music of Bard College. Each of these networks provides invaluable opportunities for programmes spread across continents or oceans to learn from each other, to connect, and to take inspiration from each other's work. The Sistema Global interface includes, among other networking opportunities, a resource portal that allows Sistema practitioners to share their instrumental resources with each other.

The third, essential stage of the Sistema movement is research and evaluation. This is vital to maintain the integrity of the Sistema movement,

106 *Orchestras Building Communities*

although as with all arts-based programmes, evaluation comes with its own vexing questions. There is a growing body of research on the Sistema phenomenon, both the original Venezuelan programme and the various international Sistema-inspired projects. Marcus has developed "SERA," an online Sistema evaluation and research archive, which is of assistance in charting and analysing the development of the Sistema movement.[5] SERA was established in 2012, following discussions with other leading Sistema experts, including Eric Booth, Richard Hallam, and Glenn Thomas.[6]

In 2013, Dr Andrea Creech was the lead author for a key research project, delivering a Sistema Global literature review, updated in 2016. Creech states that the literature review aims to reflect the international growth of El Sistema and expand understanding of Sistema-inspired projects. It also considers how Sistema and its impact relate to the wider music education ecosystem internationally, alongside a desire to share Sistema pedagogical practices.[7]

While these research portals and reviews are very positive steps in the evolution of the Sistema movement, Marcus is rightfully aware that it is a complex area to research. As he notes, researchers need to determine if the primary goals are musical, social, or a combination of both. They also need to establish how to assess the value and impact, with an understanding that to fully assess the long-term impact, studies need to be longitudinal, over a period of ten or more years.[8]

The next steps in the evaluation and research frameworks will need to include templates that are available and practicable for usage in a wide range of Sistema scenarios. With the establishment of the Sistema-focused master's programme at the Longy School of Music of Bard College and a research focus on community music at York University, new developments are afoot here that will pave the way for the next stage.

Case Study of El Sistema's Influence: United Kingdom

There are currently seven different Sistema programmes active in the United Kingdom, under the auspices of Sistema Scotland and Sistema England. With several of these programmes, symphony and chamber orchestras have taken a strategic partnership role. These include, respectively, the Royal Liverpool Philharmonic Orchestra (RLPO partnered with In Harmony Liverpool); the Royal Northern Sinfonia (In Harmony Newcastle Gateshead); the City of Birmingham Symphony Orchestra and Manchester Camerata (In Harmony Telford and Stoke-on-Trent), and both the Royal Scottish National Orchestra and the BBC Scottish Symphony (Sistema Scotland). In addition, the London Southbank Centre has been an official partner with "In Harmony Lambeth," a partnership that has allowed In Harmony Lambeth students connections with the Southbank Centre's resident orchestras, including the London Philharmonic Orchestra.

The establishment of Sistema-inspired projects in the United Kingdom was sparked by the performance of the Simón Bolívar Youth Orchestra at the London Proms in 2007. Following this performance, a campaign to establish a British model was led by leading music educators and performers. Within a year this was achieved, with the British government allocating 1 million pounds in 2008 to the establishment of "In Harmony," the British Sistema model. From 46 applicants, three pilot programmes were chosen in London, Norwich, and Liverpool.[9] By April 2009, the projects were underway, with a national steering group chaired by Julian Lloyd Webber keeping oversight of the three projects. The goals for the projects were lofty and, as with the Venezuelan model, combined social with musical aims.[10] Lloyd Webber has claimed that "[El Sistema] is surely the most extraordinary social phenomenon of our times ... In Harmony's huge potential for social regeneration has convinced me that it is the future for music education in this country."[11]

In November 2011, as part of the National Plan for Music Education, the government announced an expansion plan for In Harmony, now renamed Sistema England, and in July 2014, four new projects were confirmed at Gateshead, Leeds, Nottingham, and Telford and Wrekin. Funding was also continued for Lambeth and Liverpool but not, controversially, for Norwich. The Norwich project continues to run as an independent organisation, supported by funding from local primary schools, the Norfolk Music Hub, and local trusts.[12] While each of the UK's Sistema programmes are of interest in their own right, two have been the focus of external evaluation, which has provided valuable data on the progress and impact of the programmes. These two programmes are "Liverpool In Harmony" and "Sistema Scotland," and here an overview of these programmes and their respective impact is presented.

The Royal Liverpool Philharmonic Orchestra has a partnership role with "In Harmony Liverpool," coaching students and offering opportunities for side-by-side performances. This programme focuses on Faith Primary School, located in a low socio-economic area with issues of unemployment, crime, lack of civil engagement, and low tertiary education levels. In Harmony Liverpool has been assessed annually, with results published in detailed interim reports. It is therefore possible to track the success of this programme in achieving its stated aims, both musical and social, year by year. The most recent report reveals the many positive effects now established by the programme. With a very multicultural catchment area, students at Faith Primary were achieving lower than average scores on national literacy and numeracy tests. The programme has had significant and sustained impact on students' levels in these areas, in particular reading and numeracy, as shown in Table 5.1.

The data in Table 5.1 show the percentage of pupils in each year group who are progressing by two sub-levels or more in one academic year. This is exceeding expectation, which is for an advance of three sub-levels over a two-year period (i.e. 1.5 sub-levels per year). Although fluctuations are evident in the achievements from year to year, a significant overall improvement

108　*Orchestras Building Communities*

Table 5.1 Programme's Significant and Sustained Impact on Students' Levels and Their Results

Years 1–6	Writing (%)	Reading (%)	Maths (%)
2008–2009	56	36	35
2009–2010	59	84	75
2010–2011	48	47	48
2011–2012	61	69	71
2012–2013	68	68	66
2013–2014	59	68	69

Source: Susanne Burns and Paul Bewick. *In Harmony Liverpool Interim Report Year 5*, 2014, p. 22.

is evident from the baseline results in 2008, at the commencement of the In Harmony programme.

Musically, the students are now reaching a high level, with regular performances compulsory for all participants. These have included high-profile events, such as a side-by-side performance with the Royal Liverpool Philharmonic Orchestra in a Prom performance at the Royal Albert Hall in September 2013.[13] This performance demonstrated the progress made by the In Harmony programme, with the young Liverpool students following in the footsteps of the Simón Bolívar on the Royal Albert Hall stage. The inspiration of performing alongside the RLPO at the Proms concert in London was evident in many statements made by the participants in the *Year 4 In Harmony Liverpool Interim Report*.[14] This will be a lifelong source of pride and inspiration for these children, as well as providing a window into the reality of the operation of a world-class symphony orchestra. The children are also gaining a feeling of security and familiarity with large-scale concert halls, as both performers and audience members.

Ofsted, the nationwide education standards board, has also commented positively on the programme, making good practice visits to Sistema Liverpool in 2011 and 2013. The 2013 Ofsted Report found that the music curriculum at Faith Primary "has an outstanding impact on the personal and spiritual development of the pupils."[15] The entire teaching staff is learning instruments alongside the children and this is reported to be raising the confidence levels of the children involved.[16] As stated earlier, the children selected for this scheme come from an under-privileged sector of society with a strongly multicultural background. School for these children is often a daily challenge, working to overcome obstacles of language and cultural assimilation. By levelling the playing field between children and staff in this one area, reports have found that the children feel newly empowered. This is a valuable motivator to carry through to their learning across the rest of the curriculum.

The 2011 Ofsted Report singles out the In Harmony instrumental teachers for praise:

Every opportunity is taken to immerse pupils in musical language, and not a minute is wasted. The "In Harmony" teachers are excellent musicians and their expert modelling sets the standard for the technical and musical quality that pupils are expected to match.[17]

While effective instrumental teaching draws upon many skills, the teacher's level of technical and artistic artistry should not be underestimated. Students are able to instinctively recognise excellent playing, and a key strength of Sistema programmes linked with symphony orchestras is that students are frequently able to interact with professional players. The positive impact of the RLPO's role has been noted in the interim reports, for example:

The leadership role provided by the RLPO is proving to be potent in generating community pride. The high quality musical interventions made possible through the orchestra are arguably critical to the quality of the musical pedagogy and its impact on the children and the wider community.[18]

The programme is also evidently helping to connect the RLPO more deeply with its community. A Liverpool council member states:

For our children and staff at Faith Primary School in West Everton to be taught by musicians from the Liverpool Philharmonic, for them to become our friends, and for Liverpool Philharmonic to become like a second home in our community is something very special ... classical music is no longer a world that we are excluded from ... it's now our world, we love being in it and we love having the opportunity to share it with others.[19]

This feedback proves that the Sistema programmes are achieving a high-priority aim for all orchestral education and community engagement work: namely, to break down barriers and ensure that classical music is accessible to all sectors of the population.

Qualitative evidence in the annual reports reveals improvements in academic achievement, concentration, attendance, and motivation to learn in students in the programme.[20] The reports also note:

Increased civic pride ... Self-determination and social capita are building within the community and In Harmony Liverpool has played a key role in enabling and supporting this. The community feels a strong sense of ownership over "their orchestra" and In Harmony Liverpool as a programme.[21]

A sense of "community ownership" of an orchestra is, surely, one of the most outstanding achievements for this or any orchestral education and

110　*Orchestras Building Communities*

community engagement programme. If an orchestra can tap into the feeling of civic pride mentioned here and inspire the same passionate support and loyalty that a city offers its sporting teams, then its future is assured.

Strong efforts are made to develop community support for the programme. For example, with the "In Home" visits, a concept originally introduced by Sistema Scotland, music is brought into the heart of residential neighbourhoods. Students, together with professional musicians, perform literally in their own living rooms for family and friends. Attention is given to those families who are less familiar with classical music or who might be daunted by the procedures attached to a performance in a concert hall.[22]

A further positive benefit of In Harmony Liverpool is that the relationship between the RLPO and the Liverpool Music Support Service (LMSS) (now renamed the Resonate Music Education Hub) has been significantly strengthened. Burns and Bewick report that

> There has been a significant development in the partnership between LMSS and the RLPO through practical working and ongoing dialogue. This is clear in the development of pedagogical approaches to delivering music in schools and the link to teaching and learning in the classroom.[23]

This newly strengthened relationship will continue to benefit the citizens of Liverpool, especially with the establishment of the Music Hub model, which relies entirely on positive and effective partnership between organisations in order to function effectively. It is still too soon to determine the long-term effect of this programme on its participants, but the available data at this time points to significant positive impacts on general well-being, civic engagement, and attitude to learning. Students are continuing with pathways to high-level musical activities, with over 20 students moving on to participate in youth orchestras including the Liverpool Philharmonic Youth Orchestra, the National Youth Orchestra's Inspire programme, and the Sistema Europe Youth Orchestra.

Research undertaken on the Sistema Scotland projects, known as "Big Noise," points to similar findings. Sistema Scotland was initiated in 2008 in Raploch, Stirling, and is delivered in partnership with the BBC Scottish Symphony Orchestra. The programme has subsequently grown in scope, with a second project recently established at Govanhill, Glasgow, and plans for further expansion. The Scottish government commissioned an independent evaluation of "Big Noise," with the findings published in 2011. The report states:

> There is strong evidence from parents that Big Noise is achieving a range of short-term outcomes with the children it works with. These are primarily around personal and social development, for example it

is improving confidence, social skills and concentration in the children who engage.[24]

While these personal developments are important in their own right, they are also likely to have a positive impact on children's learning, as concentration and confidence are both essential criteria for a positive attitude towards learning. Sistema Scotland is also currently the subject of extensive research by the Glasgow Centre for Population Health, which is part of the NHS. In May 2015, the findings to date of this study were published in the report *Evaluating Sistema Scotland: Initial Findings Report Summary*. This research confirmed the findings of the Scottish government's 2011 report, stating:

> "Sistema Scotland's Big Noise programme has the potential to significantly enhance participants' lives, prospects, health and wellbeing through a variety of identified pathways in the long term."[25]

In October 2014, Sistema Scotland hosted an international Sistema teachers' conference. The aim of this conference was to bring together 150 international musicians and teachers involved in delivering Sistema-based programmes to network and share their experiences. Sistema Scotland has very strong ties with the Venezuelan Sistema. Gustavo Dudamel, the star of the Venezuelan Sistema, is a patron for Sistema Scotland and, in 2007, an official partnership was signed between the two organisations. All Sistema Scotland teaching staff have travelled to Venezuela to gain personal insight into the model, and Sistema Scotland has in turn hosted Venezuelan musicians including the Simón Bolívar Symphony Orchestra in 2012.[26]

Sceptics, Critics, and New Directions

While public opinion of Sistema to this point has been overwhelmingly positive, in the past few years there has been a growing voice of critical investigation. The most prominent critic is Geoffrey Baker, author of *El Sistema: Orchestrating Venezuela's Youth*.[27] In stark contrast to the highly positive tone of most studies of El Sistema, Baker makes critical analysis of all aspects of the programme. Baker makes several serious claims in the book, including allegations of misuse of funds, sexual misconduct between teachers and students, drug and alcohol abuse among students and staff, and vandalism by Sistema orchestral musicians on tour. It is not the place of this project to prove or disprove such claims; however, it is clearly imperative that they are thoroughly investigated by the relevant authorities. El Sistema's focus on social inclusivity and reform is also questioned, with Baker stating that reference to such elements of the project only became part of the official mission statements of the organisation in 2011.[28]

112 *Orchestras Building Communities*

Interestingly, Baker is more generous in his assessment of international Sistema-inspired programmes than of the original. He feels that, ironically, while El Sistema's social commitment may be questionable in Venezuela, it is more of a central focus to international programmes. Baker's claim is that international Sistema projects:

> are built as much on El Sistema's illusions as on its realities, and may therefore end up (and may already be) improving on the original. For example, they are taking the idea of social action through music much more seriously than in Venezuela itself.[29]

Baker questions whether an orchestra is the positive role model claimed by Abreu and his supporters. Baker notes elements of competitiveness and friction inherent in the construct of the symphony orchestra, both in Sistema orchestras and international professional orchestras. He makes mention of several studies that claim that morale in professional orchestras is concerningly low. These studies and their implications are further discussed in Chapter 9. Supporters of Sistema programmes maintain that Abreu was correct in his upholding of the symphony orchestra as a metaphor for society – a way for large numbers of people to come together to create something powerful and beautiful, based on communication, partnership, and teamwork.

Baker also suggests that there are possible patronising missionary overtones to the Sistema model, painting it as a modern continuation of insensitive efforts to impose Western culture and traditions upon developing nations.[30] While, of course, cultural imperialism is always an issue to consider, there is no evidence of a lack of connection with the musical content evident in the Venezuelan Sistema orchestras. Indeed, film footage and anecdotal evidence in DVD documentaries on El Sistema reveal a level of positive energy and commitment that many Western orchestras would do well to emulate. An oppressed culture is certainly not what comes to mind. Another, more subjective criticism by Baker is that there is too much discipline in the Sistema teaching methods. Many advocates of the Sistema model feel that discipline is, in fact, a positive element. Orchestral music demands a high level of commitment, of discipline, of self-control, and of routine application. Music education advocates often point to the many leaders across high-level professions who are musically trained as evidence of the value of the rigour of a musical background. From doctors to lawyers, politicians to engineers, you find cohorts of high achievers who devote a large portion of their formative years to playing in orchestras and ensembles.

At present, orchestral management personnel have quite a polarised view of Sistema. While many are passionate advocates, others believe that the Venezuelan model cannot translate internationally. However, as orchestras already committed to Sistema-inspired programmes continue to generate highly positive feedback, it will be interesting to see whether more

Orchestras Building Communities 113

orchestras continue to establish similar schemes in the future. The long-term impact of the current programmes will, of necessity, take time to measure. Nevertheless, at this point, one would have to say that when operated with effective planning and sincere intentions, Sistema-inspired programmes do indeed have the power to change lives.

Notes

1 https://elsistema.org.ve/, accessed 28 February, 2023.
2 Ibid.
3 www.laphil.com/education/yola/hola, accessed 15 June 2015.
4 www.sistemaglobal.org/about/el-sistema-venezuela/, accessed 10 February 2022.
5 https://marshallmarcus.wordpress.com/sera-sistema-evaluation-research-archive/, accessed 8 March 2022.
6 Ibid.
7 Ibid.
8 https://marshallmarcus.wordpress.com/2012/11/03/another-sistema-no-brainer/.
9 Stephen Hignell, Ben Sandbrook and Sophie Hollows. *Evaluation of the In Harmony Programme*, London, 2020 Arts Council England and Nordicity, retrieved from https://www.artscouncil.org.uk/sites/default/files/download-file/Nordicity%20Evaluation%20of%20In%20Harmony%20%282020-09%29.pdf, accessed 28 February 2023
10 Ibid.
11 Julian Lloyd Webber. "El Sistema: When Music Cuts Crime and Saves Lives," *The Telegraph London*, 22 December 2009.
12 https://www.norcasistema.org.uk/sistema-about, accessed 6 March 2023.
13 https://www.bbc.com/news/entertainment-arts-23932186, accessed 6 March 2023.
14 Susanne Burns and Paul Bewick. *In Harmony Liverpool: Interim Report Year 4*, Co-commissioned by Royal Liverpool Philharmonic Orchestra, Department of Education, Sistema England, 2013, Retrieved from: http://www.liverpoolphil.com/193/in-harmony-liverpool/social-action-through-music.html, accessed 12 March 2015, p. 50.
15 Ofsted inspection report September 2013, retrieved from www.liverpoolphil.com/193/in-harmony-liverpool/social-action-through-music.html, accessed 6 July 2015.
16 Burns and Bewick, *In Harmony Liverpool Interim Report*, p. 35.
17 Mark Phillips. Her Majesty's Inspector, Music, Ofsted. February 2011. Retrieved from www.sistemaengland.org.uk/in-harmony-liverpool/, accessed 20 July 2015.
18 Burns and Bewick, *In Harmony Liverpool Interim Report Year 4*, p. 7.
19 Ibid. Councillor Jane Corbett, cabinet member for education and children's services, Liverpool City Council, p. 60.
20 Burns and Bewick, *In Harmony Liverpool Interim Report Year 4*, p. 5.
21 Ibid., p. 6.
22 Ibid., p. 64.
23 Ibid., pp. 77–78.
24 *Evaluation of Big Noise Sistema Scotland*. Commissioned by the Scottish government, 2011. Retrieved from https://www.makeabignoise.org.uk/research/, p. 49.
25 *Evaluating Sistema Scotland: Initial Findings Report Summary*. Co-commissioned by Glasgow Centre for Population Health, Education Scotland, Glasgow Caledonian University, May 2015, p. 17.

114   Orchestras Building Communities

26 http://makeabignoise.org.uk/venezuela/, accessed 30 July 2015.
27 Geoffrey Baker. *El Sistema: Orchestrating Venezuela's Youth*. Oxford: Oxford University Press, 2014.
28 Ibid., p. 165.
29 Ibid., p. 306.
30 Ibid., p. 116.

6 Creative Music Making
The New Role of Animateurs and Teaching Artists

Development of the Creative Composition Workshop

The creative, composer-led workshop model of orchestral education work is one that first emerged in the United Kingdom in the 1980s, following on from the groundbreaking work of composer-teachers in the 1960s. The workshop model is a highly participatory, creative-focused model, which involves collaborative composition of a new piece of music. The group is directed and supported by a workshop leader, or animateur, who provides the framework and points of inspiration for the composition. Orchestral musicians are also often involved, lending their individual expertise on their instruments to help to guide and shape the composition process. This model of education programme has remained particularly strong in the United Kingdom from its inception in the 1980s through to the present day. Leading British animateurs have established international careers, bringing their skillset and knowledge to countries that have not explored this area in such depth. It should be noted at this point that the terminology used to refer to musicians leading these sessions has not, at the present time, found an international or permanent consensus. Rather, as the field of practice develops and international influences evolve, so the terminology is shifting and adapting. In the United Kingdom, for example, the term "animateur" was originally the main term for this role – and is still often used. However, the term "workshop leader" or "workshop facilitator" is also used with increasing frequency. In the United States, the term "teaching artist" is most commonly used to describe this role, due in large part to the impact of the work and writings of Eric Booth. It has been of great interest to watch the evolution in Australia, which has taken influence from both the United Kingdom and the United States – while both terms, and the role in general, are still taking root in Australia, there has been a clear shift over the past decade from the term "animateur" being the principal descriptor, to "teaching artist." It remains to be seen what further evolution of the defining terminology will take place over the coming decades in this cutting-edge field of work. In this book, depending on the geography and date of the work being described, the terms "animateur" and "teaching artist" are both used.

DOI: 10.4324/9781003198512-7

116 *Creative Music Making*

Orchestras take varied approaches to the creative workshop format. Some orchestras with a particular focus on contemporary composition will invite students to make their own creative responses to a particular contemporary work, using techniques utilised by the composer, and often overseen by the composer in person. This offers strong benefits to both the composer and students: the composer is able to make links with a potential new audience for their work, and the workshop leading itself provides them with a valuable source of income in a financially precarious career. Such workshops offer the participants an entry point into the challenging sound world of modern music by demystifying the aims and methods of composers, as well as helping them find their own creative voice.

Another approach to a creative workshop is to explore cross-arts possibilities, such as responding to books, paintings, or film through music. This offers clear possibilities to educators working with the new Australian Curriculum for the Arts, which encourages cross-arts links such as these. Skilled workshop leaders are able to tailor a project to match the skill level of participants. This means that alongside playing on orchestral instruments, they often make use of voice, body percussion, and percussion instruments. A tradition of workshop "games" and warm-up activities has also emerged, and there is a growing literature of resources and activities in the field. Generally, minimal reference is made to traditional music notation, with the animateur relying on their own aural memory, recordings, and graphic notation charts to document musical ideas and help shape the final product.

Australian orchestral education departments are increasingly introducing collaborative composition workshops to their programming. Over the past decade, several specialists in this field from the United Kingdom, such as Paul Rissmann, Fraser Trainer, Gillian Howell, and Matthew Barley, have passed on their skills to Australian musicians and music educators through a combination of education workshops in partnership with symphony orchestras, and training sessions for musicians and educators. In this chapter, the development of the creative workshop model in the United Kingdom is discussed, as well as an assessment of the value that such a model presents to both the practitioners and participants.

The development of this model owes much to two key figures working with UK orchestras in the late 1970s and 1980s, namely Richard McNicol, through his work with the Apollo Trust and the London Symphony Orchestra (LSO), and Gillian Moore, in her role as the first education manager at the London Sinfonietta. However, the impetus behind the establishment of this particular model of orchestra education project came from a variety of factors, and it is necessary to look further back, to the 1960s, to understand the development of creativity in the teaching of music in the United Kingdom. Developments in the classroom music education methodology of the 1960s and 1970s led to the demand for the participatory, composer-driven education projects subsequently offered by UK orchestras.

Creative Music Making 117

The 1960s was a decade of creative ferment and renewal in many sectors of society. Music education was one of these, principally led by some dynamic composers working within the school education system. This period has been well documented by Stephanie Pitts in her book *A Century of Change in Music Education*.[1] Pitts comments that

> The changing concept of music education that was beginning to emerge in the 1960s challenged the supremacy of listening and teacher-directed performance that had characterised the first half of the twentieth century... Most importantly, a reinterpretation of musical and educational aims made the connection with composition, which assumed an increasingly significant place in music teaching.[2]

Pitts also notes that

> The influence of the "composer-teacher" had been developing throughout the century ... In the 1960s and 1970s, this model reached mainstream school, as a small number of young composers took up teaching posts, so bringing their musical experience to an unprecedented number of pupils.[3]

One of the most influential of these teacher-composers, John Paynter, was instrumental in bringing about a revolution in music education with the publication of the seminal work *Sound and Silence*, published in 1970 and written with Peter Aston, his colleague at the music department of the University of York.[4] In previous decades, music education had been primarily a matter of theory and listening, of learning through studying the works of others. With *Sound and Silence* came the idea of helping children to understand music by creating it themselves. In the Introduction to *Sound and Silence*, Paynter and Aston elaborate upon this idea, radical for its time. They make the point that it is expected that children should learn about the visual arts and literature by both studying works of art and also creating their own paintings, stories, and poems. Only music education was missing this crucial element of learning through the act of creation, and it was this imbalance that Paynter and Aston sought to correct.

Sir Peter Maxwell Davies is another teacher-composer who contributed to this new method of music education. Upon taking a post as music teacher at Cirencester Grammar School in 1959, Maxwell Davies explored new possibilities for classroom composition, and the success of his methods was highly influential. Maxwell Davies has also composed major works allowing for children to participate with symphony orchestras in concert performances. The most notable of these remains "The Turn of the Tide."[5]

The development of classroom composition practice was to a large degree enabled by compositional techniques such as serialism, minimalism, and atonality. School class composition projects benefitted from the freedom

118   *Creative Music Making*

offered by modern techniques and styles which freed students from the strict rules of harmony and voice leading and, in projects using graphic scores, even from the skill of reading and notating music. George Self's work, *New Sounds in Class*, published in 1967, was a key influence on the development of graphic score notation, evolving from his work in schools in the mid-1960s.[6] *New Sounds in Class* includes a collection of graphic scores to be performed by classroom percussion ensembles. Self's views pre-empt those of Paynter and Aston, for instance when he writes:

> It is a sad reflection that although many children use their creative energies in painting and poetry, their musical activities are usually confined to performance and listening; with simplified notation it is possible for average children to compose music – and almost this alone would warrant its introduction.[7]

Following this period of rethinking how and why children should learn music in schools came a re-evaluation of education by the UK government, which resulted in the creation of the *National Curriculum* and the *Education Reform Act* in 1988.[8] This was the point at which the new impetus towards teaching music through composition gained official recognition, although not without a struggle. During the 1980s, there was a rift between those favouring traditional methods of music education, and those championing the new, participatory, approach. However, when the statutory orders for music were published in 1992, it was clear that the decision had been reached in favour of composition in schools. There were two attainment targets for music: "Attainment Target One for Performing and Composing" and "Attainment Target Two for Listening and Appraising." Ofsted (Office for Standards in Education) carries out regular inspections of teaching in all schools across the United Kingdom. The 1995 report states: "Lessons in which the teaching is good or very good usually have composing and appraising as their dominant activities, and employ performing as a supporting skill."[9]

It is clear that the official education bodies were in favour of a move towards a more participatory, creative approach to music education, and this approach gradually became established across the sector. By the mid-1990s, this approach was well developed; as Richard McNicol observed: "the quiet revolution from passive to practical classroom music in Britain and the subsequent introduction of a National Music Curriculum embracing this principle have established us as the undisputed world leader in music education."[10]

Further in this article, McNicol commented on the growing international recognition of such work, and of the admiration he had observed on his travels for the UK's decision that all children "learn to compose, to perform and, through this process, to understand music."[11]

While the decision to give children skills and confidence in composing and creating their own music was undoubtedly a positive step, it also caused

Creative Music Making   119

difficulties for teachers unfamiliar with composition and improvisation. This lack of confidence in teaching composition in the classroom directly contributed to the popularity of the compositional workshop education projects devised and offered by symphony orchestras in the 1980s and 1990s.

The London Sinfonietta was one of the key innovators of partnership work between orchestras and schools and made a significant contribution to the establishment of the creative music workshop model. In 1983, Michael Vyner appointed Gillian Moore as education officer with the London Sinfonietta, the first official post of its kind in the United Kingdom. Moore has continued to make a significant contribution to classical music and music education in the United Kingdom to the present day. She served on the government's National Curriculum Working Group in 1990, helping to create the National Curriculum for Music in England and Wales. Since 1993, Moore has been working at the Southbank Centre in a variety of roles, including head of education and, more recently, head of classical music, and she is also a visiting professor at the Royal College of Music. Here, however, it is her work with London Sinfonietta that is of particular interest.

The London Sinfonietta was established in 1968 and principally focuses on contemporary and 20th-century orchestral repertoire. While Moore's initial appointment was for one year, she stayed in her role for ten years, before leaving to work for the South Bank Centre as their head of education. Under Moore's guidance, the London Sinfonietta were pioneers of participatory orchestral education work, working closely with many of the world's leading composers and performers and setting an example which has since been followed throughout the United Kingdom and worldwide. The first decade of the London Sinfonietta's education programming (from 1983 to 1993) has been extensively researched and analysed by Julia Winterson. Winterson's article "An Evaluation of the Effects of London Sinfonietta Education Projects on their Participants" found that students involved in the London Sinfonietta education projects generally developed a positive attitude to modern music. The majority enjoyed both the workshop activities and the concert presented by the Sinfonietta at the conclusion of their project.[12] In this respect, it would appear that the Sinfonietta was therefore successful in achieving their stated aims:

> The policy was and has remained a commitment to breaking down the barriers which had traditionally existed between composers and performers on one side and audiences (or potential audiences) on the other, to making today's music available and accessible to as wide a public as possible and to handing over the rich resources at our disposal to encourage active and creative involvement in music making among many different groups of people.[13]

In an interview with Winterson in August 1995, Moore talks about her early work as education officer with the London Sinfonietta, and states that

120 *Creative Music Making*

teachers were requesting assistance with composing work, as it was newly introduced into the curriculum.[14]

In the educational workshop model developed by Moore, composers would work alongside students, using one of their own works as a blueprint, and create a new work inspired by the musical techniques used in the original composition. Often, the resulting work was then performed at the commencement of a London Sinfonietta concert. This style of education programme is highly participatory for the students involved and gives them a unique insight into the way in which a composer works. They gain a new understanding of the compositional techniques discussed as well as the various timbres and characteristics of a symphony orchestra. On conclusion of the workshop projects, students demonstrated an ability to listen to the original compositions with a new understanding and concentration. In this way, students were able to gain direct insight into major contemporary compositions, and often had personal contact with the composers themselves. The composers focused on in early London Sinfonietta education programmes included Lutoslawski, Varese, Boulez, and Stravinsky.[15]

One of the earliest London Sinfonietta education projects, begun in September 1983, was analysed by David Ruffer. This project focused on Edgar Varese, and began with workshops using his music as a model, followed by an evening with members of the London Sinfonietta. Ruffer states that a major achievement of the course was that it "brought together a group of teachers with a wide variety of experiences in teaching music to secondary-age children and had built up enough self-confidence in them for group composition to take place without the need, or aid, of notation."[16]

Clearly, the London Sinfonietta education programmes were successful in achieving a key aim of orchestral education programming, namely, helping participants to develop a connection and familiarity with the traditions and techniques of classical music.

After the initial groundbreaking period of creative-based orchestral education programming, an inevitable but necessary second phase of reflection and critical assessment followed. Interestingly, although Moore was instrumental in establishing the initial popularity of the format, she was also one of the first to recognise the importance of objective criticism, and has highlighted several issues in particular that she feels need addressing. These include the need for longer periods of contact with students[17] and the importance of including opportunities for students to perform alongside the orchestra as well as compose.[18] Most UK symphony orchestras are today taking a balanced approach to their education programming, achieved through a combination of education concerts, participatory concerts, creative music workshops, and school visits. It would, however, be a loss for the United Kingdom to not recognise the strength of its tradition in creative collaborative workshops, and its ability to assist orchestras in other countries to develop such work.

Creative Music Making 121

The Place of Creativity in Schools

Over the past 20 years, several high-profile figures in the arts and education have stressed the importance of assisting children to access their creativity. In 1992, for example, Sir Simon Rattle campaigned against a proposed review of National Curriculum that was potentially going to reduce the creative element. According to Pauline Tambling, former director of education and training at the Arts Council of England:

> It was only because Sir Simon Rattle, in his first major public intervention on behalf of music education, stood up for creative music in the primary school against the then Education Minister, Kenneth Clarke, that composition, performing and appraising remained equal parts of the new curriculum.[19]

The 1992 campaign in favour of creativity in the curriculum by Rattle and his fellow supporters was successful, although there remained a lack of consensus upon this point. The use of graphic notation in creative classroom work has been particularly divisive: some celebrate the way that it opens up the world of music composition to students regardless of their previous musical studies, while others feel that it shows a lack of respect for serious music theoretical study and tradition. Today, it is generally accepted that a balanced approach to music education must include both participatory and theoretical activities. While the question of notation can still be divisive, an approach has gradually been developed that incorporates both creativity and theory holistically. As leading American educator Eric Booth comments:

> I think musical language works like foreign language – we learn it fastest and most excitedly when we are actively immersed in the life of it, not as an exercise apart from its vitality and relevance. Yes, teach standard notation at the teachable moment, but no, don't postpone the excitement until a level of mastery is attained.[20]

In 1999, Rattle again advocated for creativity in the music classroom when he joined the National Advisory Committee commissioned by Blair's New Labour Government and chaired by leading educator Sir Ken Robinson. This committee published the landmark report *All Our Futures: Creativity, Culture and Education* (also known as the Robinson Report) in 1999.[21] The key recommendation was that education, specifically school education, needs a much stronger emphasis on creativity and culture, not only in order to ensure that students' talents and abilities in such areas are supported and fostered, but also to equip them for careers that will require such skills. The report stated that creative thinking is necessary for great achievements not only in the arts, but also in science and business. The report also claims that a standard school education relies too heavily on rote learning and

122 *Creative Music Making*

logic. Foreshadowing the Henley Report (2011), the Robinson Report also stressed the need for partnerships in order to supply children with an ideal skillset, stating: "There is a compelling argument for closer working partnerships between schools and outside organisations."[22]

The Robinson Report also noted that many organisations, including symphony orchestras, were already working in partnership with schools, but that such work was, at that time, underfunded and not given sufficient weight at management level.

In 2002, four years after the publication of the Robinson Report, the UK government implemented many of the recommendations with the "Creative Partnerships" initiative, which aimed to develop long-term partnerships between schools and cultural organisations. Creative Partnerships received substantial government funding to achieve its goals, totalling 40 million pounds between 2002 and 2011. Initially targeting 16 pilot areas, the programme rapidly expanded and reached 1 million children in over 5,000 English schools. Awarded the 2011 WISE Award from the World Innovation Summit for Education, Creative Partnerships attracted significant attention both within the United Kingdom and internationally. While it has since been superseded by the British Music Hub system, the Creative Partnerships system has a great deal to offer to other organisations looking to partner with schools. This is evident in the quantity of research undertaken on Creative Partnerships, which is archived on the "Creativity, Culture and Education" website.[23]

Sir Ken Robinson has continued to champion the importance of creativity in school education over the past two decades, using his growing public profile to highlight the issue. His 2006 TED talk on the topic "How Schools Kill Creativity," is the most viewed in TED history, with 32,994,443 downloads to date.[24] Key claims made in this speech include that "creativity now is as important in education as literacy, and we should treat it with the same status," and "we don't grow into creativity, we grow out of it."[25] Robinson subsequently presented two more TED broadcasts on related topics in 2010 and 2013, and consistently advocated for the place of the arts in the curriculum. Robinson's books are a valuable resource for educators looking to develop creativity in their classrooms and educational philosophy.

The level of international interest in Robinson's views is a clear indication that his opinions resonated internationally with both teachers and parents. The only question is to what degree arts educationalists and practitioners will partner together in order to enable students to maximise their potential creativity. Symphony orchestras can potentially continue to play a leading role in this respect: orchestral creative workshops help children to access their imagination and develop confidence in their creative skills. They provide an enjoyable, yet educative, way for students to explore their own musical voice, and thus retain their relevance to the present day.

Composition and Creativity in Australian Music Education and Orchestral Education Programmes

Creative music workshops are a relatively new introduction to Australian orchestral education programming. As noted earlier in this chapter, Australian orchestras frequently use British specialists when offering creative workshops, and it is important to ensure that the skills of these visiting artists are passed on to Australian musicians. The establishment of the new Australian National Curriculum for the Arts, which has a strong emphasis on a "Making" strand of learning, is likely to increase the market for such work. Orchestras and other arts organisations may be of assistance to schools in their approach to this element of the curriculum. This assumption is based on the rapid growth of creative music workshops in the United Kingdom between orchestras and schools following the establishment of the UK National Curriculum, which, as noted above, had a similar emphasis on composition.

A new focus in Australia on the importance of creativity in the music classroom is evident in a growing body of research on the topic over the past decade. For example, at the 2005 conference in Melbourne of the "Australian Association for Research in Music Education," Harry Burke made a presentation making direct correlations between music education in the state of Victoria in the 21st century and the work of John Paynter and his associates.[26]

The links between Australian, British, and American music education practice are also investigated in a recent article in the *Journal of Historical Research in Music Education*.[27] In this article, Robin Stevens, music education professor at the Melbourne Conservatorium of Music, observes that "The origin of school music in Australia is essentially that of transplanted British educational practice."[28] The paper also makes the point that the investigation of creative music making in the classroom had begun earlier in the United Kingdom than in Australia: "Creativity and spontaneous music making had been a focus of music education in England since the 1950s, while an emphasis on creativity did not begin in Australia until the 1980s."[29] While the article is focused on the development of classroom music education, a similar point could be made of orchestral education work in the two nations.

Australian orchestras are now starting to embrace the UK style of collaborative creative workshop. In the past, however, Australian orchestras have supported composition through other initiatives, the most common being development programmes for young composers. These are generally offered to high school students and emerging professionals and provide mentorship and performance opportunities. Such programmes include the ASME Young Composer's Award, Sydney Symphony Orchestra's Sinfonietta Programme, Melbourne Symphony Orchestra's (MSO) 21st Century Cybec Young Composers Programme, West Australian Symphony

124   *Creative Music Making*

Orchestra's (WASO) Composition Project, and the Tasmanian Symphony Orchestra's Symphony Australia Composer School. An earlier project, the "ASME Composer-in-Residence and Young Composers Project," was initiated in 1994 by Professor Gary McPherson, and analysed by Margaret Barrett. Barrett's findings were that the chief aims of such programmes were twofold: to mentor a new generation of young composers, and to create a new repertoire for performance by school and community groups. She attributes the establishment of such programmes to "the growing interest in music composition in educational contexts," which she sees

> reflected in two significant factors: a developing research culture that investigates the contexts, motivations, processes and products of students engaged in composition activity; and, in the last decade, the placement of composition as a central tenet of curriculum policy nationally (Curriculum Corporation, 1994) and internationally. (Department for Education, 1995, MENC, 1994)[30]

While the value of such programmes is unquestioned, UK-style collaborative workshops have the capacity to greatly increase Australian orchestras' impact on the composition skills of large numbers of students, not merely those who have already demonstrated talent in this area.

The term "animateur" is not generally recognised in Australia at present, although it is very commonly used in the United Kingdom. The term became popular in the United Kingdom during the 1980s, and during the 1980s and 1990s training for animateurs was gradually incorporated into the syllabus of several UK tertiary music institutions. In 2003, a landmark report into animateur practices defined the term as "a practising artist, in any art form, who uses her/his skills, talents and personality to enable others to compose, design, devise, create perform or engage with works of art of any kind."[31] In the context of this book, animateurs are understood to be orchestral education concert and workshop presenters who are skilled at engaging participants in learning, through both the performance and creation of music.

With the increasing international acknowledgement of the importance of creativity, the skills of animateurs could potentially be in greater demand in the future. It is an area of growth in Australia; several UK-trained animateurs have been engaged to work with Australian orchestras in recent years. Leading US music educator Eric Booth equates an animateur with the American role of a "teaching artist," a term recently also used by the MSO and WASO. In his seminal work *The Music Teaching Artist's Bible*, Booth states that "an animateur is basically a teaching artist placed in a position of musical leadership."[32] Booth places great importance on the role of a teaching artist, or animateur, claiming: "What teaching artists know and can do is essential to engaging new audiences for classical music, and for leading the entire field towards a culturally relevant future."[33]

Experts in the field stress the need to engage participants at the beginning of a session with a fun activity designed to put everyone at ease. For example, Booth advises teaching artists to "Start with success. Make sure the first activity is fast and fun and has an immediate experiential reward."[34]

The "warm up games" frequently involve clapping, body percussion, and call and response. They are designed to combine musical objectives with setting a positive atmosphere for the session. While they serve a useful purpose and are always popular with students, it is also important to ensure that they are only a means to an end, not the main focus of a session.

Leading animateurs such as Rissmann and Fraser Trainer combine a sense of playfulness with an underlying commitment to connect participants meaningfully with orchestral music. It is important to be able to quickly enable participants to unlock elements of works from the orchestral canon and make personal connections with them. Compositions by Igor Stravinsky are often used by animateurs as a starting point for programmes, partly because the rhythmic drive of his music is a very clear entry point. One example of this is a crowd participation activity directed by Rissmann with the LSO at a concert in Trafalgar Square, when 10,000 people clapped the rhythm of Stravinsky's Augurs of Spring.

As animateurs frequently lead projects that aim to create new pieces of music, there is often an assumption that they need to be a composer. However, a better summary of the essential skill is the ability to inspire creativity in others and respond creatively to their ideas. Another key task for animateurs when helping workshop participants feel at ease while creating music is to provide instructions that give the right balance of freedom and direction. Counterintuitively, setting limitations actually provides the confidence to engage creatively. It is the fear of the proverbial blank page that can stifle creative participation.

The 2005 Guildhall School of Music and Drama (GSMD) publication *The Reflective Conservatoire*[35] gives insight into recent practices in the animateur role and the creative music workshops they commonly lead. The chapter titled "The Creative Music Workshop: A Contextual Study of Its Origin and Practice," by Sean Gregory, current director of innovation and engagement at the Barbican, is of particular interest. Gregory notes differing ways to spark creativity at the beginning of a workshop session, such as a skeleton score of notated rhythms, melodies, or harmonies; a theme; or a narrative text. He also stresses the importance of rehearsing and refining as the new composition develops, with the animateur evaluating, listening, and guiding the process.

Peter Wiegold, a leading UK animateur who initiated the GSMD's training in this field, looks for the "third arm" between free improvisation and notated composition, for instance by giving performers prompts, or working from a skeleton score, stating: "there is a simplistic view that music is either written or improvised... But there are a thousand worlds in between."[36] Wiegold explains that he looks for aspects of a score that allow performers

126 *Creative Music Making*

to exercise their creativity and interpretative skills. For instance, he may ask for a high trill, finished with a flourish, or ask for arpeggiation of certain chords for a set number of bars. Wiegold explains: "Much of my research has been about this critical balance. What frees musicians while maintaining integrity and purpose in the music?"[37]

While visits by UK animateurs to Australian orchestras have had a positive impact, it is important for Australia to now look to develop its own workshop leaders with creative skills. This will allow Australian orchestras to offer long-term sequential programmes with a creative focus, rather than short-term intensive projects facilitated by a visiting international animateur. For this to be achieved, the visits of UK animateurs to Australia need to include professional development workshops for musicians within the orchestra with which they are working. It is also important for Australian conservatoriums to offer training in the skills required by the animateur role. Such training needs to include skills in improvisation, collaborative composition, and public speaking. Identifying within the Australian music community those individuals with the necessary combination of charisma, creative flair, and passion for music education, and offering them support and training, will potentially help to create exciting new possibilities for Australian orchestral education programmes.

American and Canadian Perspective

While, of course, there have been many contributors to the development of creative-based music education in Canada and America, here we look at two key figures who are essential to discuss in this field from an American and Canadian perspective: the first is eminent composer, writer, and educator Raymond Murray Schafer (1933–2021) and the second is the father of the teaching artist movement, Eric Booth. Murray Schafer was a highly progressive thinker on the processes and purpose of composition and music education. Some may, indeed, replace the term "progressive" with "radical." He is credited with coining the term "soundscape" and was also a practitioner of graphic notation in both his education projects and his compositions. Schafer began teaching in the 1960s, working across all levels of education from primary to tertiary. In marked symmetry with the views of John Paynter, Schafer also believed that children should be hands-on with the creation of music, and that they should be encouraged to think for themselves in their development of their musical taste and opinion. To quote from his pivotal work *The Composer in the Classroom*, first published in 1965 and subsequently reprinted in his compilation of writings *Creative Music Education: A Handbook for the Modern Music Teacher*:

> It is the duty of every composer to be concerned with the creative ability of young people. But one has to be quick to catch it. For our system of

Creative Music Making 127

music education is one in which creative music is progressively vilified and choked out of existence.[38]

If one were to replace the term "music education" with "education" here, this statement could be a direct paraphrase of Sir Ken Robinson in his scathing criticism of the lack of creative space in the education system.

The Composer in the Classroom contains a series of case studies charting educational projects delivered by Murray Schafer. They contain illuminating insight into his working process as both a composer and an educator, as well as providing insight into the ways he feels involvement in the creative process increases musical development in every facet. In one scenario, for example, Murray Schafer states that an improvisation exercise required a wind ensemble to truly listen to each other – a skill that is not always fully developed in a standard ensemble rehearsal. Schafer muses:

> It is difficult to decide whether the real value of an experiment such as that to follow is in drawing out latent talent for improvisation or merely as an exercise in ear training. Probably it serves both uses. Certainly it was discovered that most students never listen at all to one another when they play in bands and orchestras where there are twenty clarinets of sixteen flutes all tootling away at the unison lines of their Beethoven-Browns and Handel-Jacksons. Thus, to force students to listen, as was necessary here, would seem to constitute an important "breakthrough" in their musical education.[39]

In addition to the musical benefits of creative processes for students, Schafer also draws parallels with the blurring of the category of performer and composer that was occurring in the music profession through the late 20th century. The compartmentalisation of these roles impacted on music education at all levels, separating the identity of music creator from that of music performer. With the reintroduction of improvisation to composed scores, the work of Murray Schafer, Paynter, Self, Maxwell Davies, and their colleagues was pivotal in connecting the two musical skillsets at the educational grassroots level as well.

Murray Schafer's views shaped his teaching at the tertiary level as well as the projects he delivered at schools. His "Ear Cleaning" course, delivered to first-year students at Simon Fraser University, was designed to encourage them to refocus on listening, through the process of making music. Murray Schafer explains:

> I felt my primary task in this course was to open ears... As a practising musician I have come to realise that one learns about sound only by making sound, about music only by making music. All our investigations into sound should be verified empirically by making sounds ourselves and by examining the results... Improvisatory and creative

128   *Creative Music Making*

abilities – atrophied through years of disuse – are also rediscovered, and the student learns something very practical about the size and shape of things musical.[40]

Through his invention of the term "soundscape," Murray Schafer explored the fundamental question of "what is music?" In his publication *The New Soundscape*, Schafer provides a definition from the ultimate classical music radical, John Cage: "Music is sounds, sounds around us whether we're in or out of concert halls."[41] Schafer elaborates on this, with a call to arms against the casual noise pollution of the modern world:

> One of the purposes of this part is to direct the ear of the listener towards the new soundscape of contemporary life, to acquaint him or her with a vocabulary of sounds one may expect to hear both inside and outside concert halls. It may be that the listener will not like all the tunes of this new music, and that too will be good. For together with other forms of pollution, the sounds swage of our contemporary environment is unprecedented in human history.[42]

Murray Schafer passed away in 2021; however, his legacy is very much alive and vibrant. His questioning of the traditional status quo in music education continues to inspire international debate and discussion; his compositions continue to challenge and provoke audiences; and his focus on sound pollution is gaining increasing relevance in our ever-noisier world. Each time a junior primary classroom engages in a "soundscape" activity, Schafer's impact is felt. His focus on the importance of "making" is also highly impactful, resonating in the increasing proliferation of creative-based learning activities, and also at the broader level in the delivery of creative-focused curricula such as the Manhattan Music Curriculum Project and the Australian National Curriculum for the Arts.

Eric Booth has had a significant impact on creative-based music education, both in the United States and internationally. Charismatic, energetic, and highly articulate, Booth is known as the "father of the teaching artist" movement – a term that gained traction through his professional work and his landmark publication *The Music Teaching Artist's Bible: Becoming a Virtuoso Educator*.[43] Originally trained as an actor, Booth has made a significant contribution to the field of creative-based education. His impact on the music profession in itself is remarkable – like Murray Schafer, who can be credited with founding the term "soundscape," Booth has led the foundation of the field of "teaching artistry." Through his 12 years of teaching at New York's Juilliard School of Music and Drama, Booth delivered teaching skills to the elite performers of this illustrious school, creating an ongoing legacy through the generations of students who were inspired by Booth's vision of a career that combined education with performance at the highest levels. At the Juilliard, Booth started the art and education programme

Creative Music Making 129

together with colleague Edward Bilous in 1994. This was the first step for Booth in working with musicians, a genre of the arts with which he has now fully connected. Booth has also taught at Stanford University, Tanglewood Festival, and at the Lincoln Centre for 40 years. At the Lincoln Centre, Booth co-founded the "Teaching Artist Development Labs," a highly impactful training lab for emerging leaders in teaching artistry. Booth is an inspirational public speaker, and has delivered keynotes at several highly influential conferences and events, including the 2006 UNESCO Arts Education Conference in Lisbon and the 2007 conference on orchestras' connection to communities in Glasgow.

As well as being an inspiring communicator and educator, Booth is a community builder. He has established a worldwide new community of arts educators who identify as "teaching artists." This community is united through publications, all founded by Booth, including the *Teaching Artists Journal*, the *Ensemble* newsletter, and the *Ensemble Global* newsletter. In 2012, Booth co-founded the International Teaching Artist Conference, which has been held biannually in countries spanning the globe: Oslo (2012), Brisbane (2014), Edinburgh (2016), New York (2018), and Seoul (2020). Additionally, Booth also co-founded the International Teaching Artist Collaborative (ITAC) and the ITAC IMPACT – Climate, which are year-round collectives for teaching artists.

So, what is a teaching artist? This is a question that still has no finite definition. In Booth's words in the "Bible":

> There is no consensus definition of teaching artist in the evolving field of arts education. Five years ago, even the term would spark arguments from those who preferred the traditional labels of visiting artist, resident artist, or even artist educator. Part of me hopes there will never be a consensus definition for a practice so varied and dynamic.[44]

However, Booth proceeds to offer some definitions:

> an artist who chooses to include artfully educating others, beyond teaching the technique of the art form, as an active part of a career... a teaching artist is the model of the twenty-first-century artist and, simultaneously, a model for high-engagement learning in education. A teaching artist is the future of art in America.[45]

Booth then muses on how a teaching artist uses their artistic skills to help others to connect with artistic activity and processes. Booth places the emphasis on "doing," the active making of music, stating: "Art lives in the verbs as much as the nouns."[46]

While the term remains broad, an essential component of the skillset of a successful teaching artist is creativity. This includes the ability to think creatively, and to engage in creative music processes. Teaching

130 *Creative Music Making*

artistry relies on creative thinking – the ability to devise highly creative, interactive, and original learning activities that develop participation and engagement with music. Equally, confidence in exploring creative musical processes is an essential criterion in successfully delivering these learning activities.

Booth has worked in the orchestral field for over 20 years, developing these skills in orchestral staff and delivering impactful sessions and industry conferences. His contribution to the orchestral industry has included roles with the Knight Foundation's Magic of Music Programme and the Mellon Foundation's Orchestra Forum. He has delivered professional development to the New York Philharmonic's teaching artist team for over a decade – which he notes includes working with many of the Juilliard students who had emerged through his initial training.

Although Booth is teaching artistry's main spokesperson and the acknowledged leader in the field, he was not the first to use the term. The field began to develop in the 1980s, and anecdotally the term was coined by June Dunbar at the Lincoln Centre Institute in the early 1970s.[47] Booth's criteria for the essentials for teaching artistry are based on the theory put forward earlier by Howard Gardner which listed four essential roles that students should have experiences in to be a well-rounded, complete learner. These skills are creator, performer, audience, and critic. While there remain gaps in each of these areas in school-based music education, there are also gaps in the skillset of the majority of graduating tertiary-trained musicians. For example, while there is a strong focus on performing at the tertiary level, there are still few classically trained performers who are confident in the role of music creator. Booth gives the example of the musician who has a true balance in the four roles listed by Gardner: "The happiest musicians I know are those who fluidly use the range of roles in themselves."[48]

The question of the ideal training of the 21st-century musician, and the skills that are required today by the profession, are points more fully discussed in Chapter 7. One point is abundantly clear, which is that the development of creative thinking is going to play an increasing role in the training of musicians and music educators moving into the future. For that, we owe a great deal to the work of the leaders discussed in this chapter, as well as to the countless other musicians and music educators who have devoted their energies in this area.

Notes

1 Pitts, *A Century of Change in Music Education.*
2 Ibid., p. 66.
3 Ibid., p. 73.
4 Paynter and Aston, *Sound and Silence.*
5 Jolyon Laycock. *A Changing Role for the Composer in Society: A Study of the Historical Background and Current Methodologies of Creative Music-Making.* Bern: Peter Lang European Academic Publisher, 2005, p. 47.

Creative Music Making 131

6 George Self. *New Sounds in Class: A Contemporary Approach to Music*. London: Universal Edition, 1967.

7 George Self, quoted in Pitts, *A Century of Change*, p. 78.

8 *Education Reform Act*, UK Parliament, 1988.

9 Ofsted 1995 Report, as quoted in Pitts, *A Century of Change*, p. 198.

10 John Stephens. "Music in Schools," *RSA Journal*, Vol. 141(5442), August/September 1993, p. 643.

11 Ibid., pp. 642–643.

12 Julia Winterson. "An Evaluation of the Effects of London Sinfonietta Education Projects on their Participants," *British Journal of Music Education*, Vol. 11(2), July 1994, pp. 129-141.

13 London Sinfonietta. Undated document, cited in Winterson BJME article Vol. 11(2), July 1994, p. 130.

14 Winterson, *The Community Education Work of Orchestras and Opera Companies*, Appendix 6, p. 33.

15 Ibid., pp. 81–82.

16 Ruffer, "The London Sinfonietta Education Programme," p. 49.

17 Winterson, *The Community Education Work of Orchestras and Opera Companies*, p. 36.

18 Ibid., p. 33.

19 Jo Shapcott. *Orchestras and Education: A New Era*. Commissioned by the Association of British Orchestras, 1998, p. 6.

20 Booth, *The Music Teaching Artist's Bible*, p. 101.

21 Robinson, *All Our Futures*.

22 Ibid., p. 8.

23 https://www.creativitycultureeducation.org/case-studies/, accessed 6 March 2023.

24 Ken Robinson. *Do Schools Kill Creativity?* (video file), Feb 2006. Retrieved from www.ted.com/talks/ken_robinson_says_schools_kill_creativity?language=en, accessed 25 June 2015.

25 Ibid.

26 Harry Burke. "The Relevance of Creativity: John Paynter and Victorian Music Education in the Twenty First Century," in Peter de Vries (editor), *Australian Association for Research in Music Education: Proceedings of the XXVIIth Annual Conference: Reviewing the Future*. Melbourne: Australian Association for Research in Music Education, 2005, p. 51.

27 Timothy J. Groulx. "Three Nations, One Common Root: A Historical Comparison of Elementary Music Education in the United Kingdom, the United States, and Australia," *Journal of Historical Research in Music Education*, Vol. 34(2), April 2013, pp. 137–153.

28 Ibid, p. 137.

29 Ibid., p. 146.

30 Margaret Barrett. "Composing a Future for Australian Music: Perceptions of the ASME Young Composers Project [online]," In Jennifer Rosevear (Editor); Warren Bourne (Editor), *Conference Proceedings: A Musical Odyssey; a Journey of Discovery in Music Education*. Adelaide: Australian Society for Music Education, 2001, pp. 51–60. Abstract.

31 Ledgard and Odam, *The Art of the Animateur*, p. 9.

32 Booth, *The Teaching Artist Bible*, p. 249.

33 Ibid., p. 6.

34 Ibid., p. 201.

35 Odam and Bannan, *The Reflective Conservatoire: Studies in Music Education Research Studies 4*, p. 279.

36 Peter Wiegold. "But Who Will Make their Tea?" *Harmony. Forum of the Symphony Orchestra Institute*, No. 12, April 2001, p. 4.

132 *Creative Music Making*

37 Ibid., p. 5.
38 Schafer, *Creative Music Education*, p. 41.
39 Ibid., p. 33.
40 Ibid., p. 49.
41 Ibid., p. 96.
42 Ibid, p. 99.
43 Booth, *The Music Teaching Artist's Bible.*
44 Ibid., p. 3.
45 Ibid., p. 4.
46 Ibid., p. 6.
47 Ibid., p. 8.
48 Ibid., p. 58.

7 New Roles, New Skills
Implications for the Tertiary Training of Classical Musicians

The steady growth in the quantity and diversity of education and community engagement work by symphony orchestras and opera companies over the past 50 years has impacted on the skills required of musicians and administrators. Indeed, in many ways the growth of the orchestral and opera education field has necessitated a rethinking of the ideal skillset of the classical musician of the 21st century. The perplexing question is how to maintain a focus on the development of the artistic and playing skills of a young musician, as well as finding the time to develop the additional skills required to fully engage with education and community engagement activities. In April 2015, the chief conductor of the New York Philharmonic, Alan Gilbert, commented on this point:

> Orchestras need the best musicians—that will never change. But what is asked and expected of these musicians is constantly evolving. Just as the educational and outreach efforts of orchestras only achieve full resonance when they connect meaningfully and organically with who the musicians are and what they do, musicians in today's orchestras are only doing their jobs fully when they understand and invest in their expanded portfolio that is demanded by the wider definition of what an orchestra is.[1]

In order to equip emerging students with these new skills, many tertiary music schools are re-examining their course structure. Conservatories in the United Kingdom, in particular the Guildhall School of Music and Drama (GSMD), have been at the forefront of this reappraisal of tertiary music training. However, the courses currently offered by the majority of tertiary music institutions have not kept pace with the realities of the professional classical music field. Eric Booth is adamant that there needs to be more change:

> Has there been enough of a shift in the training of tertiary music students? NOOOO! Not even close!! I would say there are now some places that have recognised what needs to be done, but those places

DOI: 10.4324/9781003198512-8

134 *New Roles, New Skills*

> are few and those places that have made serious accommodation are extremely few. Most conservatories now have an elective way that you can develop some teaching artist skills while you are studying, but it is still largely Balkanised, out there on the periphery as an option if you like kids or you've heard it might generate extra income ... It has not filtered into the consciousness that the 21st Century musician has to have these skills. They are slower to evolve than the orchestras are and I'm convinced that the evolution is going to come out of market demand, not from visionary activity on high. As young people start to say I am interested in a wider range of things, the orchestral track is not necessarily the only way for me, then they will start to change. That will change it over time. There is a reason they are called Conservatories, they are very conservative.[2]

Most tertiary classical music performance degrees still focus on developing instrumental or vocal technical skills to the highest possible level, alongside coaching in chamber and ensemble skills. Little if any time is dedicated to fostering skills in teaching, improvising, composing, public speaking, marketing, or using music technology. This results in a workforce of orchestral and opera musicians with a lack of confidence in such skills, which are, however, increasingly required by education and community engagement work. Thus, many musicians have found themselves under-prepared when requested to do education or community engagement work. This is a far from optimal situation both for the morale of the musicians and for the participants in such education programmes, who deserve to be led by a well-prepared and trained team.

The solution requires action at two levels. Firstly, orchestral and opera managements need to acknowledge any skill shortages in their workforce. In-service training needs to be provided to all personnel involved in education and community engagement work, in order to equip them with the skills necessary to confidently lead and inspire participants. For example, confidence in improvisation is increasingly required of players leading education programmes, especially creative workshop models. However, this is not reflected in the typical training of an elite orchestral or opera musician, which aims to foster their ability to play precisely and accurately what someone else (the composer or conductor) requires of them. Therefore, training is needed to enable them to confidently lead creative-focused workshops. They need to re-access their creative spark and play freely, away from their precisely annotated scores.

Secondly, there is a need for readjustment at the tertiary level. Orchestral and opera musicians typically come through the music performance rather than music education degree programmes offered at tertiary institutions. Indeed, it is fair to say that within a typical music institution there exists a glass barrier dividing the performance and education streams, and their paths rarely cross. There is a subsequent lack of emphasis on pedagogy skills within a music performance degree. Leading educator, Eric Booth has commented on this issue: "I know that condescending attitudes still exist that assume any artist who chooses to also educate can't be a first-rate artist. Well, it just isn't true."[3]

Booth is speaking from experience as a member of the teaching staff of the Juilliard School of Music and Drama. Booth has also developed education skills with musicians of many leading orchestras, including the New York Philharmonic. Booth notes that in his experience: "Almost all music teaching artists feel that they have been thrust into the work before they are adequately prepared."[4]

Tertiary music performance students may take a module on pedagogy on their own instrument but they are rarely offered work experience placements, or training in group teaching or classroom work. This results in a lack of basic awareness of the skills and techniques necessary to communicate with large groups of students in an education programme. Booth also makes this point:

> I encounter hundreds of artists in the top orchestras and arts organisations who work hard to learn education skills way too late, angry that they didn't have a chance or a conservatory climate that encouraged them to learn teaching artistry during their schooling.[5]

The importance of improving the provision of education skills for artists, as well as better training in the arts for teachers, has also been emphasised by Sir Ken Robinson. This was an overall finding of Robinson's 1989 report, *All Our Futures: Creativity, Culture and Education*, and was also stated in his foreword to a 2003 publication, *The Art of the Animateur*:

> For a range of reasons, too many teachers are not well enough trained in the arts, and too many artists are not well enough trained – indeed not trained at all – to work in education. Although many artists do work in education at some stage of their careers – and often for long periods – the curricula of art schools, conservatoires and theatre schools often do little to alert them to, or prepare them for, these opportunities. In the medium and longer term, initial higher education in the arts needs to take fuller account of the multifaceted portfolio careers that many artists actually lead in the twenty first century, including work in education and the community. There is an immediate need too to provide training opportunities to practising artists who are already working, or wanting to work, in these settings. This is what Animarts was set up to do.[6]

The Animarts research project was an association between the London International Festival of Theatre (LIFT) and the Guildhall School of Music and Drama. Coordinated by Anna Ledgard from 2002 to 2003, it aimed to explore and better understand the roles and activities of animateurs

136 New Roles, New Skills

and teachers. The report *The Art of the Animateur* was published at the conclusion of the project. Key findings included the importance of effective partnership between animateurs and teachers, and the need for a valid accreditation process for personnel working in community music or orchestral community engagement and education programmes. It also stressed the need for work placements and internships:

> we are being advised that the best way for artists to learn how to work effectively in education or other settings is for them to do their learning in partnership with the people they are going to be working with, ie. teachers and other members of a school staff, community arts organisers, etc.[7]

Often, orchestral and opera education projects offered within schools will ensure that a classroom teacher is available to help with discipline and pedagogical outcomes. However, it would greatly benefit the programme if the musicians involved in education projects were first offered training in classroom pedagogy. Even programmes offered outside the classroom often require the direction of large groups of people, and here public speaking training would significantly boost the efficiency and outcome of the programme.

However, the solution to the skills shortage should ideally come before the musician is appointed to their position. The tertiary training of orchestral and opera musicians should equip them with the new skills required of musicians in the 21st century. This concern is a primary focus of the GSMD, as stated here:

> The role of a conservatoire should be re-aligned to meet the needs, expectation and potential of today's society. Reformulating the idea of what a musician could be – what he or she has beyond a technical proficiency on one instrument – is highly relevant to the workplace, as musicians now need many strings to one bow. Important qualities for musicians who want to remain employable are to be creative, multi-faceted when performing, and effective in collaborative environments.[8]

A tertiary performance degree should, of course, still aim to produce performers with a deep knowledge of the classical music canon and the highest level of performance skills. However, alongside this should be training to enable them to access and explore their musical creativity, work experience sessions with orchestral and opera education and engagement teams, training in leading creative music workshop sessions, public speaking skills, and training in teaching skills and with music technology. In his paper "Enlightenment or Entitlement," Australian researcher and Conservatorium Director Peter Tregear has commented that he feels that placing a stronger focus at the tertiary training level on the social and community role of music will, in turn, help to strengthen the conservatorium system of music education. Writing in 2014, Tregear remarks that tertiary music education is in a state of crisis. He advocates for tertiary music institutions to recalibrate their teaching in order to reinforce their relevance, stating "the case must start with a refocusing and re-energising of music's potential to play a role in the broader mission of the humanities to help sustain civil society, no less."[9] Tregear notes that the challenge for music educators will be to find the balance between the essential qualities of the discipline and the need to "engage with the rapidly changing broader cultural and political circumstances of today."[10]

This chapter focuses on institutions that are leading the way in their rethinking of their syllabus and teaching, and draws attention to the various ways in which leading conservatories are approaching the task of creating musicians who are also effective arts educators and advocates.

The Guildhall School of Music and Drama has been a leader in this area since the 1980s. In 1984, Peter Renshaw, previously principal of the Menuhin School of Music, initiated a new teaching and research programme at the Guildhall School of Music and Drama. The postgraduate "performance and communication skills" course aimed to create more versatile and dynamic musicians capable of working within a variety of musical styles and cultures. The course was focused on improvisation, communication, leadership skills, and participatory performance. In 1985, Renshaw stated his aims for the programme to be transformative for the students, to "redefine their role as musicians in society," to

> acquire the skills with which to create new audiences in the future ... and to serve the needs and cultivate the tastes of many different institutional and informal groups for whom traditional conservatoire training has not catered in the past.[11]

Peter Wiegold was appointed artistic director of the "performance and communication skills department" in 1985 and was an integral part of its success during its development years. In addition to his position at the Guildhall, Wiegold also helped to establish the workshop format within the classical music profession through training courses in workshop technique, creative leadership, and improvisation with many of the UK's orchestras and opera companies. He has made a considerable impact on the younger generation of emerging British classical musicians through his workshop training sessions with the UK's National Youth Orchestra (1996–2005), the Menuhin School, and the Southbank Sinfonia (an elite training orchestra for young professionals).[12] He also contributed to the training of Australian musicians through a partnership with the organisation Youth Music Australia in the mid-1990s, when he coached young orchestral musicians in improvisation techniques. Wiegold and Renshaw were given the freedom to create their own curriculum for the course, and it incorporated many diverse skills, described by Wiegold:

138 *New Roles, New Skills*

we included Tai-Chi, African drumming, voice, and body work, as well as many kinds of improvisation and composition. It was a wonderful opportunity to test starting from scratch. Just what is it to "make music" and be a real performer?[13]

Lord Yehudi Menuhin supported the ways in which the course structure brought students into contact with diverse sectors of society, commenting: "There is no doubt that the experience of playing in various situations other than the normal concert hall, such as at the Broadmoor Hospital and terminal homes, etc., broadens the otherwise egocentric nature of musical careers."[14]

Menuhin is speaking with experience of the often isolated and insular life of a musician, particularly at the elite solo level. The course deliberately placed students in unfamiliar situations to help them develop skills to connect and engage with a variety of different audiences. Renshaw felt that "technique, music and communication should go hand in hand ... Far too often technique is acquired in both a musical and social vacuum, divorced from any context which might give it a point."[15]

Renshaw acknowledged the conflict between the ideals of this course and the ambitions of a typical conservatoire student who is often focused on acquiring technical virtuosity, passing exams, and gaining a reputation and a professional status. However, he feels that training aimed at boosting creativity and communication skills will ultimately produce a more accomplished musician.

Initially funded for three years, the philosophies behind the performance and communication skills course have gradually become embedded in the GSMD.[16] The Guildhall department responsible for community engagement skills has had a variety of titles over the past three decades, including a period known as Guildhall Connect, founded in 2002. At this point, Sean Gregory was appointed as head of the Centre for Creative and Professional Practice. In October 2009, Gregory was appointed director of creative learning at the GSMD, bringing together the work of Guildhall Connect and the Barbican Education Department. Gregory was one of the early graduates from the original performance and communication skills course, and describes it as a seminal moment in his career. Gregory is now the vice president and director of innovation and engagement at the Guildhall. Gregory speaks of the skillset that he feels is needed for working in the community engagement field:

I think a classically trained or more formally trained musician should be confident off the written page, as well as with the written notes. It's finding a way with those musicians who are so highly trained, so highly skilled, that you don't want to put them in compromised situations. They're not jazzers, it's not why they did what they did in the first place. But I think when you're in a situation where you need to respond to what's going on, you can't just rely on the written note and the music stand in front of you. So to have the confidence to be able to use your instruments to play and respond and express through your instrument, which is your key voice, and to use that in different ways, I think is really, really important.

I think it's this spontaneity, just being able to respond to what's there. Whether it's through your voice, literally conversation, where you're listening, responding, and you're empathetic, and you can build something, and you are co-creating something all the time. One last thing is also your role in an ensemble, you might be in those situations on your own, but you're often with other musicians, your peers. You're not at that particular moment sitting in your rank and file positions in an orchestra or even a chamber group; you might be moving around, you might be sat in different places, in a hospital or wherever it is. So again, it's feeling that you can work as an ensemble in those situations, whether you're working from repertoire or not. That's a different type of teamwork, a different type of ensemble work as well.[17]

Over the past 15 years, education and community engagement skills have gradually been incorporated into the syllabus of many other leading conservatoires throughout the United Kingdom. While the Guildhall's alumni continue to make up the best part of this field of practice internationally, other institutions are increasingly taking a similar approach. London's Royal College of Music (RCM) was early to explore these issues, under the direction of Dame Janet Ritterman. Australian-born Ritterman was director of the RCM from 1993 to 2005 and was a founding member of the Creative Industries HE Forum established by the Department of Culture, Media and Sport. In 1999, the RCM established the Woodhouse Professional Development Centre (now known as the Creative Careers Centre) which aims to prepare students for entry into the profession in a variety of ways: it provides performance opportunities, experience in planning education projects, and advice on self-promotion and entrepreneurial skills. Uniquely, these services are available to students not only through their official studies at the RCM but also for five years after they graduate, providing an invaluable support and bridge for students as they negotiate their early career path. The RCM has continued to explore community music education skills and training, and the RCM Sparks Department is now a strategic partner in the prominent Tri-Borough Music Hub. The latest production from the Sparks and Tri-Borough collaboration is "Convo," commissioned by the Tri-Borough Music Hub, the Royal Albert Hall, and the Royal College of Music. This has been a two-year creative project that involved children across the three London boroughs of Hammersmith and Fulham, Kensington and Chelsea, and the City of Westminster.[18]

The Trinity Laban Conservatoire of Music and Dance, based in Greenwich, London, offers several postgraduate degrees and diplomas in

140 New Roles, New Skills

performance, workshop skills, and education skills. The master's in music education and performance is a one-year, full-time, postgraduate degree designed for any student wishing to pursue an active career as both a professional musician and a teacher or educator. In addition, Trinity Laban also offers professional development for musicians already working in the field of education in the form of "the teaching musician" postgraduate certificate/diploma/MA. While this course does not offer qualified teacher status, it is designed to bolster the skills of musicians working in education settings, including music leaders, tutors, community musicians, and animateurs, through a combination of pedagogy studies and work placements. The course is designed to fit alongside a professional career, with limited contact hours.

The University of York was the first British university to introduce a community music module to its three-year undergraduate music degree and has also offered a community music degree at postgraduate level. The University of York was also at the centre of early exploration of creative music practice in the community through the work of faculty members such as John Paynter, who joined the university in 1969, becoming head of department in 1982.[19] Also in the city of York, the York St John University has focused on community music, offering a master's in community music. This is linked to the International Centre for Community Music (ICCM) which is located within York St John University. Professor Lee Higgins is the director of the International Centre of Community Music. Higgins is a leader in the field of community music and is the author of several books including *Community Music: In Theory and Practice*, co-author of *Engagement in Community Music*, and co-editor of *The Oxford Handbook of Community Music*.

In America, the Longy School of Music of Bard College, with two campuses in Cambridge, Massachusetts, and Los Angeles, has made a clear focus on positioning its students to be socially minded and versatile, with graduate teaching degrees inspired by El Sistema. The Longy mission statement is to train "students to become exceptional musicians who can engage new audiences; teach anyone, anywhere; and use artistry to change lives in communities around the world."[20] Karen Zorn, president since 2007, has brought in a radical change of outlook and activity to Longy College, establishing partnerships with Los Angeles Philharmonic and with the Fundacion Musical Simon Bolivar. Longy students interact with public schools, community centres, prisons, shelters, and other external venues. All undergraduate students must complete a teaching artist programme, which involves them delivering an education community concert that they have designed. Elsje Kibler-Vermaas was the director of the master of arts in teaching degree at Longy College from 2010 to 2017, an appointment bookended by her appointments with the LA Phil as firstly director of education, and currently vice president of learning. Kibler-Vermaas is quite uniquely placed in this career versatility, having had direct impact both on the training of the next generation of teaching artists through the Longy master of arts curriculum

New Roles, New Skills 141

and on developing one of the most high impact avenues for teaching artist employment with the YOLA programme.

The Juilliard School in New York stands out as another innovative and forward-thinking tertiary music institution. The Juilliard is a leader in this field of training through its Teaching Artists programme, and in particular through the "Morse Teaching Artist Fellowship," as established by Eric Booth. The Morse Teaching Artist Fellowship offers experience in teaching students from Grades 2 to 12, both in classroom and instrumental teaching settings. The Juilliard also offers an educational experience to its student body through the concert fellowship, linked to its Young People's Concert series, which is offered to fourth-grade classes from New York schools. Selected students are also offered teaching experience in the Music Advancement programme, an access programme delivered to students from backgrounds underrepresented in American performing arts.

The Royal Conservatoire of Scotland and the Reid School of Music at the University of Edinburgh are also exploring ways of training musicians for versatile portfolio careers. The RCS offers BA (Hons) contemporary performance practice, with the course described as being for aspiring performance makers who wish to develop their skills as innovative and socially engaged performers, directors, teachers, and cultural leaders, who can realise their aspirations to create and shape the future of new work.[21] Nigel Osborne led the introduction of training in community music at the RCS at both postgraduate and undergraduate levels, aiming to create a new generation of workshop leaders.[22]

Richard McNicol, the maverick who pioneered the creative-based education model, feels very clearly that there needs to be a focus on two key areas: improvisation and contemporary music. McNicol states:

> I would argue they need to know contemporary music: Stockhausen, Boulez, etc., that they should know an awful lot about what other composers have done with use of masses of sound, serial technique, birdsong, nature, loud and soft blocks of sound, single line melodies, all those things. If you've got that repertoire in your head you can make what the children do work. For me, contemporary music was really the answer, because you don't need harmony and counterpoint, principles that we learned at university, but you do need creativity and imagination and self-confidence. If I were talking about training people I would be emphatic that they should learn to improvise. I would also teach them that what anybody does, you will follow, you simply are brave enough to latch on to it and improvise with them.[23]

Opera companies and symphony orchestras have a stake in the development of their future employees, and they are active in the training of young musicians alongside conservatoires. Glyndebourne Opera, for example, is making an investment in the training of young vocalists, with a focus on

142   New Roles, New Skills

diversity and inclusion, through its Glyndebourne Academy programme, which works with young singers aged 16–26 years. Through the academy programme, the singers receive training in movement and psychological support in performance and resilience, all essential qualities for a successful career.

The industry is aware that there needs to be a sector-wide effort to increase inclusivity and diversity in the classical music profession. While individual organisations are making efforts to effect change in this area, it is also essential to have diversity at the conservatoire teaching level as well. This point was made in the recently released report commissioned by Arts Council England, *Creating a More Inclusive Classical Music: A Study of the English Orchestral Workforce and the Current Routes to Joining It.* Published in 2021, the report's key aims are:

- To improve the understanding of the current profile of the classical music workforce.
- To examine talent pathways into the sector to understand what they might indicate about the diversity of the future workforce.
- To explore what learning there might be to support collective action to increase diversity and inclusion in the workforce and the pipeline.[24]

The report found that ethnical diversity decreased throughout the levels of participation in classical music – from 26% of students accessing music education through the music education hubs whole-class teaching, down to 13% at conservatoire level, and below 5% in professional orchestras. The report found that the lack of role models is a factor in this decrease in participation:

> The absence of visible role models (e.g. women or Black, Asian and other ethnically diverse role models) amongst those learning instruments or progressing in HE can negatively affect the perceptions of underrepresented groups coming through the system. Also challenging is the significant visibility which musicians from such underrepresented groups experience, and the burden of "standing out" and expectations and assumptions which come with it. Some literature reflects critically on the place of classical music in music education.[25]

Two orchestras working on developing the visibility of role models are the Chineke! Ensemble and the Paraorchestra. Chineke! is an orchestra that provides employment opportunities to black and ethnically diverse classical musicians, with a focus on performing music by under-recognised, ethnically diverse composers. Formed in 2015 by energetic powerhouse Chi-Chi Nwanoku, the orchestra plays and delivers workshops in schools and community settings as well as concert halls, bringing its performance flair and "if you see it you can be it" message directly into the communities it represents.

The Paraorchestra is performing a similar role for people with disabilities. Directed by charismatic Charles Hazelwood since 2012, this ensemble is the world's first large-scale ensemble formed by professional disabled and non-disabled musicians. These two pioneering ensembles are still at the early stages of their impact, but the hope is that they are already providing the visibility and inspiration needed to normalise diversity in the classical music profession.

Of course, learning does not stop at the conservatoire. Orchestras and opera companies have also formed close partnerships with tertiary music schools in the training of the next generation. The chief purpose of such a partnership is to provide a "bridge," or support network, in order to create the most effective possible transition for students from training to professional life. This partnership should ideally take several forms, from a discussion at management level between the orchestra or opera company and local conservatorium about the skills expected from graduates and how to achieve them, to opportunities for students to experience the realities of professional life through work experience placements or side-by-side performance opportunities.

While the benefits of such an approach to the student are clear, there are also considerable benefits to the orchestra and opera company in ensuring that graduates already have a clear idea of the standards expected of them in the professional setting. Side-by-side work and internships also serve to initiate students into the particular style and approach idiosyncratic to that organisation. All orchestras and opera companies have their own particular character and style of working, which has often been developed over centuries, and is encapsulated in subtle but important details such as the degree of playing behind the beat, approaches to rubato or a particular timbre. If organisations are able to mentor students during their formative study years, then the overall standard of performance will rise. It is also important for students to be aware of the spectrum of work undertaken by orchestras and opera companies and, ideally, are involved in all aspects of such work at the time of training, including education projects, music therapy projects, and community engagement work. One of the most high profile of these partnerships is between the London Symphony Orchestra and the Guildhall School of Music and Drama, in delivering a master's of orchestral artistry. Andra East, director of Discovery, explains:

> The whole programme [the master's in orchestral artistry] is about what it means to be an orchestral musician today. It's everything from repertoire coaching, to sitting in with the orchestra, to having a click track session so they know how to record music. Another element of what we do is have all the students take part in a training session with LSO animateur Rachel Leach, to deliver education workshops. They also have a workshop with Mark Withers who is focused on special needs and with Vanessa King who is focused on early years. So all our students

144 *New Roles, New Skills*

have those three workshops, then they have the option to shadow LSO Discovery activities. We share with them all the opportunities where we can bring them in to work with our communities and our participants, alongside LSO musicians and an animateur, so the students become part of that creative team in a shadowing role.

So, that's where we make sure that the skill set is in there. I would be really keen to see more of that happening in other similar programmes. I think it's very important that people realise it's not ancillary to, and not just adjacent to, what LSO musicians do. So many of our musicians are engaged with this, but I think many students arrive at the Guildhall not knowing that this is so core to their work. Yes – they perform on stage, but they are also delivering these sessions. And I think that is really important.[26]

East finds that having had the experience of working on these projects, under the guidance of experienced leaders in each area, the master's students are finding that they are often drawn to one or more areas of engagement, whether that be early years, working with disabled people, or working with school-aged students. The students are starting to come through the master's ready to be engaged by the LSO as "extras" in projects, and East finds that this is a smooth transition as the students are already aware of the work, understand the LSO's model, and are able to fit in.

East has focused on the skills required of the LSO musicians in delivering their pioneering education and community engagement programmes, consulting with the musicians and giving presentations on this topic to other orchestras. She feels that a diverse set of skills is clearly emerging as essential to the work:

A lot of the skills that we talk about being required for delivering effective Discovery type projects – outreach or learning and participation projects – are soft skills. Obviously, you need to be good at your instrument, of course that is very important. But perhaps the other key element of it is the improvisatory element, being able to be creative with your instrument. I think it's really, really important for us specifically in Discovery because so much of the work that we do is about creativity. And so being prepared to learn what it's like to improvise, to respond to what someone else has played, how you connect in with that – that is a very valuable skill. It's something that not all people that we see come through feel comfortable with at all. Improvisation, creativity, and flexibility are really key.

Listening, responding to visual cues and gestures, creative improvisation, creating something from nothing, decision making. Thinking once you've got an idea going, how do you then structure that and form a piece, how do you develop the idea. There's musical support for a participant as well as personal support; sometimes what you're supporting there isn't a musical thing. This adaptability and thinking on your feet, you can plan a workshop to the nth degree, but then you can be totally taken by surprise with what the young people come up with. So being able to think on your feet and be flexible around that. Teamwork, cooperation and trust: when you're working with a team of an animateur, your fellow LSO musician colleagues, and students in the room as well, you're in a team and you need to be co-operating. And then the communication, both verbal and nonverbal. Non verbal is again very important, particularly where you have participants with extreme learning disabilities, for whom verbal communication is not an option. You have to pick up on cues, work with their carer, to communicate.[27]

Kathryn McDowell CBE, managing director of the London Symphony Orchestra, feels that there is still room for improvement in finding the ideal training for emerging orchestral musicians.

There's definitely room for development – I think that will always be the case. Human nature is such that a young player coming forward wants to perfect their own skill as a musician, and they must of course do that. But there is also a question of how they can develop the broader aspects of their personality and their musicianship through their training; this needs to be a varied menu of options to suit different types of musicians – there isn't one size fits all.[28]

McDowell also feels that the Guildhall and LSO partnership in the orchestral artistry master's degree is essential in opening the eyes of the top musicians in tertiary music training to the broad picture of work available in the symphony orchestra profession. She feels that while there was much to value in previous iterations of the Guildhall's community creative training, it had one drawback – it was not connecting with the top-achieving music students. McDowell explains:

The Master of Music (Orchestral Artistry) training is trying to almost look at it from the other side of the telescope. To say to students: you know you're interested in orchestral playing, that's your vocation, but what does that look like at this time, what are the qualities that you need to have in order to be successful?

I think there are many ways to do this, you just have to try. What Guildhall School was doing through Sean [Gregory] and Peter [Renshaw] was incredibly important. What the LSO can bring through the Orchestral Artistry programme is also really important, and there will have to be other schemes and other ways to address this question as the profession changes and develops.[29]

McDowell agrees with several other leaders interviewed for this research that the training needs to continue on past the tertiary college, with musicians

146 *New Roles, New Skills*

able to readjust their goals and skillsets as they become interested in different areas of activity throughout their career. McDowell feels that this is a responsibility of professional music organisations:

> It has always been a responsibility of the education and engagement departments within the professional companies to connect with the younger players when they come in, to ask them how they would like to be involved. Sometimes the players will not be as engaged early on, but maybe later, after five or ten years, when they've become established, they look to bring some further interest and colour to their role. They look for activities to complement being a world class orchestral player and at this stage they engage further with the education and community activities.[30]

Ongoing professional development is built into the organisational structure at both operas and orchestras, with players continuing to develop the skills needed for the specific culture and activities of their organisation. The Royal Liverpool Philharmonic Orchestra has made a sizeable investment in this area, based on the findings from the report "Sound Practice," published by Associate Professor Bronwen Ackermann, Dianna Kenny, Tim Driscoll, and Ian O'Brien in 2017. In the RLPO's case, this has led to the introduction of physical and psychological support for players, but alongside this there is also financial support for players to learn new skills and undertake professional development. This is also built into the activities of the Association of British Orchestras (ABO), with Education Director Fiona Harvey feeling that it is a responsibility of the ABO to provide professional development opportunities for musicians to continue to build the skillset required to work in the full variety of roles available to them in their workplace.

The overall picture is one of an industry still in flux, but one in which the "market force" of professional activity and the demand for skills are gradually influencing the traditional training model of a professional classical musician. There will always be an inherent tension as the sheer number of hours required to become an elite – or even a professional-level – musician in this genre leaves little time for a broad curriculum. However, models of project-based work, of combining community engagement projects with performance tasks, are emerging as entirely viable and attractive to young musicians. It appears certain that within the next two decades it will become standard for a classical musician to graduate with skills in improvisation and public speaking, and experience in designing and delivering community engagement activities. They will also be accustomed to practicing their art form in a wide range of settings, which will, of course, still include the concert hall, but will also include schools, community centres, shelters, and even prisons.

To take an Australian perspective, no Australian conservatorium currently offers any specific degree or diploma in community music skills or creative leadership, and as a result Australian orchestras often engage UK experts in this field. Recognition of this skills shortage lay behind the research trip undertaken in 2009 by Nicholas Bochner, the assistant principal cellist of the Melbourne Symphony Orchestra. Bochner was awarded the Dame Roma Mitchell Churchill Fellowship in order to undertake a "Study of the use of improvisation in the teaching of classical musicians." Bochner identified the work by the LSO and the Guildhall School of Music and Drama as leaders in this field, and travelled to London to gain personal insight into the Guildhall's innovative orchestral training and the way the LSO Discovery Department puts such skills into practice. Here, Bochner summarises the aims and intentions of his research:

> During my time working in Melbourne Symphony Orchestra I have become aware of creative approaches to music education, and of a strong need for orchestras to pursue innovative techniques for community engagement ... In Australia, current training for performing musicians does not generally provide any basis for this type of innovation and I felt certain that there would be a great deal to learn from examining the practices of, and connections between, the GSMD and the LSO. I also felt that I would be well placed, through my position as a cellist with the Melbourne Symphony Orchestra, and as a member of the resident faculty of the Australian National Academy of Music (ANAM) to make good use of any lessons learnt.[31]

Bochner focused particularly on the methods of teaching improvisation at the GSMD, observing the teaching practice of David Dolan, a leader in this area. Australian orchestral musicians are generally not confident in improvisation as it is not an element of their tertiary music training. As it is a skill required for creative music workshops, it is important to address this skills gap and to look to models of best practice in the field. Dolan's methods are proven to help orchestral musicians develop confidence with improvisation which is of immediate benefit to their work in creative-based orchestral education work, but which has also been shown to develop their performance and theory skills. Further details on Dolan's approach can be found in both Bochner's Churchill Report and in an article by Dolan in the 2005 Guildhall publication *The Reflective Conservatoire*.[32]

Bochner notes that while some musicians in Australia are trained through the UK system, the significant difference in the United Kingdom is that with so many musicians trained in animateur skills there is a variety and diversity to the workforce, making it easier to engage the most appropriate leader for any particular project. Bochner's conclusion is that

> Orchestras and music colleges in Australia have much to learn from the creative approaches to teaching aspiring professionals and to engaging

148 New Roles, New Skills

with the community at large that I saw in operation at the GSMD and the LSO Discovery Programme.[33]

He is looking to implement a similar relationship between the Melbourne Symphony Orchestra and the Australian National Academy of Music (ANAM), both institutions which have shown interest in innovative approaches to creativity and communication. The ANAM, in response, has introduced a community outreach programme in which students engage in at least one project involving a performance in a non-standard context.

With increasing numbers of Australian orchestras beginning to incorporate more participatory elements into their education and community engagement activities, there is a clear need for training in creative, collaborative music making at the tertiary level. There is also a need for training orchestral musicians, classroom teachers, and instrumental teachers in this field, which could be addressed by a part-time certificate or diploma course. Alongside these specific skills, there is also a need to equip performance music majors with education and pedagogy skills and experience, in acknowledgement that most musicians will engage in teaching at some point in their careers. The need for Australian tertiary music institutions to re-examine their course structures was noted in Australia's *National Review of School Music Education, "Augmenting the Diminished,"* published in 2005. The review stated: "As musicians are increasingly called upon to work collaboratively in music education settings ... the issue of training of musicians to work in educational environments has arisen."[34]

The *National Review* noted the strength of the United Kingdom in this area, and in particular called for a greater focus on education skills to be incorporated into music degrees. Barbara Macrae, principal of the Sydney Conservatorium High School, strongly stated the need for an education component in performance degrees: "tertiary institutions educating musicians should, as a matter of course, include some teacher education components as many musicians at some point of their lives teach, either individual students or classes or both."[35]

Ten years after the publication of the *National Review*, it is concerning that no significant change has been implemented in the approach to tertiary music training in Australia. With orchestral and opera education and community engagement work currently in a growth period in Australia, it is timely to look to ways to enhance and support Australian orchestral musicians both present and future in their activities in this area.

Notes

1 Gilbert, *Orchestras in the 21st Century*, pp. 31–32.
2 Booth, interview with author.
3 Booth, *Music Teaching Artist Bible*, p. 6.
4 Ibid., p. 96.
5 Booth, *Teaching Artist Bible*, p. 7.

New Roles, New Skills 149

6 Ledgard and Odam, *The Art of the Animateur.* Foreword by Sir Ken Robinson, p. 13.
7 Animarts Report, *The Art of the Animateur.* Introduction by Patricia Clark, p. 15.
8 Odam and Bannan, *Reflective Conservatoire*, p. 298.
9 Peter Tregear. *Enlightenment or Entitlement? Rethinking Music Education.* Issue 38, Melbourne: Platform Papers, 2014.
10 Ibid.
11 Peter Renshaw. "Information: New Skills for New Audiences," *British Journal of Music Education*, Vol. 2(1), March 1985, p. 98.
12 Ibid.
13 Wiegold, "But Who Will Make Their Tea?," p. 3.
14 Renshaw, "Information," p. 97.
15 Peter Renshaw. "Towards the Changing Face of the Conservatoire Curriculum," *British Journal of Music Education*, Vol. 3(1), March 1986, p. 86.
16 Renshaw, "Information," p. 97.
17 Gregory, interview with the author.
18 www.rcm.ac.uk/sparks/, accessed 1 May 2022.
19 www.york.ac.uk.
20 https://longy.edu/about/mission-vision/.
21 https://www.rcs.ac.uk/?s=contemporary+performance+practice
22 Winterson, *The Community Education Work of Orchestras and Opera Companies*, Nigel Osborne interview, Appendix, p. 46.
23 McNicol, interview with the author.
24 Tamsin Cox and Hannah Kilshaw. *Creating a More Inclusive Classical Music: A Study of the English Orchestral Workforce and the Current Routes to Joining It.* ICM, DHA and Arts Council England, 2021.
25 Ibid., p. 19.
26 East, interview with the author.
27 East, interview.
28 McDowell, interview with the author.
29 Ibid.
30 Ibid.
31 Bochner, *The Use of Improvisation in the Teaching of Classical Musicians*, p. 1.
32 D. Dolan. "Back to the Future: Towards the Revival of Extemporisation in Classical Music Performance," in G. Odam and N. Bannan (editor), *The Reflective Conservatoire: Studies in Music Education*. London: The Guildhall School of Music & Drama, and Aldershot, England: Ashgate Publishing Limited, 2005.
33 Bochner, *The Use of Improvisation in the Teaching of Classical Musicians.*
34 *National Review of School Music Education: "Augmenting the Diminished,"* p. 34.
35 Ibid., p. 183.

8 Virtual Music Making
Classical Music Engagement Utilising Digital and Online Technology

Over the past two years, the pandemic has caused a global shift to digital and online communication and connection. Orchestras and opera companies have been a part of this seismic digital wave, with organisations forced overnight to cancel live performances and "face-to-face" delivery of programmes. While some organisations were better equipped than others to stage a rapid digital translation of their activities, all of the orchestras and opera companies consulted for this research were, at the time of writing, engaged in further exploration of digital and online technology as a means to maintain their performance platform and their connection with their audiences. At the time of writing, in 2022, we are now entering the third year of the pandemic and the global community has, to a certain extent, returned to a semblance of normality in terms of its "face-to-face" delivery of activities. However, while orchestras and opera companies have now largely recommenced live concert hall programming and their community engagement programmes have been able to reconnect face to face with participants, there remains a significantly larger digital imprint than we knew in 2019. Orchestras and opera companies, like all corporations, need to respond nimbly to rises in COVID transmission in their communities. Programmes and performances need to be ready to shift between live, digital, or hybrid delivery in the blink of an eye, and this situation is not showing any signs of being resolved in the foreseeable future.

The result of this enforced digital "trial by pandemic" has been a rapid change in the industry's awareness of the possibilities of online connection and performance. There has also been a vivid realisation, as explored in this chapter, of the limitations of the digital experience and the precious value of live, face-to-face, music making. This chapter discusses the responses of leading orchestras and opera companies through the digital COVID revolution and presents the views of key figures on the future usage of digital and online media by orchestra and opera companies. We also look at organisations that had embraced the digital possibilities pre-COVID in their connection with their audiences and communities, and had provided exemplars and resources for the demands of 2020.

DOI: 10.4324/9781003198512-9

The streaming of concerts was the initial response of the music industry to the pandemic crisis. As early as March 2020, orchestras and opera companies across the world were streaming performances that had initially been scheduled as live performances. From the Met Opera in New York to Brussel's La Monnaie and Seoul Philharmonic, the key question around scheduling for opera and orchestra managing directors was whether to stream live, new content, or look to a pre-recorded back catalogue. The Melbourne Symphony Orchestra (MSO), for example, turned a scheduled live performance of Scheherazade on 17 March 2020 into a live-stream from an empty Hamer Hall. At its peak, this performance was viewed by 5,500 people – more than double Hamer Hall's capacity. The Melbourne Digital Concert Hall is another entrepreneurial venture, which was quick to grasp the potential of the online classical viewing audience. This streaming service launched on 27 March 2020 with a ticketed viewing system, with profits going to the artists suffering from the cancellation of all the usual performance streams overnight. The concept has been a success, invaluable for the artists it has featured during the pandemic. To date, 450 concerts have been live-streamed with 2,000 musicians featured, and $1.7 million has been raised to pay the musicians from the ticket fees. In 2022, the model is still thriving, now rebranded as a national service – the Australian Digital Recital Hall. This was, of course, by no means the first paid streaming service – others have been well established for many years, including the Berlin Philharmonic Digital Concert Hall. The innovation here was maintaining the process of booking a ticket for a concert, brilliant in its simplicity and validating for the artists who knew that they were playing for a paying (although invisible) public. The Australian Digital Concert Hall has perhaps the honour of being the first concert platform to ever reverse its viewing media from online to face to face: from being a purely online platform, it is now possible to purchase tickets to view the performances live in studio as they are performed and streamed.

The decision to move online was the only option for orchestras and opera companies in 2020. The more difficult questions are still being grappled with – is the pay per view model or free streaming the best model with which to move forward? How can the visual experience be made engaging and dynamic? How can camera angles be utilised to enhance immediacy and to exploit the benefits of the filmed media? How are audiences engaging with the online performances? When and where are the performances being viewed – and on what devices?

In an article for the *New York Times* published in December 2020, at the end of the first chaotic year of the pandemic, the Boston Symphony Orchestra's video engineer Brandon Cardley gave an insight into his experiences. Cardley explains the new role that he and many others from orchestra and opera media departments were stepping into: "we went from being a nice addition to the concert to *being* the concert."[1]

The ultimate question is how to merge digital learnings with the conventional face-to-face model as we move into the next phase of the pandemic.

152 *Virtual Music Making*

Every expert interviewed for this project has stated that the future is hybrid – a fusion of the best elements of digital, but with a strong and steady focus on the magic of the live experience. This shift from face to face to online has impacted not only on the concert hall performance life of orchestras and opera companies, but also on the delivery of their diverse range of community engagement programmes. The shift brought its own array of challenges – how do you maintain connections with schoolchildren online? With patients with dementia or Parkinson's disease? How do you maintain creative-based workshops online?

Eric Booth has noted that orchestral and opera music education and community programming moved quickly through three phases of engagement with digital and online media through the pandemic.

> I watched a pattern, from last spring when the shut-downs began, there was a kind of reactive urgency to just do something, and as they moved programmes into some kind of virtual expression, it was earnest and well-intentioned but it was pretty obvious that it was not very good. The quality of our thinking on how to deliver what teaching artists do in an online medium, we were paying the price of having neglected it forever. I had been nagging about it for 20 years but we didn't go there and we looked like rotgut amateurs in our eager ways to connect with kids. The most successful thing was doing one on one lessons. Then over about 4 months of this there was a second chapter, after realising that what we had done was not very effective. This was an experimentation phase, in which we realised that people had to be creatively engaged even though it was an online medium, and you began to get some more original thinking, more creative ways of activating connections. I think it is going to lead into what I think is the third chapter of really discovering how to achieve what teaching artists need to achieve, the activation of other people's artistry so that they want to make stuff. That's going to be "hy-flex" – hybrid and flexible, and we're just at the beginning of teaching artistry's learning how to do that. It's going to become more essential because as more people encounter classical music via virtual media it's less engaging, and it's going to take more creative work to produce the kind of satisfaction that brings people back. You need teaching artist engagement to find out how to deepen the creative capacity as we develop online connection.[2]

Each of the organisations contacted through this research project is increasingly looking to widen its access through the utilisation of live-streaming, webinars, online resources, and video channels. Some have also put considerable resources into establishing educational apps and interactive digital installations, and the use of technology to enhance live concerts is also being explored. There are obvious benefits to the long-term incorporation of digital technology into education programmes. This is especially true for

Virtual Music Making 153

a country such as Australia, with vast distances between capital cities and many isolated communities. The BBC Ten Pieces programme is an example of a pioneering project that has successfully used the internet to involve children across the whole of the United Kingdom, including remote areas such as the Hebrides.

While all music organisations turned to the digital media through the pandemic, they were not all doing this from the same starting point in early 2020. Several organisations internationally had made a conscious decision to invest in digital and recorded media pre-pandemic. One such organisation is London's Philharmonia Orchestra. The Philharmonia, originally founded as a recording orchestra, is an international leader in the field of digital and online connection with a trailblazing history in this space reaching back decades prior to the pandemic. They were early to embrace the possibilities of virtual reality (VR) and have now produced three VR immersive experiences: the Virtual Orchestra (available on PlayStation VR), Beethoven's Fifth (available on YouTube VR), and Mahler's Third. With their pioneering VR soundstage installation, up to six people at a time experience a VR installation audio and visual experience that is the closest possible replication of being inside an orchestra during a performance. Eighteen ambisonic speakers project the orchestra's various sections to the participants, while the visuals seat you inside the violin section. With a bird's eye view of charismatic conductor Esa-Pekka Salonen, this experience is a highly realistic replication of the adrenalin-fuelled experience of playing in the heart of one of the world's great orchestras. To date, 350,000 people have visited the Philharmonia's installations, with over 100,000 subscribers to their YouTube channel. They have been awarded prizes including the Raindance Film Festival Award for Best VR Musical Experience, as well as three Royal Philharmonic Society Awards. As part of a consortium alongside the Royal Shakespeare Company, the Philharmonia are also co-recipients of a major government research and development grant, "Audience of the Future," which has allocated 3.99 million pounds to exploring and developing new VR and mixed reality (MR) music technology resources.

The Philharmonia Orchestra's 2009 digital installation "Re-Rite," based on a performance of Stravinsky's Rite of Spring, was the first of its kind at that time.[3] Filmed using multi-camera angles, it is designed to give an immersive experience of being part of the orchestra during their performance. This project was selected for the Royal Philharmonic Society Award for Audience Development, and has been taken on tour by the Philharmonia, both within the United Kingdom and internationally. It had a particularly strong impact in China, with 85,000 visitors in Tianjin.[4] The Philharmonia subsequently released a new digital installation project, "Universe of Sound."[5] Both Re-Rite and Universe of Sound were strongly backed by the chief conductor of the Philharmonia, Esa-Pekka Salonen, and were conducted by him. A "conductor camera" provides audiences with a musician's view of Salonen,

154   *Virtual Music Making*

revealing the way that he uses his facial expressions and gestures to draw out the music.

The Universe of Sound installation features Kinect technology (as used by X-Box) to allow visitors to try conducting the orchestra, as well as giant video displays and touch screens. Aimed at both novices and experts, it again won the Royal Philharmonic Society Award for Audiences and Engagement in 2013. Universe of Sound is based on a performance of Holst's The Planets and premiered at London's Science Museum as part of the cultural festivities for the 2012 Olympics. Also available on DVD and Blu-Ray, it is being prepared for international touring, although it requires a large space such as a concert hall, warehouse, or gallery.[6] The Philharmonia's iPad app "The Orchestra" was featured in Apple ads and was awarded the RPS Award for Creative Communication in 2014.[7] "Sound Exchange" is a further resource created by the Philharmonia, which includes 3,000 samples of music recorded by the orchestra's musicians to be used as a composing and creating tool.[8]

In Australia, the Australian Chamber Orchestra (ACO) and the Melbourne Symphony Orchestra currently lead the field in digital and online initiatives, although the Sydney Symphony Orchestra, the Queensland Symphony Orchestra, and the West Australian Symphony Orchestra are also exploring new models. The ACO's flagship programme in this area is "ACO Virtual," an audio-visual installation.[9] The 30-minute installation creates the sense of being part of the ACO in performance, with projections of 13 musicians surrounding you and sound coming from the direction of their projection. Interactive possibilities include isolating different instruments, seeing players in close up, and playing along or following along on scores. The ACO also delivered a series of digital broadcasts in response to the pandemic, known as ACO HomeCasts, which have now evolved into ACO StudioCasts.

Digitally, the MSO's key focus has been the Learn app, launched in June 2011, which explores the various instrument groups of the orchestra through graphics, interviews with 15 MSO players, and uncompressed audio.[10] In the 2011 Annual Report, it was stated that "MSO Learn is a potent symbol of our move towards a fully integrated digital future," revealing that this is acknowledged as an important area for future growth by MSO management.[11] The app has been a highly successful venture for the MSO. It has been downloaded more than 87,000 times over the past four years and has established an international profile.[12] As well as providing insight into the inner workings of the orchestra, it is helping to establish a personal connection with the musicians through interviews that cover a wide range of topics such as their choice of instrument, favourite books, and opinions on Melbourne's best restaurants. The MSO was highly impacted by the pandemic – Melbourne gained the unenviable distinction of "the world's most locked down city" – with the orchestra looking to digital broadcasts to maintain its connection with its audience.

Virtual Music Making 155

Digital engagement has been a key area of growth for the London Symphony Orchestra for some time. They have had their own recording label for 20 years and, in 2013, the orchestra made the decision to invest more heavily in audio-visual resources. However, the pandemic acted as a catalyst for the LSO's rapid digital progress. Managing director Kathryn McDowell reveals:

> I often say that our digital strategy advanced by three years in the first three months of the pandemic. We had a plan, we knew where we were aiming to go, but we didn't ever think we were going to get there so quickly.[13]

As a result of the recording label, the organisational structure of the LSO was already set for recording and broadcasting performances. Pre-pandemic, they were capturing five or six performances per year, but they had the capacity in readiness to capture all performances. The facilities at LSO St Luke's, in particular the Candide Discovery Room, were key to the growth in this area, allowing the LSO to explore digital ways of connecting with communities. The Discovery Room is equipped with ten computers, audio software, microphones, acoustic and electronic instruments, and access to the LSO's audio sample archive. Current digital and online projects include the Digital Technology Group, which is open to 13–20-year-olds from East London who meet weekly to explore ways of using technology in creating music.[14] There are also many videos on the LSO website, covering areas such as masterclasses, audition tips, interviews with visiting soloists and conductors, and A-level seminars presented by Rachel Leach and Paul Rissmann.[15]

As part of their move into the digital field, the LSO launched LSO Play in 2013.[16] LSO Play is an interactive web-based platform that features performances by the LSO of Ravel's Bolero and Berlioz's Symphonie Fantastique. By filming with multiple camera angles, viewers are able to watch up to four streams simultaneously, including a close up of chief conductor Valery Gergiev. Aimed at complementing the orchestra's education work, it is designed with schools in mind, and includes resources such as background information about the repertoire and instruments, masterclasses, and commentary by LSO players. It is differentiated from the Philharmonia's groundbreaking app, "The Orchestra," as it is free and does not require Apple compatibility, being accessible by any computer with flash.

The Moving Music appeal looked to raise 9 million pounds, which with the current 'Always Playing Appeal' can potentially make the work of the Discovery team available to the widest possible audience.[17]

McDowell notes that the LSO's digital resources are a means of making a strong connection with international audiences. She gives the example of a connection with a partner in Chile, where they had toured in 2019. The Chilean partner was keen to link with the LSO's digital community engagement, and this connection has now led to six LSO Play projects, including

156 *Virtual Music Making*

all resource materials, being translated into Spanish. The company has also licenced an initial 25 streams from the LSO platform, together with all the background digital programme notes, with the intention of building a digital library.

The LSO has also developed a digital mentoring programme, a pilot scheme with their partner company in California "Music Academy of the West." As McDowell explains:

> That for me is really interesting because it gives you a hybrid model of international engagement that could make us more sustainable for the future. We may only go to Chile once every seven to ten years, but we can keep in touch with them through the digital platform. It doesn't undermine the importance of the live connection – it complements it. The future is a hybrid form of relationships that can be expressed digitally as well as live, where there's a consistency to the presentation and content across the entire range of what we do.[18]

Andra East, head of the LSO's Discovery Department, echoes McDowell's view that the pandemic instigated an intensive acceleration in digital engagement for the orchestra. The Discovery team aimed to keep as many of their programmes running as possible throughout the pandemic with digital connection proving invaluable during lockdown and social restrictions. East explains that for some programmes the digital connection proved to have a silver lining in facilitating a closer one-to-one experience between participants and Discovery leaders. This was particularly the case with the activities they run with participants with disabilities in the "LSO Create" programme. East reflects that this programme is normally delivered in a group ensemble format, but with one-to-one Zoom sessions participants were able to connect on an individual basis with the LSO musicians, revealing more about their musical tastes and skills than in the ensemble face-to-face sessions.

The East London Academy programme also continued running during the pandemic in an online format. This programme again delivered excellent outcomes, with students working together with LSO team leader Belinda MacFarlane and composer Ayanna Witter-Johnson to create a new collaborative composition, DreamCity. For this work, Witter-Johnson worked via video link with the string students of the East London Academy, workshopping their reflections on living in London throughout the 2020 lockdowns. This resulted in themes of longing, melancholy, dreams, collective, uncertain, and versatility. From this creative starting point, Witter-Johnson then created 34 musical fragments recorded by LSO musicians at St Luke's. The recordings were then sent to the 20 East London Academy string students to learn, coached through online Zoom sessions with five London Symphony Orchestra mentors.

Through the LSO musicians' coaching, the students developed in terms of technique, posture, sound, and understanding of the recording process.

Virtual Music Making 157

At the end of the coaching process, the students had completed 480 recordings based on the initial 34 fragments. These were then edited and layered together by Witter-Johnson, using Logic software, with a video by Deon Elsworth providing a visual complement to the score. On 22 December, the participants and their families came together online with the LSO team and Witter-Johnson to listen to and watch the final production. It was a resounding success, remarkable for only two and a half months of creative endeavour.

While this was expected to be an entirely online project, it had an unexpected transition to a live, face-to-face performance outcome in 2021. On 15 August 2021, the LSO was able to return to deliver its regular high-profile performance in Trafalgar Square, the BMW Classics free open air event. For this event, the work needed to be scored and rehearsed from the original digital recording, the reverse of the usual process of recording a notated score. The 20 young musicians from the East London Academy were given the hugely impactful experience of performing DreamCity on stage with the LSO at this event, conducted by Sir Simon Rattle. In one final digital layer, this live performance was live-streamed and available for three months to view on the LSO's YouTube channel, watched by audiences around the world. Andra East emphasises how impactful this project has been:

> This project really opened our eyes to what is possible when you're forced to think differently, not just do things in a different way. There are lots of areas of our projects where we are now reassessing – should we do this project in the same way? If actually what can be achieved in a different way is much more successful, is much more interesting, is much more significant musically? I think that process has really forced us to not just accept what we know as the norm, and to see what is possible.[19]

Across the Atlantic, the Los Angeles Philharmonic was also grappling with the practicalities of maintaining their high-profile education programmes. Elsje Kibler-Vermaas, vice president of learning at the LA Phil, revealed that within hours of schools closing in March 2020 all their programmes were online, continuing in a digital space. This continued throughout the school closures and the peak of the pandemic through to September 2021. Kibler-Vermaas, like McDowell, states that the organisation gained a lot of new knowledge from their online activities.

> We've learned a lot from doing things in the digital space – and a lot of it will actually remain. Our communications to our families, how parents have been able to really show up for meetings, how we've been able to offer workshops online, how we've been able to broadcast some of our content, to bring others into our work through the digital space. That's actually been really fabulous.[20]

For the LA Philharmonic, the pandemic coincided with the construction of their new performance and rehearsal venue, the Judith and Thomas L.

158 *Virtual Music Making*

Beckmen Centre in Inglewood. This 25,000 square foot centre, the fifth site for the LA Phil's flagship "YOLA" programme, is an architecturally designed masterpiece, planned to be a truly 21st-century music education and performance space. The project, made possible through the Beckmen's generous gift, was enhanced by the contribution of architect Frank Gehry, who generously gave his time pro bono to the project. The Beckmen Centre combines a performance space with the same acoustic properties as the LA Phil's main stage performance space in Walt Disney Hall. Alongside this space are smaller teaching rooms, rehearsal spaces, and versatile communal spaces. Technology is integrated throughout, with Kibler-Vermaas stating that the pandemic prompted the organisation to upgrade their technology investment. There are now Zoom installations in each of the large ensemble rooms and Internet2, which provides a strong platform for digital music making. The space is intended to work as a national and international centre for music education, with capabilities for rehearsal recording, distance learning, and live-streaming. This is enabling the YOLA programme not only to connect their students together in the various YOLA sites, but also to link in music students from across the United States and overseas.

The centre also acts as a focal point for providing connection and professional development to music educators. From 20 to 23 October 2021, the Beckmen Centre hosted a pioneering national symposium on the theme of "Change," delivered in a hybrid face-to-face and online format. This will be a continuing format for future symposia, offering the opportunity for an international gathering of music educators, music administrators, arts advocates, and stakeholders in arts engagement and music education. Kibler-Vermaas looks forward to the Beckmen Centre continuing to act as a physical and digital hub of music education. In practical terms, with Chief Conductor Gustavo Dudamel taking up a new role as music director of the Paris Opera, she sees the digital capabilities of the centre as key to maintaining Dudamel's intense contact with the YOLA students. The LA Phil's utilisation of Internet2 is making hopes of transatlantic rehearsals and masterclass sessions between Paris and Los Angeles a very real proposition. Internet2 was originally introduced in 1996; however, it is its most recent developments in low latency audio that has music educators most excited. Running at only 5ms latency, this is making possible international masterclass coaching events and links between orchestras and remote conductors.

The New World Symphony has also been quick to grasp the exciting possibilities of Internet2. The New World Symphony has gained attention for its pioneering approach to integrating technology with the classical music experience for over a decade. Its $160 million concert hall, the New World Centre, has been internationally recognised as a leading example of how technology and architecture can be used to enhance a concert experience. Designed by Frank Gehry in consultation with Michael Tilson Thomas (music director of the resident New World Symphony), and constructed

Virtual Music Making 159

between 2008 and 2011, the New World Centre is designed to create maximum involvement between the audience and performers, including sail-like panels on which images can be projected.[21] The centre also includes a 7,000 square foot projection wall on the outside of the building, on to which performances are live-streamed for an external audience, complete with 155 speakers. The New World Symphony has been using Internet2 with LOLA (low latency) for masterclass sessions since 2004, linking cellists from the New York Philharmonic and Cleveland Orchestra with young, early career cellists in Miami. By 2015, the latency had reduced to a level that allowed Tilson Thomas to conduct musicians from the Atlanta Symphony Youth Orchestra in a side-by-side performance.[22]

For Glyndebourne, one project was born out of the pandemic's new "global online" interface. Glyndebourne's learning and engagement department had an existing link with Minnesota Opera Company's education department. In 2020, Minnesota Opera performed Glyndebourne's 2017 youth opera "Belongings," and the two companies had been in discussions about staging a production together over the following years. The pandemic offered the catalyst for the collaboration to move ahead – working online together the two opera learning departments could work outside the limitations of travel logistics. Their online project "A Place Beyond Tomorrow" was an intense meeting of ideas and visions with a large impact from current affairs. The pandemic itself brought awareness of a shared global community to the forefront, perhaps never more fully since World War II. In Minnesota, the concepts of community and hopes for the future were brought sharply to life with the death of George Floyd, which had occurred just around the corner from the Opera House. The result was a dynamic outlet for the voice of youth in terms of visions for the future.

The international organisation representing education departments within opera and dance companies, RESEO, is currently leading a large-scale project aiming to assist in the development of a digital arts education space. Titled "Mind the Gap: Building Digital Bridges to Community," the project is led by RESEO in Brussels, running from 2021 to 2023 with funding from the Erasmus Foundation. Partners in this project include Garsington Opera (UK), Les Clés de l'écoute (France), Irish National Opera (INO) (Ireland), Western Norway University of Applied Sciences (Norway), and Materahub (Italy). The project is a continuation of a specific focus on this area by RESEO, following its 2015 publication "European Overview of the Use of Digital Media for Opera, Music and Dance Education." The digital focus by RESEO is a double recognition of both the immense possibilities in the utilisation of digital media by arts education programmes, as well as the challenges faced by companies in setting up digital programmes.[23]

RESEO states that given the impact of COVID it is now more urgent than ever to overcome these issues, as vulnerable communities were significantly impacted by the pandemic from an economic, health, and psychosocial perspective.[24] The Mind the Gap project has three key aims: to produce

160 *Virtual Music Making*

a database of case studies that illustrate best practice in the utilisation of digital media for community engagement programmes by arts organisations; to create a knowledge "hub" of resources that will be available to future programmes; and to publish a research report outlining the project, its findings, and outcomes. Each of the partners in Mind the Gap brings a high degree of expertise to the digital space.

Garsington Opera, for example, has delivered two high-profile digital opera programmes, "Person 181" and "Dare to Dream." "Person 181" is a 360 degree film made in collaboration with the BBC. This innovative project featured 180 community members in the cast of a new opera commission, "Silver Birch," a production based on the poetry of Siegfried Sassoon with the score composed by Roxanna Panufnik and a libretto by Jessica Duchen. The production was recorded with 360 degree video, alongside ambisonic audio, to allow the viewer of the film to feel that they are on stage with the cast – that they are "Person 181" in the production.[25]

"Dare to Dream" premiered in March 2019 at the Royal Albert Hall. This newly commissioned children's opera featured digital delivery in both the creation of the work and in the performance production. The project was an ambitious international collaboration, connecting 740 children from Buckinghamshire in the United Kingdom with children from Syria, Uganda, and Bangladesh. Through Skype workshops, they created themes and poetry that explored the challenges that they were experiencing in their lives, alongside a shared vision of hope for the future. The performance incorporated multimedia film of the young poets from Syria, Uganda, and Bangladesh, bringing their voices and images directly into the production. This project is a pioneering exploration of the possibilities in digital co-creation across nations, as well as the possibilities of multimedia performance delivery in opera.

"Out of the Ordinary" is another pioneering project working at the cutting edge of digital possibilities. Developed by Irish National Opera, this project is a Virtual Reality Community Opera project working with communities in Inis Meáin, Tallaght, and rural Ireland. Created in partnership with production company Algorithm and Virtual Reality Ireland, the project is connecting communities with little or no experience of opera with the digital and creative engagement team of INO. The final product will be a virtual reality opera composed by Finola Merivale with director Jo Mangan, to be delivered in June 2022. The virtual reality experience is designed to be an immersive and high-impact engagement with the art form, which is intended to appeal to new opera audiences. The project was awarded the 2021 Fedora Digital Prize, a 50,000 euro award that aims to celebrate and support innovative programmes that deliver access to opera and ballet through digital innovation, connecting audiences through digital means. Peter Maniura, chair of the Fedora Digital Prize jury, stated that the jury was highly impressed by the project's goal to redefine community engagement through such an innovative digital project.[26]

Virtual Music Making 161

"Out of the Ordinary" is part of Irish National Opera's participation in the TRACTION international project. TRACTION is an EU Horizon 2020–funded research and innovation project with nine key partners, including Dublin City University, Vicomtech, Centrum Wiskunde & Informatica, Universitat Autònoma de Barcelona, SAMP music school, Liceu Opera House, François Matarasso, and Irish National Opera. TRACTION is running three pilot programmes with opera companies, with the underlying aim to utilise opera to connect with and benefit communities that are at risk of exclusion. Through the same process, the aim is for opera companies to reinvigorate their connection with communities and to speak for their time and place. The TRACTION project acknowledges the challenges faced by the art form but feels hope for its future in maintaining its place in reflecting and renewing culture.[27]

The digital creation process of the opera was highly practical given the challenges of face-to-face connection over the past two years. Composer Finola Merivale was able to conduct regular creative workshops each week with participants direct from her home in New York. With Zoom meetings now an accepted part of life worldwide, the projects are setting an early example of the potential for international co-creation projects in the arts.

François Matarasso is the creative, artistic, and social manager of TRACTION. Matarasso brings 40 years of experience working in community and participatory art projects. His research covers the historical development and current practice in the community and participatory art field, exploring the importance of cultural identity. His 2019 book *A Restless Art*, published by the Calouste Gulbenkian Foundation, covers key case studies in the development of participatory art, including in the music space the work of Gareth Malone, The Sixteen, Philharmonie de Paris, and Sage Gateshead (UK). Matarasso's summary of the current situation echoes my evaluation through research for this book: that participatory art, defined by Matarasso as a "practice that connects professional and non-professional artists in an act of co-creation" has now become normalised.[28] That is not to say that every citizen across the globe has taken part in one of these projects; however, the trend is now firmly established and there is significant international cross-fertilisation between organisations with rich experience in the practice and those newer to the concept. With the extra possibilities offered by digital media connectivity, I feel that there will be an exponential rise in the availability of participatory art projects to even the world's most remote communities.

To those who worry that developments in technology will make live performance obsolete, Peter Wiegold reminds us that the live performance will always have its own unique strength: "We have one ace up our sleeve. The sense of occasion. The unique moment that could only happen there and then, in that hall, in that community, between those people."[29]

This point was reinforced by every leader interviewed for this project, despite the value that the digital interface brought to their work

162 *Virtual Music Making*

throughout the pandemic. For example, Peter Garden, executive director of performance and learning at the Royal Liverpool Philharmonic Orchestra, shares:

> One year on from the start of the pandemic we're continuing digital streams with full orchestras, we've just announced our latest digital season. I think now it will always be part and parcel of what orchestras do, I think we'll always have that live offer and digital offer because there are different things that you get from it, different experiences and access that audiences can engage with through digital, and we've learned a lot about how to do it. I think the business models are still up in the air on whether this is an investment in audience development and engagement, or is there actually also an opportunity from this around monetising your product and changing your content, there are still massive questions and opportunities.
>
> I think what we've been reminded of is the importance of the collective live experience, both onstage and for audiences. That sense that one of the beauties of music is the ability to bring people together for a shared experience. You can't beat having 1500 people in a concert hall and that real excitement, and we have this with Domingo's [Hindoyan] first official concerts as Chief Conductor – we were at the BBC Proms last Sunday with 5 000 people in the Royal Albert Hall with a full orchestra bouncing off the stage. I think it actually has reminded us all what we took for granted. We've learned to really appreciate that live experience.[30]

Garden also notes the limitations for the delivery of their education programme through the online medium:

> I think around learning and participation, again, we will always now have a blended model of live and digital. We've learned some really interesting things about how effective some of those things can be, for example through engaging people experiencing mental ill health digitally who were feeling isolated or were vulnerable during the pandemic, or through positively engaging parents as part of online instrument lessons with young people, but equally the limitations. For example, with some choral singers coming back to in-person rehearsal, singing at home into a laptop for many months can affect musical aspects such as ensemble skills, vocal projection, intonation, blending, and it has taken fantastic effort and skill by singers and their music leaders to successfully return to their high standards.[31]

Several interviewees have spoken of the challenges of "digital poverty," with inequitable access to devices and the internet across their communities. There were also challenges with children online when the children were receiving their entire schooling through Zoom; they wanted the music making to return to the live experience. As Garden notes:

> The importance of your identity, community and social networks through music massively came to the fore again, because it's such a social thing with like-minded people working together in an ensemble. And when you take that away, you lose a massive part of the musical experience.[32]

The City of Birmingham Orchestra (CBSO) has filmed a ten-piece ensemble for an education programme, with every orchestral family represented. This recording is then taken to schools, with a CBSO musician presenting the programme, playing along with the video live, and leading participatory activities with interaction between the film and the presenter. This model, which is highly efficient and effective for schools, is a good model to look to for other organisations. The initial contact of the school visit can then be transitioned on to further engagement with the orchestra.

Overwhelmingly, the view of interviewees for this book, and of the author, is that in a world that is increasingly influenced by digital and online media, the potency of a live experience is important to retain. While digital media certainly has the potential to allow for greater access to orchestral and opera education programmes, their primary role should still remain to disseminate and enhance live experiences, not to replace them.

Notes

1 www.nytimes.com/2020/12/17/arts/music/classical-concerts-coronavirus-stream.html, accessed 10 January 2022.
2 Booth, interview.
3 www.philharmonia.co.uk/re-rite/.
4 Ibid.
5 www.philharmonia.co.uk/universeofsound.
6 Ibid.
7 https://www.wisemusicclassical.com/news/2962/Classical-Apps-win-RPS-Award/, accessed 6 March 2023.
8 https://philharmonia.co.uk/resources/sound-samples/, accessed 6 March 2023.
9 www.aco.com.au/about/acovirtual, accessed 8 July 2015.
10 https://itunes.apple.com/au/app/mso-learn/id441422027?mt=8, accessed 1 August 2015.
11 2011 MSO Annual Report, p. 2.
12 2014 MSO Annual Report, p. 29.
13 McDowell, interview.
14 http://lso.co.uk/lso-discovery/community/digital-technology-group, accessed 20 May 2015.
15 http://lso.co.uk, accessed 20 May 2015.
16 http://play.lso.co.uk, accessed 21 May 2015.
17 LSO Moving Music, https://www.youtube.com/watch?v=qRDxUrxMPAQ, accessed 6 March 2023.

164 *Virtual Music Making*

18 McDowell, interview with the author.
19 East, interview.
20 Kibler-Vermaas, interview with the author.
21 www.nytimes.com/2011/01/27/arts/music/27open.html?_r=2.
22 Christine Senavsky. "What is Internet2 and How Can Music Education Programs Use It?" Carnegie Mellon University, 2019.
23 RESEO website www.mindthegap-project.org/, accessed 25 January 2022.
24 Ibid.
25 Garsington Opera website www.garsingtonopera.org/news/person-181-bbc-garsington-opera-collaborate-360-film, accessed 20 January 2022.
26 Irish National Opera website www.irishnationalopera.ie/news/2021/out-of-the-ordinary-wins-fedora-digital-prize, accessed 20 January 2022.
27 www.traction-project.eu/about/, accessed 10 January 2022.
28 Matarasso, *A Restless Art.*
29 Wiegold, "But Who Will Make Their Tea?" p. 8.
30 Garden, interview with the author.
31 Ibid.
32 Ibid.

9 Music, Health, and Wellbeing
Benefits for Both Musicians and Participants

Music's potential to enhance health and wellbeing is one of the major areas of research and practice across the professional and academic music field in the 21st century. With findings based on cutting-edge neuroscientific research, we are beginning to understand more about the unique way that the human body processes and responds to music, literally a "full brain workout" as memorably coined by Australian expert Dr Anita Collins. A key area of focus is music's potential to reduce dementia, Parkinson's disease, and Alzheimer's disease symptoms, with research showing remarkable results for patients based on music interventions in these areas. Orchestras and opera companies are highly engaged in this area, providing programmes aimed at delivering direct and tangible improvements in health and wellbeing for a variety of sectors of their community. Programmes have been devised aiming to support people with various disabilities and health conditions, both mental and physical. Programmes are being delivered in partnership with health services in many countries, often with government health funding supporting the activities; programmes are also being delivered in partnership with care home and nursing home providers.

A landmark report, *Orchestras in Healthcare*,[1] was published in February 2021. This report was co-authored by Sarah Derbyshire, Fiona Harvey, and Matthew Swann, representing Orchestras Live, the Association of British Orchestras, and the City of London Sinfonia, respectively. Their decision to undertake the research for this report grew from an Association of British Orchestras conference in January 2020. At this conference it became clear that orchestras and medical professionals were passionate about the benefits of music for health, but that what was lacking was a clear understanding of practical steps that could be taken. The report aimed to address this issue by providing a comprehensive picture of current activity in the field. A survey was sent to 54 Association of British Orchestras member orchestras, opera companies, and choirs which captured their programmes connecting with the public health space between April 2019 and March 2020. The report showed that 63% of the UK's orchestras were engaged in health and social care activities, with others very keen to start work in this space. Orchestras were connecting with the health-care sector in a variety of levels,

DOI: 10.4324/9781003198512-10

166 *Music, Health, and Wellbeing*

from formal partnerships in hospitals, through to programmes in the community. Ten orchestras worked in hospital acute settings and a further six in hospital chronic settings. Seven orchestras worked in mental health settings, 10 in social care settings, 24 in community settings, and 20 in care settings. Funding of 1.6 million pounds was allocated to the work, the majority raised by orchestras themselves.

In parallel to the activity in this area from within the orchestral and opera community, there has been a growth in initiatives to support and facilitate partnerships between arts and health. An example of this in the United Kingdom is the National Academy for Social Prescribing, launched in October 2019, which aims to create partnerships across the arts, health, sports, leisure, and the natural environment. In 2014, the All-Party Parliamentary Group on Arts, Health and Wellbeing (APPGAHW) was established in the United Kingdom, aiming to improve awareness of the benefits of the arts for health and wellbeing. From 2015 to 2017, the APPGAHW conducted an inquiry into the role of the arts in health, culminating in the publication of reports highlighting current and future directions in the area, as well as acting as an advocacy voice for the value of the arts in health.[2]

The ABO Report notes that there is a sense of a new energy from the health-care sector in proactively connecting with the arts:

> GP practices, in their role as Clinical Care Commissioners, are now contractually obliged to prescribe social activities, legitimising social prescribing within primary care for the first time ... Targeted initiatives such as Thriving Communities have been launched with the aim to bring together place-based partnerships to improve and increase the range and reach of available social prescribing community activities – especially for those people most impacted by COVID-19 and health inequalities.[3]

There is a clear opportunity for the health-care sector to engage more proactively with orchestras and opera companies in the delivery of artistic, creative programmes with core benefits for community health and wellbeing. Internationally, there is a sense that we are shifting into a new phase in the creation and partnership delivery of such programmes. With the impact of COVID, the positive impact that orchestras and opera companies can make on people's physical and mental health has arguably never been more necessary.

In response to the needs of the pandemic, three opera companies have begun to offer specific programmes assisting patients suffering from "long COVID." The English National Opera's (ENO) "Breathe" programme is using singing techniques to combat symptoms of breathlessness and anxiety in patients with COVID-19. The programme is simple in design and execution, delivering six weekly group lessons focused on breathing exercises and singing lullabies to participants, led by an ENO vocal specialist. Participants

Music, Health, and Wellbeing   167

are then provided with digital resources, including exercises, song sheets, and audio and video excerpts, to assist them in maintaining progress. The pilot programme was delivered in October and November 2020, after England had been hit by the first major COVID wave. The programme is available to patients eight weeks after their COVID diagnosis, who are still suffering from ongoing symptoms. The pilot programme, delivered to people from their thirties to their seventies, was extremely successful, with 90% of participants reporting that the programme had reduced their feelings of breathlessness, and 91% reporting that they had seen a reduction in their anxiety levels. With the core partnership between the ENO and Imperial College Healthcare Trust, the programme has developed to now collaborate with 63 specialist long COVID clinics. The programme is currently only available to people living in England; however, the ENO is currently exploring an expansion of the programme across the United Kingdom and with international partners.[4]

Further north, Scottish Opera is running a similar programme, "Breath Cycle." Scottish Opera initially devised this programme in 2013 to work with patients with cystic fibrosis, focusing on developing classical singing techniques to assist with developing more efficient breath control. This project was documented for both artistic and clinical outcomes, showing positive results in both areas (albeit with a small initial sample size of participants). Scottish Opera has now adapted this programme for use by patients suffering from long COVID symptoms. In a point of difference from the ENO Breathe programme, Scottish Opera is offering song writing sessions to assist with emotionally processing the COVID experience, in addition to singing sessions developing classical breath techniques.

In America, Los Angeles Opera's Connect programme also adopted the ENO's approach. Working in partnership with UCLA Health, LA Opera Connect is running a programme that works on breathing, mindfulness, and relaxation through the medium of vocal sessions led by two teaching artists. The programme is being researched by UCLA Health to measure outcomes and effectiveness, with early reports being positive. In a recent article, a member of the medical team spoke of the parallels to their existing therapy treatments, stating that in addition to developing lung health the exercises also help " the mind and brain with the power of music and song ... My patients have absolutely loved it."[5]

While these programmes are gaining much attention in matching music resources to one of today's great medical challenges, there are other initiatives of strong interest. One key area of growth is programmes focused on inclusivity and diversity. Bournemouth Symphony Orchestra's Resound Ensemble, part of Arts Council England's Change Makers initiative, is setting new precedents for inclusivity. Established on 12 January 2018, the Resound Ensemble is the first disabled-led ensemble of any UK mainstream orchestra. Conductor James Rose leads the group, developing an innovative head baton conducting technique. Under his direction, the ensemble

168 *Music, Health, and Wellbeing*

delivered its debut performance at the BBC Proms on 27 October 2018, an astonishing nine months after its inception. This performance made history as the first disabled-led performance at the Proms in its entire history. The Resound Ensemble is only part of the Bournemouth Symphony's focus on inclusivity and diversity; another key part to their community engagement programme is the Recovery Orchestra, delivered with the Bristol Drugs Project for people with alcohol or drug addiction.[6]

The Adelaide Symphony Orchestra (ASO) and Pittsburgh orchestras are among organisations that have recently developed an inclusive concert model which is suitable for children with sensory needs. The ASO's Relaxed Concerts have been devised in partnership with community groups working with children with disability and sensory needs, including Can Do: 4 Kids, Access2Arts, and Tutti Arts. Considerations for the concerts included the layout of the space, the lighting design, breakout rooms, and a visual storybook explaining the concerts for families to access before attending. Children are encouraged to be comfortable with beanbags on the ground, and are also free to move around and dance if they so wish. The concerts have proven to be very successful and popular. Pittsburgh Symphony has also been delivering sensory concerts since 2014, with a similar consideration for making the concerts sensitive to the needs of children with autism spectrum disorders or who have sensory sensibilities. Pittsburgh Symphony also pays attention to the lighting, keeping low levels of light throughout the performances. They also aim to reduce sudden loud sounds, provide fidgets, earplugs, and noise cancelling headphones, and have a designated quiet area with relaxing activities. The activities of orchestras in paying such sensitive and practical care to ensuring their performances are accessible to families with sensory needs are a welcome and highly positive step.

Many orchestras and opera companies are delivering programmes for people living with dementia and their carers. These include Opera North, which has delivered opera performances for people with dementia and Alzheimer's disease in partnership with a local Leeds dementia charity. The work of Glyndebourne Opera with dementia patients and their caregivers has been discussed in the case study in Chapter 4. Canberra Symphony has been delivering a "Music and Memory" programme in which musicians perform live music for people with dementia, in partnership with Goodwin Aged Care Services and ActewAGL. Some interesting points in this programme include that the participants were involved in selecting the music to be performed – an important factor, researchers believe, as music has been shown to activate long-term memories and increase alertness and social interaction. This programme is being researched to determine both its short- and long-term effects.

"The Lion's Face" is a significant work that focuses on Alzheimer's disease and its impact on patients, carers, relatives, and clinicians. Commissioned by The Opera Group (London), the opera is composed by Elena Langer with a libretto by Glyn Maxwell. The premiere performance was in Brighton in

Music, Health, and Wellbeing 169

2010, with performances in London at the Linbury Studio, Royal Opera House, Covent Garden. The creation of this work was influenced by input from Professor Simon Lovestone and his colleagues at the Institute of Psychiatry, King's College London, the Biomedical Research Centre for Mental Health at South London, and Maudsley National Health Service Foundation Trust, UK.[7]

In 2013, the Philharmonia Orchestra commissioned a one-act opera, The Bargee's Wife, in partnership with Mind Song and the Three Choirs Festival in Gloucestershire. The libretto by poet Karen Hayes was movingly inspired by the words of local people living with dementia, with a powerful score by John O Hara. The community opera featured a chorus of 150 singers, mostly drawn from the local community, and the storyline was also local – the tragic tale of a girl who drowned in the Gloucester canal in the 1930s.

These are only a few examples of organisations engaging with their local communities to create, through music, moving and community building experiences. With research on the benefits of music for people with a range of illnesses and disabilities, these programmes are each worthy of scrutiny, support, and further structural partnership support. The performance commission model discussed above also offers the opportunity to share and amplify the voices of vulnerable and disadvantaged communities – a powerful contribution that, delivered well, will allow for stronger understanding and empathy across society.

The primary focus for orchestral and opera education programmes to date has been their ability to be of service to the community. However, there is also a growing recognition of the positive impact that participation in education programmes can have on the personal development and job satisfaction of musicians themselves. A member of the London Symphony Orchestra involved in its education programming has observed: "I now feel like a musician again, rather than an instrumental operative."[8] Education programmes allow players to freely express their individual musicality, a welcome outlet for players who usually need to put their personal opinions aside in deference to ensemble cohesion.

Several surveys of orchestral musicians have revealed low levels of job satisfaction, despite the high competition for such positions. In 1991, a survey of orchestral musicians from selected US, UK, and German orchestras placed orchestral players' job satisfaction at a lower level than federal prison guards. Professional string quartets, on the other hand, reported extremely high levels of job satisfaction, placing first in the survey.[9] The obvious inference to be made from these data is that the higher level of independence and responsibility required by chamber music contributes to greater work satisfaction. As many orchestral education programmes involve performances by small chamber ensembles, orchestral musicians are thus able to access the benefits of chamber music within their orchestral career.

While most research in this area has come from the United States, there is also clear relevance for Australian orchestras. A recent survey of Australian

170   *Music, Health, and Wellbeing*

orchestral musicians returned concerning data regarding levels of psycho-logical stress and job dissatisfaction. Many participants also reported problems with alcohol and drug dependency. Findings from this survey were published in the report "Psychological Well-Being in Professional Orchestral Musicians in Australia: A Descriptive Population Study."[10] The report warns: "This study has identified a significant pattern of anxiety, depression and health behaviours that require attention in occupational health and safety policies and programmes for this workforce."[11]

From 377 participants drawn from all of Australia's professional orchestras, 32% gave a positive depression screen and 22% answered affirmative for a question screening for post-traumatic stress disorder.[12] In light of these issues, it is clearly important to seriously consider the current orchestral career and ways that it can be modified to improve quality of life and job satisfaction. The benefits of participation in education work for orchestral musicians deserve to be carefully considered by orchestral management.

In addition to the benefits of taking part in chamber music performances or creative-based workshops, there is also the eternal truth of teaching: in explaining music or techniques to others, the teachers themselves gain a better understanding of their practice. For example, Eric Booth discusses the results from an American survey of orchestral musicians involved in education work: "Being a teaching artist makes you a better artist."[13] Booth goes on to state: "Teaching, most of the respondents stated, changes you as a performer. The change mentioned most frequently was becoming freer in performance, looser and braver at improvisation."[14]

As well as helping players in their sense of personal fulfilment, participation in education programmes can also help to achieve a better understanding of a composition, and can help to shape an interpretation. It can be an opportunity for orchestral musicians to play together in different formats from the usual, quite rigid, orchestral seating code. Workshops based on an orchestral score can also be an opportunity for musicians to identify melodies or rhythms in common, across instrument families. The large number of players in a symphony orchestra can hamper connections such as this between different sections of an orchestra, and players therefore largely rely on a conductor to draw such connections to their attention. It will undoubtedly make for a stronger performance, as well as a more engaging experience for the musicians, if they are fully aware of their place in the overall construction of the piece they are performing.

A recent study tested the hypothesis that participation in education programmes is beneficial for the wellbeing and job satisfaction of orchestral musicians. Researchers Abeles and Hafeli compiled data from 47 musicians from two US orchestras relating to their participation in education programmes.[15] Abeles and Hafeli note the implications of an earlier study by Parasuraman and Purohit (2000), which "identified the lack of artistic integrity – which leads to 'boredom stress' – as a major contributor to the stress orchestra musicians report."[16] They suggest that part of the problem is a dichotomy

Music, Health, and Wellbeing 171

between orchestral musicians' training and work life.[17] The typical education of an orchestral musician has traditionally focused on the development of solo performance skills, including expression and individual interpretation.

This loss of independence could be surmised to principally affect string rank-and-file players. Hafeli and Abeles' research returned promising results. Their interviews and observations of the 47 musicians led them to the conclusion that participation in education programmes resulted in an increased feeling of autonomy and self-expression. The report included a quote from a musician known as "Amy," who commented: "

> To play in an orchestra is to sacrifice individuality in favour of group blend, and this program provides a creative outlet to fill that artistic void."[18]

While this is a field that would benefit from further quantitative data, anecdotal responses such as these would seem to prove true the prediction made by Peter Renshaw in 1992, as the industry was first emerging. Renshaw envisioned that

> As orchestras become transformed into an integrated community of musicians and management, the players will have an increasing opportunity to play a central role in major decision making ... This constitutes nothing less than a renaissance for orchestral players. They will rediscover who they are as individual musicians.[19]

Recognition of the benefits of education and community engagement work for orchestral musicians continues to grow. While this should not be the primary motivation in planning an orchestra's education and community engagement programming, it is a significant consideration. Orchestras are staffed by talented and creative people and, as in all workplaces, it is important to ensure that their skills are being effectively utilised. However, it is important to note that care should be taken to match players to the style of education programming to which they are best suited. Additionally, in order for musicians to fully experience the benefits of education and community engagement activities, they need to feel suitably equipped with the knowledge and skills necessary, and here earlier points regarding training and professional development are relevant. When fully prepared and confident in their roles, orchestral musicians can find education programmes a welcome chance to express their personal musicality. The leadership, collegiality, creativity, and engagement required in leading education programmes can balance the conformity often required of an orchestral career.

Notes

1 S. Derbyshire, F. Harvey, and M. Swann. *Orchestras in Healthcare*, Report. Association of British Orchestras, City of London Sinfonia, Orchestras Live, London, 2021.

172 *Music, Health, and Wellbeing*

2 www.culturehealthandwellbeing.org.uk/appg-inquiry/.
3 Derbyshire et al., *Orchestras in Healthcare*, p. 16.
4 www.eno.org/eno-breathe/who-is-the-programme-for/.
5 www.uclahealth.org/u-magazine/opera-gives-voice-and-breath-to-patients -recovering-from-covid.
6 https://bsolive.com/news/a-year-of-bso-resound/.
7 David Fuller. "Dementia at the Opera: *The Lion's Face,*" *The Opera Quarterly*, Vol. 24(4), 2011, p. 509 – 521.
8 Renshaw, "Orchestras and the Training Revolution," p. 62.
9 J. Allmendinger, R. Hackman, and E. Lehman. "Life and Work in Symphony Orchestras," *The Musical Quarterly*, Vol. 80(2), Summer 1996, p. 201.
10 Kenny et al., "Psychological Well-being in Professional Orchestral Musicians in Australia," pp. 210–232.
11 Ibid., abstract.
12 Ibid.
13 Booth, *The Teaching Artist Bible*, p. 42.
14 Ibid., p. 43.
15 Abeles and Hafeli, "Seeking Professional Fulfilment," pp. 35–50.
16 Ibid., p. 36.
17 Ibid.
18 Ibid., p. 45.
19 Renshaw, "Orchestras and the Training Revolution," p. 69.

10 A Second Pillar, or Working on the Fringe?

A Summary of the Current Situation and Examination of Future Developments

The need for education and community engagement programmes to be closely aligned with orchestral and opera main stage work was emphasised by many interviewees consulted for this project. At this time, there remains a danger that education and community engagement programmes may operate as satellite activities, disconnected from a company's main performance series. This issue is gaining attention across the international sector; in 2015, it was a focal point for the League of American Orchestras National Conference. In his opening address, Jesse Rosen, the chief executive officer (CEO) of the League of American Orchestras, noted the need for orchestras to "Integrate community engagement in all activity; it's a value, not a programme."[1] Rosen also commented:

> "Community engagement", though, is a problematic term. We often use it to describe ancillary activity that often has little or nothing to do with the orchestra in its essential form, giving concerts of classical music in its main stage series.[2]

Here, Rosen has encapsulated the problem: while orchestras may wish to engage with the community, this connection has not truly developed unless the activities of education departments are truly linked to the heart of the orchestra. The closing session of the conference, chaired by Eric Booth, also focused on this issue. With the theme: "The Next Frontier is Center Stage [sic]: Enhancing the Relevance of our Core Artistic Work," this session was devoted to looking for ways to correct this situation and achieve a closer alignment between the experimental activities of orchestral education departments and main stage concert performances.

The main requirement for this integration to occur is close dialogue and collaboration between managing directors, artistic directors, and education managers. This will enable education programmes to enhance and support a company's long-term artistic and strategic planning. This point was first raised more than two decades ago by Peter Renshaw, who had a pivotal role in establishing education training for British musicians. According to Renshaw:

DOI: 10.4324/9781003198512-11

174   *A Second Pillar, or Working on the Fringe?*

> The success of any training and development programme depends initially on the conviction and enthusiasm of the Managing Director and key Board members ... The long-term aim, then, must be to integrate this developmental work into the central artistic policy of the orchestra. This can only be realised with the full support and active involvement of the Music Director.[3]

Although Renshaw was writing in 1992, this "long-term aim" cannot yet be said to have been established sector-wide.

However, there are positive indications that education managers are increasingly being given greater support by their board members, senior management, and chief conductors. In Australia, for instance, the Melbourne and West Australian Symphony orchestras have both recently established new departments for community engagement, with the result that their education managers are now senior management staff. The support of the chief conductor is another key factor in the position of the education department within the orchestra. Here, again, there are significant developments – when conductors of the calibre of Sir Simon Rattle, Gustavo Dudamel, and Alan Gilbert throw their collective weight behind the importance of education programming, then a serious statement is being made to both the industry and the public. As shown in this book, Rattle and Dudamel's appointments as chief conductor at the Berlin Philharmonic and the Los Angeles Philharmonic were catalysts for a large shift in the community engagement programming of the companies. Their support has given status, weight, and a platform for this work that has paved the way for structural and funding boosts to the education and community engagement programming of the company. By choosing to personally conduct performances and rehearsals for education and community engagement projects, they have also brought such programming into alignment with the flagship performance activities of the organisation. Clearly, it is to the benefit of the entire organisation, as well as participants in the education programme, if the education programmes are as closely entwined with main stage events as possible. In this way, participants feel truly connected with the company's personnel and are offered realistic insights into their daily activities.

Another indicator of the importance placed on education work is the number of personnel allocated to education and community education departments within the management team, although this is, of course, influenced by the available budget of the organisation. Internationally, the London Symphony Orchestra (LSO) has the greatest number of education positions, with 17 personnel working in various education roles. However, this is by no means a typical situation. Most orchestras and opera companies allocate between two and five positions to their education and community engagement programming. With some, there is a single, part-time appointment. While each orchestra and opera company work to achieve strong results with the personnel available, there are, of course, limits to

A Second Pillar, or Working on the Fringe? 175

what can be achieved through a single, part-time position in comparison to a well-staffed department.

Alongside the above points in regard to the support of general management and adequate staffing, the next step is to understand how education and community engagement programmes can be centrally aligned within the orchestra or opera company. Over the course of this study, a number of ways in which this can be achieved have emerged. Firstly, it is important that the programmes involve core members as much as possible, rather than relying on casual musicians. Ideally, a personal connection should be developed between participants and orchestral musicians and opera singers. While programmes often make use of a freelance workshop leader or animateur, ideally this position should also be connected with the company's core musicians as closely as possible.

A second important point for possible connection is through programming: for instance, by structuring education events around a main stage concert programme. Examples of this approach have been noted through this research, such as the creative music projects based on main stage programmes. The creative workshop model programme invites participants to make a personal connection with the music, to understand it from the inside. It is then important to link this connection back to the main stage performance of the work by the symphony orchestra or opera company.

The key place for establishing alignment, however, lies with the decision makers at the top of the organisation. When the managing director, CEO, or artistic director of an organisation places true importance on the community engagement activities of their company then alignment and impact naturally follow. Richard McNicol, who has worked with key orchestras including the LSO and the Berlin Philharmonic, firmly believes that the support of the organisational leadership is essential. McNicol states:

> It entirely depends on the leadership of the orchestra. Totally. With Scottish Chamber Orchestra, when Ian [Ritchie] was there and Kathryn [McDowell] was there as Education Manager, it really was a crucial, central issue for them, and a lot of the players were involved. Kathryn set up projects all over the place, in museums, in wonderful venues, and we commissioned music from James Macmillan and others. It was fantastic, and the LSO is the same. But, you know if the management's not interested, then it's really, really hard.[4]

When McNicol first worked with the LSO, Clive Gillinson was the manager. McNicol speaks highly of the support and trust that Gillinson placed in the work delivered by the newly established LSO education team:

> Clive gave us complete freedom – total freedom. So if I said I wanted to do Firebird and Petruchka for a kids' concert, the answer was yes. I think it's incredibly rare that they are willing to give control over to the

176 A Second Pillar, or Working on the Fringe?

department. I think we were the only ones that he didn't sort of keep an eye on, because the two managers were just wonderful. They were so incredibly competent.[5]

One of the most interesting developments in recent years has been the ascent of the original pioneers of orchestral and opera community engagement work to key leadership roles in the classical music industry. At the London Symphony Orchestra, we find Kathryn McDowell as managing director. At Glyndebourne Opera, Stephen Langridge is the artistic director. Gillian Moore is director of programming at the Southbank Centre, and Katie Tearle is head of new music at Peters Publishing Company. At the Royal Liverpool Philharmonic Orchestra (RLPO), Peter Garden has been promoted to a position co-ordinating performance across the orchestra as a whole. At the Los Angeles Philharmonic, Elsje Kibler-Vermaas is now vice president of learning. Each of these leaders brings with them their passion for community engagement, as well as their understanding of the realities involved in creating and delivering programmes with true impact. They are, individually and collectively, reshaping how orchestras and opera companies function from key positions of influence and power.

Fiona Harvey, from the Association of British Orchestras (ABO), has reflected on this progression. She believes that the skillset developed by education managers brings a holistic understanding of how the organisation runs and how it connects with its community. Harvey explains:

> The Chief Executives of the future are Education Managers because of all the work you do. You're working with musicians, composers, conductors, you're much more engaged with orchestras than say marketing or fundraisers are. You are dealing with sponsors, boards, teachers, you've got a broad range of skills and you have to run your own budgets and fundraise for work. So you're doing a General Manager job, not just being an Education Manager, so I think that's why it's been an easier move for some of them.[6]

Kathryn McDowell feels that the integration of community engagement into the main stage life of an orchestra or opera company is essential. In an interview with the author, McDowell discusses this point, both from her perspective in her current position as well as her views formed through her previous career steps. McDowell explains:

> One of the things that I've always felt was essential is that education and community programmes have got to be central to the activities of the organisation. I was fortunate at the Scottish Chamber Orchestra where that was the case, because it was led from the top by the Managing Director. Other staff were questioning about the programme, but he was clear that this is central to what the Company is doing, it's the

A Second Pillar, or Working on the Fringe? 177

future and we've got to go there. I realised that if this work was to be integrated into the core of what orchestras do, I could only do that from a senior position. I took a job after the SCO in general management with the Ulster Orchestra, and that was quite salutary because even though I was effectively the number two in the organisation I found that while Education had its important place, it was in a silo. I wanted to broaden that out, to do all sorts of community-based projects with the whole orchestra. Whilst people were very welcoming and respectful, and we made considerable progress, I realised I couldn't really make it integral to the thinking of the organisation as a whole from that position.

When I then took up the role of Managing Director of the LSO in 2005, the question of integration was absolutely top of my agenda. I would say it took a few years to really get that to the place I wanted it, of a real understanding across the organisation that the education and engagement work is central and integral to who we are. When we develop international residencies, sometimes those have been driven as much by what we could bring on the education side as the performance side. A great example of that is our residency at Aix-en-Provence. When that was set up in 2010/11, the Festival Director, Bernard Foucroulle, wanted the LSO to share our practice in education community work, to enable them to build their own education programme in Aix, which they have done spectacularly well. From our first conversations with Bernard I knew he was absolutely serious about wanting to change the whole perspective of that festival to something that was really rooted in their community, in the south of France.[7]

From an American perspective, Eric Booth feels that there is still much progress to be made in terms of the integration of community engagement programming into the core business of orchestras and opera companies. Booth states:

It's still very separate. The LA Phil is a good exemplar of reconceiving performances that have more attractive entry points. The creativity of their programming, and when they include video, dance, singing, they do it in a way that is attractive to the hard core traditionalist and welcoming to a wider embrace. That is an example of expanding the core offering of an orchestra. They are out on the lead of that saying that this can be your main identity.

The main identity is that the education endeavour is a separate thing, it gets half the usual rehearsal time, musicians often condescend to it and bring their least alive artistic self to it. The big exception in this country is Carnegie Hall's LinkUp, which has a kind of vitality to even wake up the musicians to the fun of it. The key to LinkUp is that it is Teaching Artistry at the heart of it, kids performing with the orchestra and kids being already involved in the themes the orchestra is working

178 *A Second Pillar, or Working on the Fringe?*

on, so it is teaching artistry turned into a whole programme. It is no accident that the head of Carnegie Hall's teaching artistry programme is a teaching artist, one of the great teaching artists of Juilliard and then Philadelphia. Teaching artistry informs everything she does, consequently it informs everything Carnegie Hall does.[8]

At the Royal Liverpool Philharmonic Orchestra, Peter Garden is part of a new effort to reshape the culture of the organisation. Garden explains the impetus behind a major review in 2015:

> The idea was to create a more musician-centred culture, supported by a multi-disciplinary team around the players – managers, physios, coaches, a range of specialists – along with investment in the individual and collective development of the musicians, their skills, well-being, drawing from their expertise and embedding a more positive, supportive working environment. The goal was to generate a shared vision or strategy for the artistic growth of the Orchestra, including greater autonomy, a sense of one team focused on achieving the mission and vision of the organisation. A recognition of the equal value of wide ranging artistic, performance and learning activities, how they operate, bring benefit to the organisation, and most importantly maximise the positive impact for, and meaningful engagement with, our audiences, participants and local communities. An important change was creating project structures that better empower and draw upon the creativity, artistry and extensive leadership capabilities of our musicians working side by side in collaboration with project managers, benefiting from the collective experience and skills of the totality of the Liverpool Philharmonic workforce.
>
> Liverpool Philharmonic's vision is to be a UK and international ambassador for our City and meaningfully engaged with our local community. The full range of performance and learning activities are required to achieve this vision, to deepen relationships with our existing audiences, be creative and ambitious in developing future audiences, to be relevant and open, to be a trusted partner, play to our strengths and learn from others, to play our full role in the musical, cultural, educational, heath and community life of our city and wider region. Learning and community engagement activities are not limited to one part of the vision. They have a vital ambassadorial role through our reputation, impact and track record in music education, long term community engagement and partnerships, for example, orchestral concerts for schools since the 1940s; 14 years of In Harmony Liverpool; extensive youth talent development programmes supporting young music creators and performers; 14 years working in partnership with the NHS supporting adult service users experiencing mental ill health, dementia, people going through cancer treatment. This strengthens the value of the institution in the

A Second Pillar, or Working on the Fringe? 179

City, whilst also supporting and enhancing Liverpool's wider reputation for the arts and culture at the heart of the city's overall strategic plans.[9]

Looking to the future of where the industry is moving, there is consensus that there will be further change, and that the pandemic's impact will be long-lasting and deep. However, many of the industry leaders feel that this impact is not necessarily entirely negative. For example, Eric Booth feels that it is a catalyst for transformation, experimentation, and needed reflection within the industry:

> As a result of the pandemic, I think there is going to be significantly more experimentation in the short term, and more individuation of orchestras. That this notion of an identity that is beyond just "playing the best Beethoven that anyone ever heard" is going to become a marketing advantage. The LA Phil is already playing into "we do the most creative programming of any US orchestra". It's all going to be expansions of the current traditional model – without giving any of that up. To pull that off they are going to need musicians who can do more than play and get every note right. They are going to need musicians who are passionate advocates and have their own projects and communities, to create the vitality that is going to be the new value proposition of orchestras. That is my ambitious hope, and I think teaching artistry is going to be more at the centre of it, certainly multiple modalities of connecting with audiences is going to be much more present. I think virtual connection to larger communities is not going away, and it is a huge opportunity for development of ongoing relationships – not just pasted in until you can get back to the orchestra hall.[10]

Booth feels that there is a new and welcome focus on establishing meaningful relationships between orchestras, opera companies, and their communities – relationships that focus on a smaller group having deeper contact with the organisation. He feels that

> In the last 10 years in orchestras, there is a recognition that the broad and shallow model is defunct. That in fact measuring your success by how many little heads you have touched is almost embarrassing at this point, it is again the condescending model of the assumption of largesse, rather than the recognition that if you want to have impact it doesn't happen quickly, especially if you are moving into strange communities like schools that are largely arts unfriendly. This evolution was largely driven by the funders. The funders were the first ones to start to say, you know this drive by "wide and shallow" – we don't want to put millions of dollars into that any more.[11]

While there are undoubtedly still funders who appreciate seeing large numbers of participants reached, there is certainly a growing momentum towards

180 *A Second Pillar, or Working on the Fringe?*

a more intimate, concentrated approach. This can be seen in the Sistema programmes across Asia, Europe, America, and Australia that devote considerable resources to a connection with a small body of students. The "Beacon Schools" initiative of the Aurora Orchestra, the students mentored through Glyndebourne Academy, the East London students mentored by the LSO, each of these programmes is focused on personal connections through the longitudinal development of skills and sequential steps of activity.

Evaluation is an essential element in determining the effectiveness of current activities, as well as determining directions for future changes and growth. The Association of British Orchestras has addressed this issue in conferences and through publications which have been of great value to British and international organisations. The issue was first raised by the ABO in 1989 when Sue Robertson (then director of programmes at the South Bank Centre) presented a paper at a meeting of ABO education managers on the subject of evaluation. Robertson raised eight key points for reflection:

- What are our terms and what do they mean (aims, objectives, targets)?
- What are we trying to evaluate?
- Whose experience are we trying to evaluate?
- Who are we evaluating for?
- How do we evaluate? What methods do we select and why?
- How long should the period of evaluation be in relation to a particular project?
- What do we do with the results of our evaluation?
- What are the practical considerations of evaluation for all arts organisations?[12]

Robertson's points on the evaluation of orchestral and opera education programmes remain applicable today, more than 25 years after her presentation. In 1997, the topic was raised again by two key figures at the ABO, Pauline Tambling (director of education and training at the Arts Council of England) and Jo Shapcott (education adviser to the ABO). Tambling commented:

> While most education managers recognise the importance of evaluating individual projects, the regular evaluation of the programme as a whole is not undertaken as a matter of course; nor are similar standards, aims or expectations applied across the profession as a whole.[13]

Shapcott who, like Robinson, worked as an education officer at the Southbank Centre during the 1980s, contributed a paper on the subject to the 1997 ABO *Workbook*, titled "Conversations about Evaluation: Have We Moved On?"[14] In this paper, Shapcott presents her response to Robertson's provocative presentation and questions whether sufficient progress has been

A Second Pillar, or Working on the Fringe? 181

made in the area. Robertson makes the point that it is crucial for education managers to be clear and honest about the aims of their work:

> We all make enormous claims for education work and heavy demands for its resourcing, so we have to be able to say why it is important in more than simply superficial terms. We have to find the language and the data to support our claims.[15]

This point remains true, and at the front of the minds of today's education managers. The question of how to evaluate their programmes effectively is still a live matter. Considerations of the chief intended impact raise pivotal questions about the essential purpose of the work. The issue of effective evaluation has also remained a focus of the ABO in more recent years. In 2008, the Paul Hamlyn Foundation funded a publication on qualitative evaluation after a meeting in April 2008 had identified evaluation as an area in which ABO members still required assistance. The publication, titled *Make the Difference: Evaluating Education Projects*, is a substantial 53-page examination of the aims of evaluation and ways to incorporate evaluation into all stages of an education programme, from initial planning to post-event reflection. Various methods for evaluation are examined, including observation, written surveys, telephone surveys, and face-to-face surveys. The relative benefits and weaknesses of each method are presented, as well as a breakdown of the specific tasks involved in carrying out the survey in each category. Further valuable advice is presented in writing questionnaires that are clear, precise, relevant, and neutral. Finally, methods of analysing the data, compiling an evaluation report, and disseminating the reports are suggested.[16] This publication remains of great value to organisations today in establishing their evaluation processes. It is also increasingly common for orchestras and opera companies to partner with university researchers in order to commission external evaluation of their work. This has been a strong model for programmes including the Los Angeles Philharmonic and its YOLA programme, for Sistema Scotland, for the RLPO, and for the Adelaide Symphony Orchestra, to name but a few.

While we are still at a pivotal stage of evolution in the nexus of the connection between classical musicians and their communities, it is possible at this point to make assessments of the next stages of development. As previously stated, the education department must have the full support of the board, senior management, chief conductor, and music director. It is also increasingly the case that these leaders will have direct experience in the delivery of community engagement programmes themselves. It is also essential for musicians to have relevant training – both in their initial tertiary degrees at conservatoires, and then through continued, targeted professional development sessions as required throughout their careers. This professional development must match the programmes that they work on – a programme connected with dementia patients, for example, requires

182   *A Second Pillar, or Working on the Fringe?*

different training and support than a programme working with teenagers at a local school.

As addressed above by Eric Booth, there is a need for programming to connect impactfully and over a sustained time period with a specific community. There is also, arguably, a place for programmes to connect with a wider cross section of society, to ensure that equity of access is maintained. Therefore, a future model could well be one with two main components: one being flagship year-long projects centred around participation, partnership, and co-creation, and the other being a range of shorter-term programmes. These could include performances with multilevel participation, education concerts, early years programming, workshops with secondary school students, open rehearsals, adult lecture series, partnerships with local music colleges and youth orchestras/opera companies, digital and online resources, and programmes delivering health and wellbeing support. While these programmes depend on the company having sufficient resources, both financial and personnel, they would enable the orchestra or opera company to make a significant contribution to their community, as well as enhance the music education of a wide range of age groups. In this way, they would be achieving two key aims: firstly, establishing community relevance; and secondly, supporting a wide sector of society in participating and engaging with music.

Strategic, quality partnerships are key to the success of programming. Partnerships generally fall into three main categories: schools, community groups, and vocational training. Partnerships with schools are essential to bolster music education and help to establish more equitable access to music for children. Partnerships between orchestras, opera companies, and schools are becoming deeper and more impactful. The international community has already paid close attention to the formal partnership within the British Music Hub model. Now, those orchestras taking up residence in, or forming schools, will be paid equal attention – what is the impact and the long-term legacy for children if they have attended a school with a resident first-class music organisation? The minimum impact expected will be an increased interest in and participation in learning orchestral instruments. Strength at the grassroots level of music education is essential to the overall music ecosystem, and there remains further room to develop programming that supports this level. Partnerships with the community enable orchestras and opera companies to support lifelong learning, music therapy, rehabilitation, and social regeneration.

Effective partnerships between professional orchestras, opera companies, tertiary music departments, and youth orchestras are essential to ensure that future musicians are identified and supported on their journey. At the time of writing in Australia, the Melbourne Symphony Orchestra has announced a new training and mentoring programme that will link with students at the Australian National Academy of Music (also based in Melbourne) as well as early career graduates. Young musicians will receive masterclasses, opportunities to play alongside the sections, and tutoring in a bid to smooth the pathway from training to the profession. This model is similar to others, longer established. The Hallé Orchestra, for example, has a close relationship with the Royal Northern College of Music (RNCM), which was also originally established by Sir Charles Hallé. Since 2003, the orchestra has offered opportunities to string, brass, wind, and percussion students. The opportunities begin with workshops, progressing through observing the section, to playing in a rehearsal, then a concert, then being placed on an extra list. The String Leadership programme is targeted at the most talented recent graduates from conservatoires, offering a stipend, mentoring, chamber music opportunities, and involvement in education programmes. These programmes have resulted in several appointments to the core membership of the orchestra, with the students thoroughly vetted, up to speed in the artistic and social culture of the orchestra. This is a model for others to look to.

Notes

1 Jesse Rosen. Opening address at 2015 National Conference of the League of American Orchestras, 28 May 2015, accessed http://americanorchestras.org/conferences-meetings/conference-2015.html.
2 Ibid.
3 Ibid., p. 66.
4 McNicol, interview with the author.
5 Ibid.
6 Harvey, interview with the author.
7 McDowell, interview with the author.
8 Booth, interview with the author.
9 Garden, interview with the author.
10 Booth, interview with the author.
11 Ibid.
12 Fiona Lockwood (editor). *Workbook*. Association of British Orchestras, 1997.
13 Pauline Tambling. *A Year in the Life: The ABO's National Education Programme*. Commissioned by the Association of British Orchestras, 1996–7, p. 16.
14 Lockwood, *Workbook*, p. 27.
15 Ibid., p. 28.
16 Annabel Jackson. *Make the Difference: Evaluating Education Projects.* Commissioned by the Association of British Orchestras, 2009.

Conclusion

This book has aimed to provide an overview of the myriad ways in which orchestras and opera companies are connecting with their communities – and are strengthening these communities – through their education and engagement programmes. While the industry has experienced severe challenges over the past three years, the overwhelming consensus is that fresh shoots of innovation are emerging from the crisis. It is clear that the education and engagement departments of these companies were central to maintaining relevance through the dislocations of the pandemic – the rapidity with which these departments are able to adapt programmes and quickly adjust logistical planning was central to maintaining musical activity when main stage programming was no longer an option.

Realisation is growing sector-wide of the importance of education and community engagement programmes. The position of the education department is steadily growing closer to the central management and activity of the orchestra and the opera company. The support of chief conductors, chief executive officers (CEOs), and board members is helping to raise the profile of orchestral and opera education programming both within the music industry and with the general community. There is a recognition that if education and community engagement programmes fail to be aligned with main stage programming then organisations run the risk of creating a second tier of activity unrelated to their main concert performances. While significant progress has been made in this respect over the past decade, there remains room for further development, and it is likely that in coming years education managers will continue to play a more prominent role in strategic planning. In this way, further points of intersection between education and community programmes and main stage performances can be established, thereby fostering meaningful relevance between orchestras, opera companies, and their communities.

Over the course of research for this book, the passion and energy of the interviewees consulted has created, for the author at least, a sense of deep optimism for the future of orchestras and opera companies and their ties to their communities. Despite the significant challenges posed by COVID, the commitment of these organisations to maintain their community

DOI: 10.4324/9781003198512-12

Conclusion 185

engagement programming and the ingenuity with which they have honoured these commitments, have been deeply moving. A model for best practice and future developments has emerged. Key points include the full support of the management, the chief conductor and the board and the establishment of a well-staffed education and community engagement department. The managers of this department must be involved in strategic planning in order to integrate their work with the long-term planning of the company. The most important growth areas identified are participation and co-creation: the importance of linking people in a hands-on immersion with the art form in projects that are co-devised between the community and the organisation. Evaluation must continue to chart, rigorously and methodically, the impact and progress of programmes in order to provide feedback both to the organisation and to the wider community.

The musicians of the future need to be trained in the skills necessary to advocate for their art form and engage their communities. This training is gradually starting to appear in tertiary institutions, but there remains a need for a wider rethink of the course structure and assessment procedures. Internationally, the Guildhall School of Music and Drama, the Royal Academy and Royal College of Music, the Juilliard School of Music and Drama, the New England Conservatorium of Music, and Longy School of Music are leading the way in terms of their incorporation of community engagement training into their degree structure. Over time, a cyclical effect is developing where students who participated in programmes as children move on to build their skills as teaching artists and animateurs through their tertiary training. This generational cycle is already making its mark internationally – a key example is the Los Angeles Philharmonic, which is now employing students from its YOLA programme as teaching artists.

While many would take a bleak view of the future of classical music at the time of writing, others are optimistic, feeling that the efforts being made by organisations to connect with their communities can, in fact, usher us into a brighter future. Alan Gilbert, chief conductor of the New York Philharmonic, presented this view at his 2015 Royal Philharmonic Society Lecture, commenting:

> In these turbulent times there are wonderful and inspiring examples of orchestras that are getting it right. What they share is a site-specific understanding of what their communities need, and what they can uniquely provide with their musical powers ... What orchestras can be for their audiences is changing, and that actually presents a wonderful opportunity for us to grow.[1]

It is now no longer a question of whether orchestras and opera companies *will* do such work, but rather *how* they can achieve maximum impact with their finite resources, and how they will continue to respond to the ongoing challenges of the next stage of the pandemic. To help make these decisions,

186   *Conclusion*

evaluation is key, both in order to add quantitative data to the body of research on such work, and to ensure that best practice is being developed. From early, somewhat self-centred motivations of building audiences and maintaining funding, orchestras and opera companies are now aware of the immense value of their work for their communities. The education and community managers interviewed for this work were uniformly altruistic in their aims and approaches, focused on achieving maximum benefit for their communities and their organisations through their programming, with a focus on planning and delivering the projects together in partnership.

The following key findings were established throughout the writing of this book:

1. The scope of orchestral and opera activities has shifted from an original focus on school education to now encompass the whole community.
2. A participatory element is essential in order to break down barriers, engage, and inspire.
3. Training for orchestral musicians and opera singers in education and creative skills is essential in order for them to confidently contribute to programmes.
4. Partnerships between orchestras, opera companies, and other institutions ensure that all contributors to the musical ecosystem are working together, and that resources are used to their best advantage.
5. It is essential to thoroughly evaluate programmes, to ensure that best practice is being established, to ascertain whether key aims are being met, and to provide data to funding bodies.
6. A shift is developing towards programmes that establish a close personal connection between musicians and participants over an extended time period.
7. Creative-based programmes are a growth area internationally, long established in the United Kingdom.
8. There is a growing recognition of the possibilities for orchestras and opera companies to be of benefit to disadvantaged sectors of society.
9. Orchestras and opera companies are increasingly exploring the possibilities inherent in digital and online technology.
10. The choice of venue can make a significant impact on the result of a programme.

This final point is worth exploring further. As stated in the Introduction to this book, and explored throughout these chapters, orchestras and opera companies can be found in a diverse range of venues. These still include large concert halls and opera theatres, but today's workplace includes church halls, schools, prisons, hospitals, train stations, art galleries, museums, libraries, community centres, and even, through digital media, the lounge rooms of participants. Each of these venues influences the outcome of the education or community programme undertaken.

Conclusion 187

For the purposes of education and community programming, a concert hall is used to best effect in programmes with a participatory element, ideally with participants sharing the main stage. In this way, participants are able to experience the excitement of a main stage concert hall first hand, and their achievements can be celebrated through performance and applause. Care needs to be taken to maintain a connection when presenting performances from the main stage and the participants are seated in the auditorium. It is still possible to maintain a participatory element – as the City of Birmingham Symphony Orchestra (CBSO) admirably achieves with Steve Pickett for example – and the use of video and multimedia screen projections can also serve a useful purpose.

A specific education venue owned and operated by the company is highly desirable – and even more so if it is connected with the main concert hall. The impact of such a venue on education and community engagement programming is clearly evident in the work of organisations such as the London Symphony Orchestra (LSO), the Hallé, and the LA Philharmonic. This facility can overcome any potential scheduling difficulties, provides a welcoming and intimate environment for education activities, and allows an orchestra and opera company to fully develop their education and community activities without encountering logistical issues.

Events held in schools bring the orchestral and operatic experience directly to students in their own environment. These events also offer the potential for an effective partnership to be established between the orchestra or opera company and school teachers, enabling a strong degree of articulation and collaboration between the two institutions. This is being taken to the next step with the establishment of schools with an orchestra on site – and even schools being developed by orchestras. The world will be watching with interest on the development of these schools as a model of bringing elite musical performances naturally and organically into the everyday lives of children. Ideally, all school-based programmes should also contain many opportunities for the students to experience a main stage concert. School-based activities should feature full-time members of the company, who the students would then see performing on stage. This will create a new feeling of connection and intimacy for the students when watching the performance, and will also enable them to experience the unique power of an orchestra or opera company in full performance.

Events scheduled at other community venues, such as art galleries, museums, libraries, and residential homes, help to link the orchestra directly to its community and to take away the invisible barrier that many feel a large concert venue represents. These programmes, as with school-based events, should aim to connect the participants with the central music making of the orchestra or opera company. This can be achieved when programmes include core performance members of the orchestra or opera company, as well as linking the activities by theme to main stage programming.

188 *Conclusion*

Musicians, administrators, and communities now need to explore together what a 21st-century orchestra or opera company can and should achieve and contribute to society. In Alan Gilbert's words:

> I want to see orchestra musicians held up as heroes in their communities – both for their brilliance as musicians, but also for how they use that talent to touch the lives of those around them through music. How this redefinition is seen by the audience is equally critical: people must get used to seeing musicians as the crucial agents of change in communities, as teachers, leaders, and role-models.[2]

With the advocacy and support of leading figures in the industry for the excellent work being undertaken by education and community engagement departments, a redefinition of the role of a musician may now be imminent. This redefinition would see the skills of an orchestral musician or opera singer being used to create a positive impact on society through their performances and teaching, and their involvement in health and wellbeing programmes and social regeneration programmes. Indeed, this is already happening – we have English National Opera singers prescribed by the NHS, orchestral musicians partnering with nursing homes, and brass bands in juvenile detention centres setting troubled youths onto a more positive path. Ultimately, the goal of orchestral and opera education and community engagement programmes is to establish a broader, more equitable level of access to the power and the joy of music. The managers of these programmes seek to enable people of all ages and backgrounds to find personal connections with music, enhancing their everyday life. In Eric Booth's words:

> The number one job of an artist is to create worlds, and to invite others to enter that world and have this powerful experience. The number one job of a teaching artist is to activate the artistry of other people. And when that innate birthright capacity is awakened, it is so powerful, it can be channelled into any number of different purposes.[3]

As this vision comes to fruition – as the doors to the world of music are opened for all – then orchestras and opera companies can look forward to a vibrant future in which they are valued and integral to their communities.

Notes

1 Gilbert, RPS Lecture, p. 4.
2 Ibid.
3 Booth, interview with the author.

Index

**Page numbers in *italics* reference figures.

ABC *see* Australian Broadcasting
   Corporation
ABO *see* Association of British
   Orchestras
Acland Burghley School 58
ACO *see* Australian Chamber
   Orchestra
ACO HomeCasts 154
ACO StudioCasts 154
ACO Virtual 154
Adelaide Symphony Orchestra (ASO)
   5–6, 81–88; Big Rehearsal 86;
   The Bush Concert 87; Edward
   and Edwina project 87; Elder
   Conservatorium of Music 84; Floods
   of Fire *79–80*, 83; Relaxed Concerts
   168; Silos and Symphonies 84–85
Adwan, Moneim 100
Agreed, Glyndebourne Opera Company
   81, 97
Akiki, Bassem 100
Algorithm 160
*All Our Futures: Creativity, Culture
   and Education* 121
All-Party Parliamentary Group on
   Arts, Health and Wellbeing
   (APPGAHW) 166
'Always Playing Appeal' 155
Alzheimer's disease 168
America, creativity 126–130
ANAM *see* Australian National
   Academy of Music
Andrews, Kerry 77
Animarts 135–136
animateurs 5, 32, 115, 124–125
Apollo Trust 33

APPGAHW *see* All-Party Parliamentary
   Group on Arts, Health and Wellbeing
applause 31; *see also* clapping
Arts Council, education policy 32
ASME Composer-in-Residence and
   Young Composers Project 124
ASO *see* Adelaide Symphony Orchestra
Association of British Orchestras (ABO)
   10, 180; professional development
   146; "The Turn of the Tide" 68
Aston, Peter 117
Attainment Target One for Performing
   and Composing 118
Attainment Target Two for Listening
   and Appraising 118
Aurora Orchestra 64
Australia: creativity 123–126;
   Curriculum of the Arts 116; early
   orchestral education 44–50; teaching
   artists 115; Tony Foundation 19
Australian Broadcasting Corporation
   (ABC) 9, 46; National Training
   Orchestra 51
Australian Chamber Orchestra
   (ACO) 154
Australian Digital Recital Hall 151
Australian National Academy of Music
   (ANAM) 148
Australian National Curriculum for the
   Arts 123
Australian Proms 49–50
Australian symphony orchestras,
   financial troubles 26–27

Barbican 57, 72, 89
The Bargee's Wife 169

190   *Index*

BBC orchestras, Ten Pieces 75–81, 153
BBC Proms 168
Beacon Schools initiative 180
Beckmen Centre 90–91, 158
Belongings, Glyndebourne Opera
    Company 82, 97
Benedetti, Nicola 59–60
Benedetti Foundation 59–60
Benedetti Sessions 59
benefits of music 165–166
Berg, Airan 83, 100
Berlin Philharmonic 25
Berlin Philharmonic Digital Concert
    Hall 151
Bernstein, Leonard 12
"Big Bang Show" 42
"Big Noise" 110–111
Big Rehearsal, Adelaide Symphony
    Orchestra 86
Bochner, Nicholas 11, 147
Booth, Eric 13, 56–57, 126, 128–130,
    133–135, 152, 170, 177–179
Borda, Deborah 88
Boulez, Pierre 23
Bournemouth Symphony Orchestra:
    Recovery Orchestra 168; Resound
    Ensemble 167
Boyle, Stephen 9
"Breath Cycle," Scottish Opera 167
Breathe programme, English National
    Opera (ENO) 166–167
"A Bridge Between Two Worlds" 101
Brink Productions 83
British orchestras, community
    engagement 25–26
"The Bush Concert," Adelaide
    Symphony Orchestra 87

Canada, creativity 126–130
Canberra Symphony, Music and
    Memory programme 168
CBSO *see* City of Birmingham
    Symphony Orchestra
Chi-Chi Nwanoku 142
children's concerts 30–31
Children's Hospital Programme,
    London Symphony Orchestra 69
Chineke! Ensemble 142
choirs, London Symphony Orchestra 69
choral programmes, London Symphony
    Orchestra 73–74
City of Birmingham Symphony
    Orchestra (CBSO) 58–59, 72,
    163, 187

clapping 125; *see also* applause
classical music 4
classroom composition practice
    117–118
Clyne, Anna 77
Cochran, Emma 8
co-creation music programmes 14
collaboration 58; *see also* partnerships
collaborative composition
    workshops 116
collaborative partnerships 57–58
Community of Musicians 11, 13,
    20, 22
community ownership 109–110
composers 75, 127; Nancy and Barry
    Sanders Composer Fellowship
    Programme 92
composer-teacher 117
conductor camera 153
conductors, school concerts 32–33
"Connect It" (Meredith) 77
Connect programme, Los Angeles
    Philharmonic 167
"Convo" 139
COO *see* "Creating Original Opera"
Country Fire Service and State
    Emergency Service 83
Covent Garden 38, 40
COVID pandemic 2, 26, 150–151,
    166, 179; phases of engagement
    152; RESEO (European Network
    for Opera and Dance Education)
    159–160
Craigmillar Festival 43–44
"Creating Original Opera" (COO) 39
Creative Careers Centre, Royal College
    of Music (RCM) 139
creative composition workshop
    115, 116
creative music workshops,
    Australia 123
Creative Partnerships initiative 122
creative workshops 24; digital
    technology 161
creativity 5; America 126–130;
    Australia 123–126; Canada 126–130;
    in schools 121–122
Creech, Andrea 106
cross-disciplinary education model 42
"Crossing Borders" 43
Curriculum of the Arts, Australia 116

Damrosch, Frank 45–46
Damrosch, Walter 30, 45

Index   191

"Dare to Dream," Garsington Opera 160
Davidson, Jane 41–44
Davies, Sir Peter Maxwell 117
"Decisions" 39
dementia 168–169
depression 170
Deutsche Kammerphilharmonie Bremen 58
digital engagement, London Symphony Orchestra 155–157
digital mentoring programme, London Symphony Orchestra 156
digital poverty 162–163
digital technology: Australian Chamber Orchestra (ACO) 154; City of Birmingham Symphony Orchestra (CBSO) 163; digital poverty 162–163; Garsington Opera 160; Glyndebourne Opera Company 159; Irish National Opera 160–161; Los Angeles Philharmonic 157–158; MSO 154; New World Symphony 158–159; Philharmonia Orchestra 153–154; RESEO (European Network for Opera and Dance Education) 159–160; virtual reality (VR) 153
Discovery Days, London Symphony Orchestra 69
Discovery Department, London Symphony Orchestra 33–38, 67–68, 75, 147
Discovery Room, London Symphony Orchestra 155
diversity 142
Dixon, Dean 50
Dolan, David 147
Donatella Flick LSO Conducting Competition 72, 86
Dove, Jonathon 96
DreamCity 156–157
Dudamel, Gustavo 88, 90, 104, 111

"Earth" (Zimmer) 76
East, Andra 143–145, 156
East London Academy, London Symphony Orchestra 71, 156
education departments, Sydney Symphony Orchestra 50–53
education managers 22, 174, 176, 180–181, 184

education programming 174; shift in 24
Education Reform Act (1988) 118
education skills 134–136
"Edward and Edwina" project, Adelaide Symphony Orchestra 87
Edward Heath Assistant Animateur Scheme 36
El Sistema 3, 89, 104–106; critics 111–113; United Kingdom 106–111
Elder Conservatorium of Music 82, 84
elitism 27
engagement, COVID pandemic 152
England, music education programmes 61–62
English National Opera (ENO), long COVID 166–167
ethnical diversity 142
European Network for Opera and Dance Education (RESEO) 44
evaluation 180, 186; SERA 106
events 187

Faith Primary School 107–108
Ferraretto, Julian 85–86
financial troubles 26–27
Finnish National Opera (FNO) 42
flagship programmes 4
Fleischmann, Ernest 11, 20, 22, 35
Floods of Fire, Adelaide Symphony Orchestra 79–80, 83
FNO (Finnish National Opera) 42–43
Foccroulle, Bernard 101
Forman, JoAnn 38, 40
Fundacion del Estado para el Sistema Nacional de las Orquestas Juveniles e Infantiles de Venezuela *see* El Sistema
funding *see* government support for arts

Garden, Peter 57, 162–163, 178
"Gareth Goes to Glyndebourne" 96–97
Garrett, David 9
Garsington Opera 160
Gilbert, Alan 23–24, 133, 185, 188
Gillinson, Sir Clive 35, 37, 175–176
Glydebourne Opera 93–99
Glyndebourne Academy 99
Glyndebourne Opera Company 44, 141–142; "Agreed" *81*; "Belongings" *82*; dementia programmes 168; digital technology 159; "Raise Your Voice" 99

192 Index

government support for arts, United Kingdom 60–63
graphic notation 121
Greater Manchester Hub 63–64
Gregory, Sean 57, 125
Gronowski, Simon 101
Guildhall School of Music and Drama (GSMD) 37, 78–79, 95, 133, 135–139; London Symphony Orchestra 71–72, 143–145, 147
The Gypsy Violin 71

Hallé Orchestra 58, 64, 183
Harmlet School for the Arts 39
In Harmony Lambeth 106–107
In Harmony Liverpool 110
In Harmony programme 107–109
Hart, Philip 13
Harvey, Fiona 10, 60–61, 63, 176
Hastings Spring, Glyndebourne Opera Company 96
head baton conducting technique 167–168
health 165–168, 188
Heinze, Sir Bernard 30, 44–49
Henley, Darren 60–61
"The Hogboon" 73
In Home visits 110
Hopkins, John 49
hy-flex 152

ICCM see International Centre for Community Music
identity 177
Imago 97
improvisation 134, 147
inclusivity 167
in-service training 134
integration of community engagement 176–177
International Centre for Community Music (ICCM) 140
internships 136, 143
iPad app, "The Orchestra" 154
Ireland 43
Irish National Opera, "Out of the Ordinary" 160–161

jam sessions 24
Juilliard School (New York) 141

"Kalevala" 42
Kibler-Vermaas, Elsje 89–91, 140, 157

Kinect technology 154
Knight Crew, Glyndebourne Opera Company 96

La Monnaie de Munt 100–101
Langridge, Stephen 94–96, 98–99
Layla and Majnun 101
League of American Orchestras 173
Lee, Jennie 31
LIFT see London International Festival of Theatre (LIFT)
"The Lion's Face" 168–169
live performance 161
Liverpool In Harmony 107
Liverpool Music Support Service (LMSS) 110
LMM see London Music Masters
LMSS see Liverpool Music Support Service
lockdown music-making 2
London, Philharmonia Orchestra 153
London International Festival of Theatre (LIFT) 135
London Music Masters (LMM) 85
London Sinfonietta 119, 120
London Southbank Centre 106
London Symphony Chorus 69
London Symphony Orchestra (LSO) 6, 25, 67–68; Children's Hospital Programme 69; choral programmes 73–74; Community Choir 69; Community Gamelan Group 69; Create programmes 69, 76; digital engagement 155–157; digital mentoring programme 156; Discovery Choir 69; Discovery Days 69; Discovery Department 33–38, 67–68, 75, 147; Discovery Friday Lunchtime 69; Discovery Room 155; East London Academy 71, 156; Guildhall School of Music and Drama (GSMD) 71–72, 143–145, 147; Nancy and Barry Sanders Composer Fellowship Programme 92; opera 73–74; "Rites of Passage" 71; Singing programme 69; Soundhub 72; String Experience 72; "Take A Bow" 6, 71; On Track programme 70–71, 77–78
long COVID, English National Opera (ENO) 166–167
Longy School of Music of Bard College 140

Index 193

Los Angeles Philharmonic 25, 88–93;
  Beckmen Centre 90–91; Connect
  programme 167; digital technology
  157–158; "Mahler Project" 92;
  "Take a Stand" conference 91–93;
  Youth Orchestra Los Angeles
  (YOLA) 88–89, 158
LOVA ("La Opera, un Vehiculo de
  Aprendizaje") 41
LSO Create 156
LSO Music Education Centre 37
LSO Play 155
LSO St Luke's 37

"Mahler Project" 92
main identity 177
"*Majnun and Orfeo*" 100
Malone, Gareth 69–70
Marcus, Marshall 105–106
Master of Music (Orchestral Artistry)
  training 145
Matarasso, François 161
Maxwell Davies, Sir Peter 73
Mayer, Sir Robert 30–31
McDowell, Kathryn 35, 67–68, 74–75,
  145–146, 155, 176–177
McGinn, Mary Ruth 40
McGuire, Marshall 12
McNicol, Richard 32–34, 36, 116, 118,
  141, 175–176
Meet the Music school concerts, Sydney
  Symphony Orchestra 53
Melbourne Digital Concert Hall 151
Melbourne Symphony Orchestra
  (MSO) 148, 151, 154
Menuhin, Lord Yehudi 138
Meredith, Anna 77
Merivale, Finola 161
Metropolitan Opera 40
Mind the Gap 159–160
Misper, Glyndebourne Opera
  Company 96
"The Monster in the Maze" 73
Moore, Gillian 13, 25, 116, 119
Morrison, Richard 59
Morse Teaching Artist Fellowship,
  Juilliard School (New York) 141
Moving Music appeal 155
MSO *see* Melbourne Symphony
  Orchestra
MSO Learn 154
MU (Musicians Union) 62–63
Murray Schafer, Raymond 126–128

Music Academy of the West 156
Music Advancement programme,
  Juilliard School 141
Music and Memory programme,
  Canberra Symphony 168
music education 18–19
music education programmes 3, 5, 117;
  El Sistema 3; value of 27
Music Hub model 60, 62–65
Music Hub system (UK) 4
music participation 19, *21*
Music Services 62
Music Viva 52–53
Musicians Union (MU) 62–63

Nancy and Barry Sanders Composer
  Fellowship Programme 92
National Academy for Social
  Prescribing, United Kingdom 166
National Centre for Music, Scotland 60
National Curriculum, United Kingdom
  118, 123
National Curriculum for Music in
  England and Wales 119
National Plan, United Kingdom
  61, 107
National Training Orchestra 51
National Youth Orchestra, United
  Kingdom 64
New Sounds in Class 118
New World Centre 158–159
New World Symphony, digital
  technology 158–159
New York Philharmonic 45
New York's Metropolitan Opera 38
New York's Metropolitan Opera
  Guild 39
Nexus Arts 83
"Night Ferry" (Clyne) 77
"No Place Like" (Andrews) 77
Northern Irish Arts Council 43

Ofsted (Office for Standards in
  Education) 118
Open Music Academy 83
"Opera, A Vehicle for Learning" 41
opera, London Symphony Orchestra
  73–74
opera education programmes,
  development of 38–44
The Opera Group (London) 168–169
Opera North, dementia
  programmes 168

194 *Index*

operat education programmes 19–20
"The Orchestra," iPad app 154
orchestral education programmes
19–20, 22, 44–50
Orchestra of the Age of
Enlightenment 58
Orfeo and Majnun project, La Monnaie
de Munt 100–101
organisational leadership 175–177, 185
Orquesta Sinfonica Bolivar *see* Simon
Bolivar Symphony Orchestra
"Out of the Ordinary," Irish National
Opera 160–161
outreach, United Kingdom 24

Panufnik Composers Scheme 72
Paraorchestra 142–143
participation in venues 187
partnerships 57–60, 64–65, 182–183;
orchestras and opera companies
143–145; Strategic Partnership for
the Tri-Borough Hub 63; *see also*
collaborative partnerships
Paynter, John 117, 140
performance and communication
skills course, Guildhall School
of Music and Drama (GSMD)
137–138
performers 127
"Person 181" 160
personnel allocated to education
174–175
phases of engagement, COVID
pandemic 152
Philharmonia Orchestra 153; dementia
programmes 169; "Re-Rite" 153;
"Sound Exchange" 154; "Universe of
Sound" 154
Pittsburgh orchestras 168
Pittsburgh Symphony 168
The Place Beyond Tomorrow 97, 159
polymorphous groupings 23
professional development 146
programming 181–182; structuring
education events 175
Proms: Australian Proms 49–50;
"Toddler Proms" 50
"Push," La Monnaie de Munt 101

"Raise Your Voice," Glyndebourne
Opera Company 99
Rattle, Sir Simon 33, 72–73, 75, 121
RCM *see* Royal College of Music

RCS *see* Royal Conservatoire of
Scotland
Recovery Orchestra, Bournemouth
Symphony Orchestra 168
Redbridge Music Service 72
Reid School of Music 141
Relaxed Concerts, Adelaide Symphony
Orchestra 168
Renshaw, Peter 137–138, 171, 174
"Re-Rite" 153
RESEO (European Network for
Opera and Dance Education)
44, 101; digital technology
159–160
Resonate Music Education Hub 110
Resound Ensemble 167
resource kits, Sydney Symphony
Orchestra 52–53
Rissmann, Paul 36–37, 86
"Rites of Passage," London Symphony
Orchestra 71
Ritterman, Dame Janet 139
RNCM *see* Royal Northern College of
Music
Robertson, Sue 180–181
Robinson, Sir Ken 122, 135
Robinson Report 121–122
ROH *see* Royal Opera House (ROH),
London
role models 142
Rose, James 167
Rosen, Jesse 173
Royal College of Music (RCM) 139
Royal Conservatoire of Scotland 141
Royal Liverpool Philharmonic
Orchestra (RLPO) 107–109,
146, 178
Royal Northern College of Music
(RNCM) 183
Royal Opera House (ROH),
London 38–44

Sargent, Malcolm 30–31
school concert model 31–33
schools, creativity 121–122
Scotland, National Centre for Music 60
Scottish Opera 41–42; "Breath Cycle"
167; Craigmillar Festival 44
Seattle Opera Company 38–39
Self, George 118
Sellars, Peter 98
sensory needs 168
SERA 106

Seven Seeds project, Tri-Borough Hub 63
Shapcott, Jo 180
Shaw, Roy 32
Shireland CBSO School 58
Shireland Collegiate Academy Trust 58
Silos and Symphonies, Adelaide Symphony Orchestra 84–85
"Silver Birch" 160
Simon Bolivar Symphony Orchestra 92, 104, 106
Sinfonietta 47
Sing Up 60, 70
Singing programme, London Symphony Orchestra 69
Sistema England 107
Sistema Global 105
Sistema Scotland 107; Big Noise 110–111; In Home visits 110
Slatkin, Leonard 11
"Sound Exchange" 154
Soundhub, London Symphony Orchestra 72
soundscape 128
SSO see Sydney Symphony Orchestra
SSO Proms 49–50
St Luke's 37–38
Stevens, John 33
Strategic Partnership for the Tri-Borough Hub 63
streaming concerts 151, 162; see also digital technology
String Experience, London Symphony Orchestra 72
structuring education events 175
support from organisational leadership 185
Sydney Opera House 51
Sydney Symphony Orchestra (SSO) 8; education department 50–53; Meet the Music school concerts 53
symphony orchestra model 23
Symphony Society of New York Orchestra 45

"Take A Bow," London Symphony Orchestra 6, 71
"Take a Stand" conference 105; Los Angeles Philharmonic 91–93
Taylor, Bruce 38
teacher-composers 117
teaching artists 5, 56, 115, 124, 129; see also animateurs

Teaching Artists programme, Juilliard School (New York) 141
Tearle, Katie 94–98
"Ten Pieces," BBC orchestras 75–81, 153
tertiary music training 133–137
tertiary performance degree 136
Thriving Communities 166
"Toddler Proms" 50
"Tony Foundation" 19
On Track programme, London Symphony Orchestra 70–71, 77–78
TRACTION 161
training 148, 185; in-service training 134; Master of Music (Orchestral Artistry) training 145
Tri-Borough Hub 63, 139
Trinity Laban Conservatoire of Music and Dance 139–140
"A Trip to the Moon" 73
"The Turn of the Tide" 42, 68
Tutti Arts 83

UCLA Health 167
United Kingdom: animateurs 115; El Sistema's influence 106–111; government support for arts 60–63; Music Hub system 4; National Academy for Social Prescribing 166; National Curriculum 123; National Plan 61; National Plan for Music Education 107; outreach 24; Sing Up 70
"Universe of Sound," Philharmonia Orchestra 153–154
University of Adelaide, Open Music Academy 83
University of Edinburgh 141
University of York 140

van der Harst, Dick 100
Varese, Edgar 120
Venezuela, El Sistema 3, 104
venues 186–187
virtual reality (VR) 153
Virtual Reality Community Opera 160
Virtual Reality Ireland 160

Wainwright, Christopher 10
Walking the Downs, Glyndebourne Opera Company 96
warm up games 125
Webber, Lloyd 107

196   *Index*

wellbeing 169–171, 188
Wider Opportunities 60
Wiegold, Peter 125–126, 137–138
Winterson, Julia 7–8
Witter-Johnson, Ayanna 156–157
Woodhouse Professional Development
    Centre, Royal College of Music
    (RCM) 139
work placements 136
workshop facilitators 115
workshop leaders 115
workshop model 8, 120
workshops: collaborative composition
    workshops 116; creative composition
    workshop 115; creative music
    workshops 123

YOLA *see* Youth Orchestra Los
    Angeles
YOLA at HOLA (Heart of Los Angeles)
    158
York of St John University 140
"Young Wonders Incorporated"
    (Searchinger) 39
youth concerts, Australia 47–49
Youth Orchestra Los Angeles (YOLA)
    88–89

Zimmer, Hans 76
Zoe (2000), Glyndebourne Opera
    Company 96
Zoom 158

Printed in the United States
by Baker & Taylor Publisher Services